DELINQUENCY
IN
PUERTO RICO

**Recent Titles in
Contributions in Criminology and Penology**

Police Administration and Progressive Reform: Theodore Roosevelt as
Police Commissioner of New York
Jay Stuart Berman

Policing Multi-Ethnic Neighborhoods: The Miami Study and Findings for
Law Enforcement in the United States
Geoffrey P. Alpert and Roger G. Dunham

Minorities and Criminality
Ronald Barri Flowers

Marijuana: Costs of Abuse, Costs of Control
Mark Kleiman

Doing Time in American Prisons: A Study of Modern Novels
Dennis Massey

Demographics and Criminality: The Characteristics of Crime in America
Ronald Barri Flowers

Taking Charge: Crisis Intervention in Criminal Justice
Anne T. Romano

Beyond Punishment: A New View on the Rehabilitation of Criminal Offenders
Edgardo Rotman

Police Pursuit Driving: Controlling Responses to Emergency Situations
Geoffrey P. Alpert and Roger G. Dunham

Vigilantism: Political History of Private Power in America
William C. Culberson

Chinese Subculture and Criminality: Non-traditional Crime Groups in America
Ko-lin Chin

A Sword for the Convicted: Representing Indigent Defendants on Appeal
David T. Wasserman

DELINQUENCY IN PUERTO RICO

The 1970 Birth Cohort Study

Dora Nevares,
Marvin E. Wolfgang,
and Paul E. Tracy

with the Collaboration of Steven Aurand

Foreword by Miguel Hernandez Agosto

Contributions in Criminology and Penology, Number 31

GREENWOOD PRESS
New York • Westport, Connecticut • London

Library of Congress Cataloging-in-Publication Data

Nevares-Muñiz, Dora.
  Delinquency in Puerto Rico : the 1970 birth cohort study / Dora
Nevares, Marvin E. Wolfgang, and Paul E. Tracy with the
collaboration of Steven Aurand ; foreword by Miguel Hernandez
Agosto.
    p.   cm.—(Contributions in criminology and penology, ISSN
0732-4464 ; no. 31)
  Includes bibliographical references.
  ISBN 0-313-27456-8 (lib. bdg. : alk. paper)
  1. Juvenile delinquency—Puerto Rico—Longitudinal studies.
I. Wolfgang, Marvin E., 1924-   . II. Tracy, Paul E. III. Title.
IV. Series.
HV9124.A5N48   1990
364.3′6′097291—dc20   90-32108

British Library Cataloguing in Publication Data is available.

Copyright © 1990 by Dora Nevares, Marvin E. Wolfgang, and Paul E. Tracy

All rights reserved. No portion of this book may be
reproduced, by any process or technique, without the
express written consent of the publisher.

Library of Congress Catalog Card Number: 90-32108
ISBN: 0-313-27456-8
ISSN: 0732-4464

First published in 1990

Greenwood Press, 88 Post Road West, Westport, CT 06881
An imprint of Greenwood Publishing Group, Inc.

Printed in the United States of America

The paper used in this book complies with the
Permanent Paper Standard issued by the National
Information Standards Organization (Z39.48-1984).

10 9 8 7 6 5 4 3 2 1

Contents

FOREWORD	vii
ACKNOWLEDGEMENTS	ix
1. BACKGROUND FOR THE CURRENT STUDY	1
Juvenile Delinquency Research in Puerto Rico	1
Official Statistics of Juvenile Delinquency	3
Defining the Cohort	7
The Site of Intervention	7
Capturing the Cohort	11
Collecting the Data	14
Coding the Data	15
The Importance of Birth Cohort and Longitudinal Studies	17
2. PREVALENCE	19
A Methodological Note on Prevalence	19
Delinquency Prevalence in the 1970 Cohort	22
Prevalence Summary	41
3. INCIDENCE	45
Incidence and Severity	45
Violent Offenses	53
Weapon Offenses	59
Narcotics Offenses	66
Incidence Summary	91
4. AGE AND DELINQUENCY	93
Age-At-Onset	93
Age-At-Offense	105
Age and Delinquency Summary	119

Contents

5. DELINQUENT RECIDIVISM 121
    Chronic Offenders 121
    Offense Probabilities 124
    Offense Transitions 134
    Recidivism Summary 143

6. POLICE AND COURT DISPOSITIONS 145
    Police Dispositions 145
    Court Dispositions 150
    Court Sentences 159
    Disposition Summary 170

7. COHORT COMPARISONS 173

8. SUMMARY AND IMPLICATIONS 177
    Summary 177
    Policy Implications 178

ENDNOTES 181

REFERENCES 183

APPENDICES
1. Order of the Court Authorizing Access 185
   to Juvenile Records. (Orden y Solicitud de
   Análisis y Estudio al Amparo de Art. 37(D) de
   la Ley -88 de 9 de Julio de 1986).

2. Form PPR36, Police Juvenile Records Card. 190
   (Tarjeta de Record de Menores en la Policia).

3. Form OAT110, Index Juvenile Card. 192
   (Tarjeta de Indice Juvenile en el Tribunal).

4. Form PPR116, Police Intervention Report. 194
   (Intervención con Menor).

5. Form PPR113, Supplementary Police Report. 197
   (Supplementario de Intervención).

6. Offender Demographic Form. 199

7. Offense Form. 200

8. Coding Instructions. 205
   (Instrucciones para Codificación).

9. Definition of Coded Variables. 223

INDEX 231

Foreword

Juvenile delinquency research in Puerto Rico has been conducted for nearly a generation. But having learned about longitudinal, birth cohort research, that seeks to answer the basic question of how many of our children are arrested at least once or more times before reaching adulthood, I and the Senate asked the pioneer of such research, Professor Marvin E. Wolfgang, of the University of Pennsylvania, and Professor Dora Nevares de Aponte, his former doctoral student, of the Inter American University to conduct a Puerto Rican birth cohort study.

The Senate and I are grateful for this research, the first of its kind in Puerto Rico, and a major contribution to longitudinal studies.

The research findings show that Puerto Rican delinquency is much less than in the mainland United States or elsewhere. They also suggest that our present programs are effective and our social services for first-time juvenile offenders work well.

The message is that our Government should more fully support all of our delinquency prevention programs, especially to deter early delinquents from becoming chronic, career juvenile and adult offenders.

Miguel Hernandez Agosto
President, Senate
Commonwealth of Puerto Rico

Acknowledgements

We wish to acknowledge the strong support from the President of the Senate, the Honorable Miguel Hernandez Agosto, for the initiation and conduct of the research.

We appreciate also the personal assistance given by the Secretary of the Senate, Mr. Ramon Garcia Santiago, in providing us with all the necessary support and facilities of the Senate. Were it not for his close attention to many complex details concerned with the project, this final product would be much diminished. His personal touch is a major part of this study.

The project was carried out under the auspices of the Senate's Special Crime Commission, and was funded by the Senate in a cooperative agreement with the Executive Branch, in which the Secretary of Justice, the Honorable Hector Rivera Cruz participated along with the Secretary of Social Services, the Honorable Carmen Sonia Zayas, the Secretary of Public Education, the Honorable Awilda Aponte, and the Police Superintendent, Mr. Carlos Lopez Feliciano. To all of these people we wish to express our sincere appreciation.

The Governor's Office of Juvenile Affairs gave us a grant for the partial funding of the project. We give our acknowledgement to the Director at that time, Mrs. Evelyn Cole de Irizarry, and her successor, Mrs. Norma Perez, Acting Director. The Director of the Puerto Rican Criminal Justice Automated System, Mr. Jose Perez Rodriguez, kindly provided all the requested data of the 1970 cohort available in the information system.

Acknowledgements

The Director of the Demographic Office, Mrs. Mercedes Ortiz de Martinez, kindly provided the registration printouts of the 1970 birth cohort and further verified for us the birth date of some cases in which we had doubts. Our thanks to her.

The Commonwealth's Office of Right to Work provided some funds for the hiring of research assistants. We offer our acknowledgements to Ms. Ilena Echegoyen and Mrs. Jane Temes for their cooperation.

The President of Inter-American University, Dr. Pedro Jose Rivera, authorized a partial reduction of the academic load of one of us (Dora Nevares) in cooperation with this research.

The Superior Court Judges in charge of the Juvenile Court in San Juan, Carolina, and Bayamon, Honorable Justices Jose Aponte Perez, Flavio Cumpiano, and Juan Arill, kindly assisted in the coordination of the data collection and provided valuable cooperation to the research assistants. We thank them for this important assistance.

At the Police District Offices of Juvenile Assistance, in San Juan, Carolina, and Bayamon, their Directors, Mr Gilberto Diaz Pagan, Mrs. Maria Carrasquillo, and Mr. Jorge Alicea, deserve our acknowledgements for facilitating the police data collection.

The research assistants who collected and coded the data deserve our sincere appreciation for the high sense of responsibility and enthusiasm with which they carried out their tasks. They are law students--Jose Velazquez, Jorge Gordon, Carlos Padilla, and Yolande Figueroa--who worked on this project from its beginning. Sandra Fuentes resigned after two months and Magda Lanza was then recruited as research assistant.

At the later stages of the research, law students Hilda Rodriguez and Santiago Martinez joined as assistants in the coding process. Law student Naomi Diaz also joined us, and with great dedication and efficiency typed the Spanish report.

Three recently graduated lawyers from the Inter-American University supervised the process of data coding. We offer deep appreciation and acknowledgement for their dedication and excellent work. They are Glorimar Acevedo, Ivan Encarnacion, and Maribel Sanchez.

Dr. Mercedes Cintron, Administrator of Juvenile Institutions, advised us on the services provided by the juvenile institutions. Dr. Miguel Valencia also deserves our appreciation for his advice on the selection of the prevalence denominator.

Finally, we are pleased to acknowledge our thanks to Steven Aurand, who was responsible for the extensive computer programming and assisted in the data analyses.

DELINQUENCY
IN
PUERTO RICO

1
Background for the Current Study

JUVENILE DELINQUENCY RESEARCH IN PUERTO RICO

Until the late sixties literature on juvenile delinquency in Puerto Rico was limited to official reports published by government agencies that included mostly statistics from the police and court administrations, proceedings from professional conventions, research papers, and graduate dissertations.[1] In subsequent years, most research studies presented the incidence of delinquency for a set of selected years and profiles of juvenile offenders. No longitudinal study of juvenile delinquency had ever been done in Puerto Rico.

Kupperstein (1969), in collaboration with Toro-Calder, conducted a cross-sectional study utilizing data from court records. The research analyzed the processing of juvenile court cases in San Juan and established a socio-cultural and legal profile of the juvenile delinquent who was indicted and processed in the San Juan Juvenile court in 1966. Eighty-five percent of juvenile delinquents in the sample were males between ages fifteen and seventeen. Females accounted for only 15 percent of the sample, but were referred to court at a younger age than males. Sixty-five percent of the sample subjects lived in urban slum areas or public housing, characterized by high social pathology, while 11 percent lived in rural areas. Eighty-seven percent of the families of the juveniles reported income levels below the Puerto Rican average.

Kupperstein's study also found that 43 percent of the juveniles were in school at the time of committing the offense, and 56 percent had dropped out of school before graduating from high school. Among those that had left school, only 39 percent had finished sixth grade and 6 percent had finished the ninth grade. The median age for dropping out of school was 12 years, while 60 percent of drop-outs had a two-year academic backlog. Among the population of school dropouts, unemployment was very high.

The offense characteristics of Kupperstein's sample comprised 1,046 events committed by 1,399 juvenile offenders. Seventy-three percent of the criminal events were carried out by an offender acting alone, while only 27 percent involved two or more delinquents. Gang behavior did not prevail in these acts of delinquency. Among offenses in which the victim was injured (30 percent of the sample), 85 percent involved victims and offenders who were either known or related. Most cases of personal injury were carried out by females between sixteen and nineteen years of age. Property offenses accounted for 31 percent of the sample cases: 11 percent were robberies and 23 percent were auto thefts or damage offenses.

Mercedes Otero de Ramos (1970) also used court records to study the relationship between delinquency and school dropouts. The sex and age breakdown of the juvenile delinquent, taken from court records from 1960 to 1964, is slightly different from that of the previously mentioned study--87 percent of the sample were males, while 13 percent were females. Among them, 52 percent were dropouts. Most of the delinquents were sixteen or seventeen years old.

Lopez-Rey, Toro-Calder, and Cedeno-Zavala (1975), in a major cross-sectional study of crime and delinquency in Puerto Rico, analyzed official police and court statistics on juvenile delinquency for the fiscal years 1965-66 to 1969-70. They provided rates for Type I and Type II offenses[2] per 1,000 persons between seven and seventeen years old, by sex. Lopez-Rey et al. reported that for both sexes, the rates during that period fluctuated between 18.74 and 15.15, and that the average rate for males was 29.9, while for females the rate was 2.8.

Lopez-Rey et al. also found that the rate at which juveniles were intervened by the police increased gradually with age, but was highest at age seventeen, followed by ages sixteen and fifteen.

An experimental research study was conducted by Ferracuti, Dinitz, and Acosta (1975) and was aimed at identifying the differences between official delinquents and nondelinquents living under the adverse conditions of the slum area ("arrabal and caserio") in metropolitan San Juan. They studied 101 matched pairs of male delinquents and nondelinquents, aged eleven to seventeen. The delinquents were juveniles who had cases pending in the juvenile court in San Juan between 1966 and 1969. The matching variables between the control and experimental groups were: area of residence, socioeconomic level, family income, and age. The members in the control group had no known criminal history.

The Ferracuti et al. research revealed that the families of nondelinquents were cohesive and stable, had greater economic aspirations, and had more firm religious interests than those of the delinquent group. Nondelinquents had better school performances and more positive social attitudes than did delinquents. Juvenile delinquency appeared to be only one element of a multi-problem family syndrome characterized by broken homes, instability, subsistence standard of living, and physical and mental disabilities. After analyzing police and court records they found that offenders were mostly loners and that gang involvement was minimal, but personal violence was high. The authors argued that official records underestimated the problem of hard drugs.

Vales and Ayala (1986) have provided a profile of the institutionalized juvenile offender in 1984-85. They found the following characteristics. Two out of three juveniles were between 15 and 17 years old, with an average age of 16.3 years. Fifty-one percent had attended elementary school, and 65 percent were school dropouts who were unemployed. Seventy-four percent lived in urban areas, while the remaining 26 percent came from rural sections. Forty-nine percent lived in greater metropolitan San Juan, and three out of four lived in socio-economically deprived areas. Fifty-five percent came from welfare homes, and 81 percent lived in broken homes, with most living with their mothers (37 percent). Sixty-five percent were institutionalized for Type I offenses, of which 82 percent were property offenses and 18 percent were crimes against the person.

OFFICIAL STATISTICS OF JUVENILE DELINQUENCY

Police statistics on juvenile interventions suggest that during a twenty-three year period from 1964 to 1987, juvenile delinquency has not significantly increased in Puerto Rico. Table 1.1 provides data for the number of police interventions with juveniles for Type I and Type II offenses for fiscal years 1964-65 to 1984-85, and for natural years 1986 and 1987. The number of juvenile interventions fluctuates, but there is no discernable trend.

Delinquency in Puerto Rico

TABLE 1.1   Police Interventions with Juveniles for Type I and Type II Offenses 1964 to 1987

Years	Total Juveniles
1964-65	11,931
1965-66	11,982
1966-67	14,051
1967-68	14,943
1968-69	14,066
1969-70	13,740
1970-71	12,969
1971-72	12,013
1972-73	10,974
1973-74	9,737
1974-75	8,753
1975-76	11,347
1976-77	12,568
1977-78	12,213
1978-79	11,469
1979-80	10,848
1980-81	11,410
1981-82	10,535
1982-83	10,680
1983-84	10,904
1984-85	10,332
1986*	10,749
1987*	11,354

Source: Police Statistics
* Refers to natural years

When the rates of police interventions per 1,000 population at risk (7 to 17 years old) for Type I and Type II offenses are considered, a reduction is shown throughout the years. Table 1.2 shows that in 1961-62 the rate of police interventions was 19.3, while in 1980-81 the rate decreased to 15.2

TABLE 1.2   Rates of Police Interventions with Juveniles for Type I and Type II Offenses

Fiscal Year	Population age 7 to 17	Police Interventions	Rate
1961-62	686,452	13,254	19.3
1970-71	732,400	12,969	17.7
1980-81	749,774	11,410	15.2

Source: Police Statistics; Bureau of Census

Background for Current Study

Table 1.3 provides a breakdown by Type I and Type II offenses of the number of police interventions from 1980 through 1987.

When the number of police interventions for Type I and Type II offenses is compared with the juvenile population, aged ten to seventeen, as provided by the 1980 Census (550,016) and the Puerto Rico Planning board, interventions represented approximately two percent of the juvenile populations for the years 1980 to 1987. This figure is a slight reduction from the period 1959-60 to 1962-63, during which police interventions represented approximately 2.5 percent of the juvenile delinquency population (see Kupperstein and Toro-Calder, 1969).

TABLE 1.3   Type I and Type II, Police Interventions with Juveniles for both Sexes in Puerto Rico

Year	Type I	Type II	Total
1980	4,543	6,553	11,096
1981	4,708	6,228	10,936
1982	4,525	6,239	10,764
1983	4,091	6,473	10,564
1984	3,998	6,940	10,838
1985	4,102	7,446	11,548
1986	3,717	7,032	10,749
1987	3,522	7,832	11,354

Source: Police Statistics

Court referrals of juveniles during 1960-61 represented only one percent of the child population, aged ten to seventeen. Two decades later, in 1980-81, court referrals of juvenile cases still represented only about one percent of the juvenile population.

Table 1.4 compares police interventions with cases of juveniles processed in court for fiscal years 1980-81 to 1984-85. The ratio of police interventions to court cases processed was approximately two to one.

Table 1.5 provides the number of police interventions of juveniles for Type I and Type II offenses in the Greater Metropolitan San Juan area, for each of the police districts and for the whole island.

Police interventions in Greater Metropolitan San Juan have constituted approximately one-third of the total police interventions in all of Puerto Rico during the last seven years.

Delinquency in Puerto Rico

Table 1.5 also shows that police interventions during that period in Puerto Rico have fluctuated between 10,564 for 1983 and 11,548 for 1985. But, if we consider the end points of the seven-year period for the Greater Metropolitan San Juan area, the number of interventions differs from 3,386 in 1987 to 3,390 in 1981.

TABLE 1-4   Police Interventions for Type I and II Offenses referred to Courts 1980-81 to 1984-85

Year	Police Interventions	Court Complaints	% of Cases referred
1980-81	11,410	6,240	55%
1981-82	10,535	5,777	58%
1982-83	10,680	5,159	48%
1983-84	10,904	4,714	43%
1984-85	10,332	4,836	47%

Source: Police Statistics;
Court Administration Reports

TABLE 1-5   Police Interventions: Type I and II, Both Sexes in San Juan, Carolina, and Bayamon

Year	Police Districts San Juan	Carolina	Bayamon	Greater San Juan	Puerto Rico
1981	1,298	612	1,480	3,390	10,936
1982	1,129	620	1,366	3,115	10,764
1983	1,141	592	1,314	3,047	10,564
1984	1,096	664	1,431	3,191	10,838
1985	1,081	671	1,543	3,295	11,548
1986	1,058	695	1,263	3,016	10,749
1987	1,070	784	1,532	3,386	11,353

Source: Police Statistics

The official statistics given above support the initial general statement that juvenile police interventions have not increased throughout the years exhibited here. This is true despite the fact that both police resources and the juvenile population have increased over these years.

Background for Current Study

DEFINING THE COHORT

The cohort delinquents of this study are comprised of all males and females born in 1970 who, before reaching their eighteenth birthday, either had at least one arrest record or were officially declared status offenders in the Greater San Juan Metropolitan Area of Puerto Rico.

In selecting this particular birth year, we were interested in having a cohort that reached maturity nearest the year of this research study. This choice allowed us to have the most recently available data. Moreover, the research findings for so current a cohort would have currency and the greatest transferability for producing conclusions relevant for public policy and legislation. The specific provision (Article 37 (3)) of the Juvenile Statute that requires the destruction of police records once the juvenile attains age eighteen was another decision-making factor in our selection of the present cohort.

In accordance with these above considerations we selected 1970 as the birth year of the cohort. The upper age limit of the cohort was set at age seventeen, for once juveniles attain eighteen years of age, they are considered adults for purposes of criminal responsibility unless they are waived to adult court while still juveniles. Thus, the 1970 birth cohort has allowed us to trace offender status and police and court records up to age seventeen.[3]

The Site of Intervention

In selecting the site of official intervention, we limited the geographic area to that comprised by the police districts of San Juan, Carolina, and Bayamon. Although pragmatic reasons of accessibility to the data influenced our decision, other considerations contributed as well. The chosen area is mostly urban and its residents move throughout greater San Juan in their contacts with the police courts, schools, and other social agencies that deal with juveniles. However, the area has several different levels of physical and economic styles, like urban slums, public housing projects (some being quite large), private residences and condominiums, and rural barrios which include both very expensive and low-cost homes. Further, this San Juan Metropolitan area comprises about one-third of Puerto Rico's population and has one of the greatest population densities in the hemisphere.

Until 1978, our site of intervention was a sole police district known as the Greater San Juan Metropolitan Area.

Delinquency in Puerto Rico

In 1978, Special Order 78-1 issued by the Commonwealth's Police Superintendent divided the Greater San Juan Metropolitan Area into three geographically based units or police districts: San Juan, Carolina, and Bayamon. Each of the three areas has a Juvenile Justice Division to investigate offenses in which juveniles are involved. The municipalities covered by each of the three police districts, which form the site of our cohort delinquent behavior, are included in Table 1.6.

TABLE 1-6 Municipalities Covered by the Greater Metropolitan San Juan Police Districts

POLICE DISTRICTS		
San Juan	Carolina	Bayamon

MUNICIPALITIES		
San Juan	Carolina	Bayamon
	Trujillo Alto	Catano
	Canovanas	Guaynabo
	Rio Grande	Toa Baja
	Loiza	Toa Alta
		Naranjito
		Corozal
		Dorado
		Vega Alta

According to the Census of 1980, the San Juan Standard Metropolitan Statistical Area (SMSA) was comprised of the following municipalities: San Juan, Truillo Alto, Carolina, Canovanas, Loiza, Guaynabo, Bayamon, Catano, and Toa Baja. The population of this area was 1,086,376 out of a total Puerto Rican population of 3,196,520. The urban population of the San Juan Standard Statistical Metropolitan Area was 1,044,978, while the rural population was 41,398. The percentage of juveniles under age eighteen years in 1980 was 35.1 percent in that area, while for the whole island it was 38.2 percent.[4]

In order to have perfect correspondence with the geographical area covered by the three police districts that comprised the Greater Metropolitan San Juan Area, the municipalities of Rio Grande, Naranjito, Corozal, Toa Alta, and Dorado had to be added to the Bureau of Census definition, and to the figures of the San Juan Standard Metropolitan Statistical Area. The specific area of this research is outlined in Figure 1.1.

Figure 1.1
Puerto Rico Districts

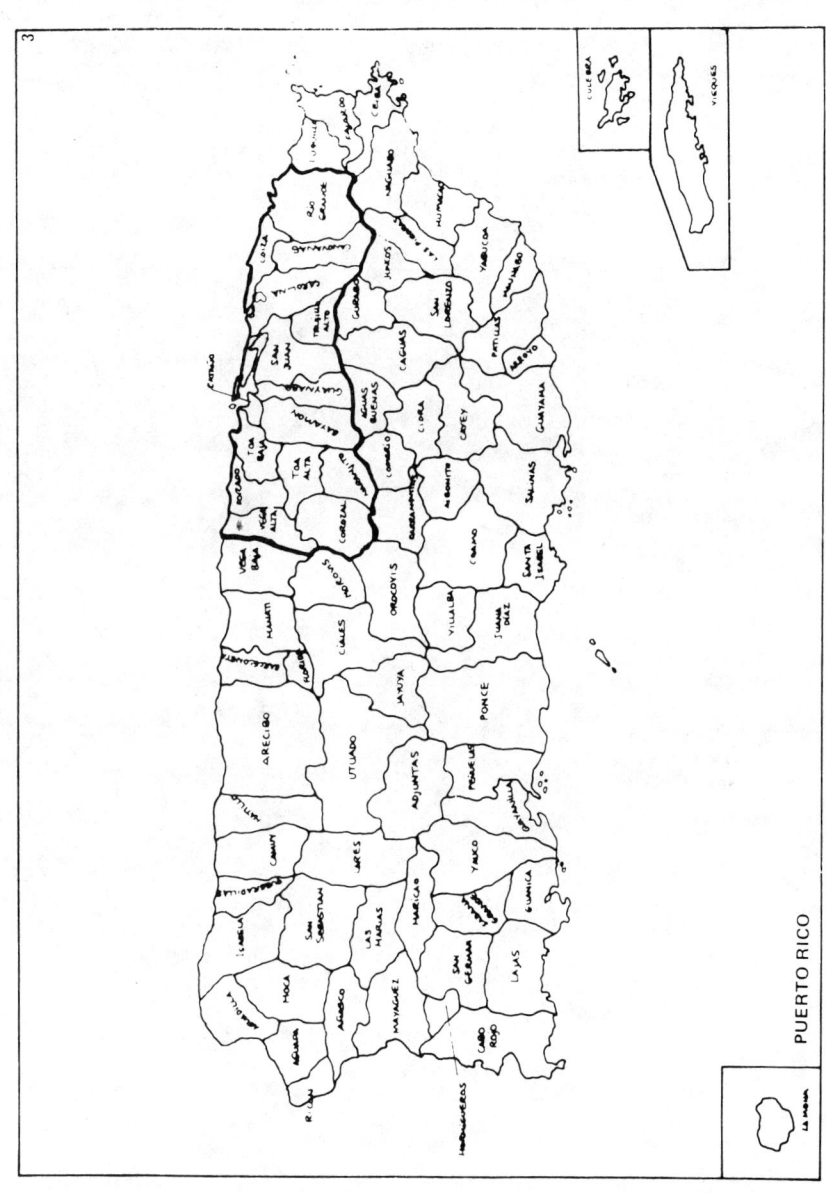

Delinquency in Puerto Rico

This process increased the 1980 population of our site of study to 1,299,934, or about 38 percent of the total island population of 3,196,520. The distribution between urban and rural population was nine to one. Table 1.7 provides the urban and rural population for the municipalities of Greater San Juan according to the 1980 Census.

TABLE 1-7   Urban and Rural Population in Greater San Juan, 1980

Police District and Municipality	Urban	Rural
San Juan		
San Juan	433,901	948
Carolina		
Carolina	159,055	6,899
Truillo Alto	47,884	3,505
Canovanas	19,549	12,331
Loiza	19,074	1,793
Rio Grande	19,253	15,030
Bayamon		
Bayamon	189,753	6,453
Catano	26,243	-----
Guaynabo	76,378	6,436
Dorado	19,075	22,332
Carozal	5,889	20,784
Naranjito	2,849	12,754
Toa Alta	19,156	15,754
Toa Baja	73,141	5,105
Vega Alta	20,531	8,165

Source: Bureau of Census, Population 1980, Puerto Rico, Table 32.

As shown by Table 1.7, except for the municipalities of Corozal and Naranjito, the Greater San Juan area is mostly urban. People used to travel throughout the whole area, both for employment and schooling, particularly in the case of attending private schools (notwithstanding the requirement of the public education system that students register at the school to which their place of residence is assigned).

Table 1.8 includes data on the population served by the Police Districts of San Juan, Carolina, and Bayamon for the years covered in this study, 1980 through 1987. Over

Background for Current Study

the course of these years, the population increased overall by approximately 100,000 people. Carolina had the biggest increase, about 70,000 people, while Bayamon increased by about 27,000 people and San Juan decreased by about 7,000.

TABLE 1-8   Population by Police Districts in Greater San Juan

POLICE DISTRICTS

Year	San Juan	Bayamon	Carolina	Total
1980	432,973	518,774	303,748	1,255,495
1981	410,058	523,218	311,996	1,245,272
1982	390,682	518,686	321,290	1,230,658
1983	386,156	534,288	331,241	1,251,685
1984	405,111	553,249	339,252	1,297,612
1985	424,065	572,206	347,262	1,343,533
1986	424,065	572,206	347,262	1,343,533
1987	425,751	545,661	380,873	1,352,285

Source: Division de Estadisticas, Negociado de Servicios Technicos, Policia de Puerto Rico

Capturing the Cohort

Police and Court Records of juveniles are confidential as set forth by the Juvenile Statute. But provision 37 (d) of the statute allows examination of these records for official and legitimate purposes, including scientific research, in accordance with an order of the Juvenile Court. In order to have access to the official delinquency records of our cohort we had to obtain a court order, (see Appendix 1). The Senate President also signed a cooperative agreement with the various government agencies that, among other things, provided us access to agency data files.[5] Privacy guarantees were properly given and these guarantees have been maintained throughout the collection, coding, and processing of data.

Our next step was to identify the juveniles born in 1970 who had at least one official contact with the police which also resulted in a written report in the greater San Juan area.

The Juvenile Aid Division of the Police Superintendency maintains in each of its district offices a local master record file of those juveniles who have had police contact within their police district and which resulted in a written report. This master file consists of a series of cards arranged in alphabetical order. The file is divided into active and inactive cases. A case is considered inactive once the juvenile reaches age eighteen, and it is moved from the active to the inactive file. Every five years the inactive cards are destroyed, but the police records of those persons are separated for destruction once they attain age eighteen.

The card in the master file of police interventions with juveniles includes the following information: name, nickname, age, sex, race, address, birth place, and birth date; father and mother's name, living status, and address; name of person with whom the juvenile lives, relationship and reason for living with that person; student status, school, grade attending or last grade completed; working status, occupation, and employer. The back side of the card records information related to the offense or offenses charged (that is, legal label of offense, date, place, intervention report number, and police disposition (see, Appendix 2, form PPR-36).

Our research assistants examined the active master file in each of the three Juvenile Aid Division offices of Greater San Juan and photocopied the cards of both males and females born in 1970. While they were photocopying the cards, a cohort number was assigned to each juvenile for identification purposes. Simultaneously, in the office of the research project at the Senate, master lists of the cohort were being prepared for each police district with the following information taken from the police cards: the cohort member's identification number, name, parent's names, birth date, birth place, and police disposition.

The master lists were used to verify both birth date and offenders who had official records in different police districts. The master lists were also used as a guide to look for the court records of the cohort members that were referred to the court by the police.

The record of each juvenile in the master list who was born in Puerto Rico was manually examined in computer printouts supplied by the Commonwealth's Demographic Office of those born in 1970. Those juveniles born in Puerto Rico who were not included in the demographic lists, and whose cases were not referred to court, were sent to the Demographic office for further verification of birth date.

If the juvenile was referred to Juvenile Court, the records included proof of his/her birth date. We further verified the birth date of those juveniles once we began the collection of court data. When the juvenile was not born in Puerto Rico, we verified the date of birth by

Background for Current Study

looking for a birth certificate in the court record. For those cases in which the juvenile was not born in Puerto Rico and the case was not sent to court, we relied on the birth date included in the police report.

Through this process, we obtained a cohort of males and females who: a) were born in 1970; b) had at least one police contact in which a written report was filed before the subject reached eighteen years of age; and c) resided in the three police districts of San Juan, Carolina, and Bayamon.

We further increased our cohort lists by checking two other sources: 1) the Puerto Rico Automated Juvenile Justice Information System (PRAJJIS) and 2) the Court Master Files. The PRAJJIS procedure was particularly necessary in the case of the police district of Bayamon, because in that district the police records dated before 1984 were destroyed to make space available for more recent records. This information had to be recovered from the court files. Despite the general availability of data in the court files, those police records of juveniles who had been disposed remedially by the Bayamon Juvenile Aid Division before 1984 are missing from our cohort. However, we did record the offense date and the name of the offender for these missing remedials. Moreover, looking at the court's master files was another means of capturing members of our cohort, who for some reason, were missing from the police master file.

PRAJJIS provided a list of offenders born in 1970 plus pertinent offense and socio-demographic data. We verified the PRAJJIS lists against our master lists and added those cases from the former that were not included in the latter.

The Juvenile Court also maintains a master file of juveniles who are referred. This file is arranged alphabetically and includes a card for the juvenile offender with the following information: name, address, birth date, parents' names, juvenile case number, other concurrent case numbers, and previous court cases by date, case number, type of offense, and disposition (see, Appendix 3). In San Juan a master file exists that covers the whole island. We further verified our cohort master lists against this file, looking for juvenile offenders born in 1970 who were not included in our cohort master lists and who had been arrested by the police for offenses in the Greater San Juan Area.

In the case of status offenders, PRAJJIS provided a list of males and females born in 1970 who were classified as status offenders, had conduct problems, or were school dropouts and runaways (respectively, S2 and S3, S1, and S5 according to PRAJJIS codes). Because PRAJJIS only has records beginning in July 1984, we missed incidents of juveniles who had conduct problems who were neither referred to the police nor to the court, but instead were referred to the Department of Social Services. However, we obtained status offenders from the court's master file, because by law an offender has to be declared as such by the court.

Collecting the Data

The police reports provided data regarding the contacts that our cohort members had with the police, and these reports contained enough information to trace the case throughout the court system, when the case was referred for prosecution. These reports are included as Appendices 4 and 5 (Intervencion con el Menor; Suplementario).

The police offense report (Appendix 4) is prepared by the officer who intervened with the juvenile for the offense. Each report includes a vast array of descriptive information concerning the offender and the victims and witnesses. This information includes: report number assigned by the police district; complaint number assigned to the delinquent event; police area and police division that intervened with the juvenile; Social Security number of the juvenile; title of the offense involved in accord with the law (including status offenses); classification of the offense based on the Uniform Crime Reporting (UCR) system of the Federal Bureau of Investigation (FBI) with its corresponding code number; date of the event; date, time, and place of the police intervention; the name, sex, race, address, telephone number, nickname, place and date of birth of anyone taken into custody as offender or suspect; the juvenile's parents' names, address and living status, as well as the person with the whom the juvenile is living and the reasons for the arrangement; the juvenile's school status, school name, grade registered or last attended, school address; when employed, provision is made for the juvenile's occupation and the name and address of the employer; name, sex, race, age, and addresses of complainant, victim, and witnesses; name of the officer who intervened with the juvenile, and his police district or division, name of the officer receiving the report, and police district and division; and disposition (that is, remedial or referred to court, to the juvenile prosecutor, or to another agency).

In addition to the above information, the police report includes data pertaining to the offense itself. These data include: the presence of weapons and narcotics; a detailed description of the event--it usually includes

Background for Current Study

information secured by the police when intervening the juvenile, and describes how the offense took place, losses or injuries sustained by the victim, and action taken by the officer who took the juvenile into custody.

The Supplementary Intervention Police Report (Appendix 5) is prepared by the Juvenile Aid officer after meeting with the suspect's parents and the victim(s) or witnesses. This supplementary report provides additional information regarding the event, and a detailed description of the final action taken, such as: clearing of the offense by remedial disposition because the case was either unfounded or the victim was not interested in further action; dismissal of the case by the court; or clearing by arrest and jurisdiction turned over to the Juvenile Court; or any other pertinent action. When the action taken was further police investigation, a second supplementary report was filed when the case was finally cleared.

Guided by the master lists of cohort members, the research assistants photocopied the police offense reports of arrests of the cohort members in the police districts of San Juan, Carolina, and Bayamon. These records were transferred to the Senate's research project office, in accord with the court order, for later coding. Those cases that were disposed remedially by the police or dismissed by the court were ready for coding.

After this step, some assistants went to the juvenile courts to examine the records of those cohort members whose cases were referred to them. In these cases, valuable information was obtained, including data related to the disposition of the case by the court, and the exact sentence or treatment ordered by the court. We also examined social, psychiatric, and sociological reports, which provided additional information to be used in coding. Moreover, some of the information collected from court records is extremely valuable for further research concerning the behavior of the cohort members, who are now entering adulthood.

The research assistants collected official intervention data of cohort delinquency up to December 31, 1987. Those cases were followed through the juvenile justice system for disposition data through February 1988.

Coding the Data

The directors of the research team, with the assistance of their computer analyst, developed two coding forms. One, titled "Offender Demographic Form," included for each cohort member the identification number, birth date, birth place, and color (see Appendix 6). The other form, titled "Offense Form," provided for coding information related to each offense committed by the cohort member, and relevant demographic information at the time of the commission of the offense. This form coded for each offense the following information: type of school attended or attending; whether in school when arrested; highest grade completed at time of arrest; members of household; occupation of head of household; sources of household income; number of siblings; and mental retardation, or insanity.

The offense variables coded were: court number, case number, date of offense, type of offense, number of victims, characteristics of victims and type of injury, presence of weapons, dollar value of theft or damage losses, number and type of premises forcibly entered, number of co-offenders and co-offenders' characteristics, possession of drugs, type of drug or alcohol used or under the influence of at the time of the arrest.

The disposition variables coded were: date of arrest; type of police disposition; date and number of days of pretrial detention; date of court disposition; reason for jurisdiction waiver and adult court disposition when appropriate; type of sentence; number of weeks served on probation, in diversion program, or custodial institution; type of treatment; amount of fine and restitution; date of discharge, and whether the juvenile was a fugitive at the time of the offense, had pending charges, or was on probation.

In the preparation of coding forms, we included all the available variables relevant to the offense description and the computation of scale scores of the severity of each offense as derived from the <u>National Survey of Crime Severity</u> (Wolfgang <u>et al</u>., 1985).[6] This system of evaluating the comparative severity of a delinquent event gives us a complete picture of the exact seriousness of the crime which would not be possible using only the legal labels attached to the crime by the police. Further, the severity scaling system permits the classification of offenses in this Puerto Rican cohort according to the same procedure as used in the two major longitudinal cohort studies of delinquency in Philadelphia conducted by Marvin E. Wolfgang and his associates at the University of Pennsylvania. With these classifications, we can compare the delinquencies in this cohort with the two in Philadelphia, thus increasing our knowledge of the comparative severity of delinquency in Puerto Rico.[7]

The coding forms also provided for the inclusion of the PRAJJIS identification number, but we could not code it because PRAJJIS did not include it in the records given

Background for Current Study

to us. Nonetheless, some of the items were coded using the same variables and codes as used by PRAJJIS.

The process of data coding was personally directed and supervised by the project directors. The coding was performed by recently graduated lawyers and present law students in accordance with a detailed coding manual that included specific instructions in Spanish for each item in the coding form (see Appendix 8). Also, detailed definitions of variables, as well as an explanation of the coding for open-ended items were prepared to assist the persons who entered the data into the computer from the code forms (see Appendix 9). The computer processing of the data files was done at the Sellin Center for Studies in Criminology and Criminal Law, Wharton School, University of Pennsylvania.

THE IMPORTANCE OF BIRTH COHORT AND LONGITUDINAL STUDIES

Cross-sectional analyses that simply ask how many juveniles in any given year were delinquent do not answer the important question of what may be the probability or chance that a person born in any given year may be arrested before reaching adulthood. Only a longitudinal study which traces persons from birth can answer this simple, but important question.

A birth cohort--that is, persons born in a given year and followed through records throughout their juvenile years--is the most sophisticated research tool available to researchers in criminology. The first such study in the United States was conducted in Philadelphia (for a cohort of persons born in 1945, Wolfgang et al., 1972) by the Sellin Center for Studies in Criminology and Criminal Law at the University of Pennsylvania. The Center has recently completed a second birth cohort in Philadelphia with a 1958 birth year (Tracy et al, 1990).

One of the principal virtues of a longitudinal birth cohort study is that probabilities of delinquency over a juvenile lifetime can be calculated and analyzed. Moreover, because the age and time of events in the personal biographies of the juveniles can be recorded and sequenced, stronger causal inferences about the relationships between delinquency and the many possible factors that we think are associated with delinquency can be made more carefully and confidently.

Longitudinal, birth cohort research thus provides the field of criminology with the best data available for conducting analyses of delinquency and, consequently, of making scientifically based recommendations for policy and legislation.

2
Prevalence

A METHODOLOGICAL NOTE ON PREVALENCE

Instead of first searching the school records for the total number of children born in 1970 and then checking the names of these subjects with the police files, this Puerto Rican birth cohort study first obtained the names of all persons born in 1970 who were contacted by the police in the three districts of the Greater San Juan Metropolitan Area.

In order to obtain a population base of all persons born in 1970 so as to create a denominator to calculate a rate or proportion of arrestees among the population at risk of delinquency, we first obtained information about the school population for grades four through twelve for San Juan, Bayamon, and Carolina. We soon realized that these school data were only public school data and that data on private school enrollments were inaccurate or unavailable, and that the number of school dropouts was unclear for each grade and age. Hence, we sought to construct a more valid population base.

We obtained the information we needed from a Bureau of the Census publication (1983). In this report, the number of males and females who were ten years old in 1980 and who were born in 1970 is presented by separate communities that correspond to the police districts available for this research. The distribution by sex of this population is represented in Table 2.1. The combined population of the 1970 cohort subjects by sex and district appears in Table 2.2.

TABLE 2.1 Persons Born in 1970, Aged 10 Years in 1980 by District and Sex

District	Male	Female	Both
San Juan			
San Juan	3,605	3,530	7,135
Carolina			
Carolina	1,808	1,784	3,592
Trujillo Alto	559	498	1,057
Canovanas	369	377	746
Loiza	237	225	462
Rio Grande	398	393	791
Total	3,371	3,277	6,648
Bayamon			
Bayamon	1,951	1,908	3,859
Catano	284	276	560
Guaynabo	825	808	1,633
Dorado	255	275	530
Corozal	291	345	636
Naranjito	294	288	582
Toa Alta	369	325	694
Toa Baja	869	860	1,729
Vega Alta	338	325	663
Total	5,476	5,410	10,886
Total (All Districts)	12,452	12,217	24,669

There are several caveats to be considered in the use of this particular population base of ten-year-olds in 1980 who were born in 1970. These are: 1) the mortality rate between ages ten and seventeen is very low; 2) some children may have migrated from Puerto Rico during the ages ten to seventeen; 3) some children in the three police districts may have left during ages ten to seventeen for other parts of Puerto Rico (but these are thought to be few in number); and 4) some children may have migrated into the three areas, but these are also believed to be few in number because most mobility is within these areas rather than movement in or out. In general, therefore, we believe that the population base of 12,452 males and 12,217 females, in a total population of ten to seventeen year-olds of 24,669 for the three areas is a valid base for calculating the prevalence of delinquency in the 1970 birth cohort.

Prevalence

Comment should be made about the relatively low delinquency prevalence of 11 percent for males, 2 percent for females, and an overall delinquency rate of nearly 7 percent. The corresponding prevalence rates for males in the Philadelphia birth cohorts of 1945 and 1958 were 35 percent and 33 percent, respectively. These rates are similar to other longitudinal studies elsewhere. Thus the question, why the low rates of delinquency in the densely populated Greater San Juan Metropolitan Area?

We can only surmise. The fact that some juveniles who are found to have committed offenses are only informally handled by the police, and thus, are not officially recorded as delinquents occurs in all jurisdictions. We have no reason to believe that this process is more extensive in Puerto Rico than in other jurisdictions on the mainland or in Europe. Based on our interviews with agency representatives of the juvenile justice system in Puerto Rico, we believe that it is a valid conclusion that fewer children commit delinquent acts on this island than elsewhere.

Moreover, the rate of one-time offenders--or the desistance rate after the first offense--is much higher than elsewhere, nearly two times that of Philadelphia, for example. Again, based on our observations, we believe that the juvenile justice services for delinquents in Puerto Rico function with exceptional efficiency in discouraging recidivism. Something is working very well in the processing and handling of first-time offenders that promotes future conformity to legal and communal laws, so that very few first-time delinquents go on to the second, third, or subsequent delinquent acts. We are not certain why this is, because we have not researched the effectiveness of the system, but we do know that the system functions well.

Because of the very low recidivism, as we will point out in a later chapter, our definition of the chronic offender has been modified from that used in the two Philadelphia birth cohorts, in which chronic delinquency was defined as the commission of five or more offenses before age eighteen. We had to change the definition in the 1970 Puerto Rico cohort, to include only three or more arrests, in order to have a sufficient number of cases for the analysis of chronic recidivism. This, however, is not just a statistical decision. The distribution of delinquency in the Puerto Rico cohort is concentrated at the lower end of the continuum, and thus, a lower threshold of chronic delinquency (three or more offenses) appears to be warranted on substantive grounds as well as statistical.

In short, Puerto Rico is blessed by a social system that produces or fosters a very low rate of juvenile delinquency, and by a juvenile justice system that seems to be functioning very productively to deter further delinquency beyond a first encounter with the police or the courts.

DELINQUENCY PREVALENCE IN THE 1970 COHORT

Through a variety of methods we have been able to identify and capture the delinquency data for a cohort of persons, born in 1970, and resident in three areas of Puerto Rico. The layout of cohort subjects by the three police districts is given in Table 2.2.

TABLE 2.2   Distribution of 1970 Cohort Subjects by District and Sex

District	Male	Female	Both
San Juan	3,605	3,530	7,135
	14.6%	14.3%	28.9%
Carolina	3,371	3,277	6,648
	13.7%	13.3%	26.9%
Bayamon	5,476	5,410	10,886
	22.2%	21.9%	44.1%
Total	12,452	12,217	24,669
	50.5%	49.5%	100.0%

Percentages are of total cases.

Table 2.2 indicates that the 1970 cohort consists of 24,669 subjects. The cohort breakdown by sex reflects a very even distribution, with about 51 percent males and 49 percent females. By area the data show that the largest percentage of subjects come from Bayamon (44 percent), followed by San Juan (29 percent), and then last by Carolina (27 percent).

Because we have subject data by sex we have been able to compute population-based offender and/or offense rates in our analyses that include subject's sex. This is not possible, however, for color categories because we have color data only for delinquents not for cohort subjects.

We are aware that most Puerto Ricans have the perception that racial discrimination, bias, or prejudice, have virtually disappeared from the island. Most public officials make proud assertions about the absence of discrimination, and there is ample evidence that these assertions are reasonably correct.

The tables and text in which we refer to color are based on the classification used by the police for identifying and investigating purposes. This same color classification, which has no physical anthropological validity, is transmitted to the juvenile and criminal court systems. As authors of this report, we did not create this classification of color categories; we have only accepted what we received from the police. The data we have collected and analyzed suggest differences in the commission of delinquency, and differences in the responses to juveniles by the police and the courts.

The most basic measure surrounding delinquency concerns the proportion of a subject population that has had official contact with the justice system. This measure is generally referred to as <u>prevalence</u>.

Before discussing the various analyses of prevalence, it is instructive to show the breakdown of delinquency by the two prime demographic variables of sex and color. These data are given in Table 2.3. These data indicate that the vast majority of delinquents in this study are males (83 percent) compared to females (17 percent). The data further show that more delinquents are white (54 percent) than either of the other color groups--trigueño (38 percent) and nonwhite (8 percent).

Table 2.4 presents the delinquency prevalence data by sex, based on cohort subjects as the denominator. These results indicate that males (11 percent) are about five times more likely than are females (2 percent) to be designated as delinquent. The male to female ratio (based on percentages) is lowest for one-time offenders (3.6:1) and is highest for recidivists (12:1). Thus, males are more likely to be recorded as delinquent in the first place, and as the frequency level of delinquency increases, the male versus female differential increases as well.

Table 2.5 is similar to Table 2.4, but instead of basing the percentages on the number of subjects, the data show the sex breakdown of the various delinquency status categories with the delinquent subset as the base.

These data clearly point out the sex differences in delinquency in this cohort.

TABLE 2.3   Distribution of 1970 Cohort Delinquents
            By Color and Sex

COLOR OF OFFENDER

Sex of Offender	Nonwhite	Trigueño	White	All
Male	116	540	748	1,404
	6.9%	31.9%	44.3%	83.1%
Female	19	95	171	285
	1.1%	5.6%	10.1%	16.9%
Both Sexes	135	635	919	1,689
	8.0%	37.6%	54.4%	100.0%

Percentages are of total cases.

TABLE 2.4   Number and Percentage (of Total Cohort) of
            Delinquents by Frequency Category and Sex

SEX

Category	Male	Female	Both
Subjects	12,452	12,217	24,669
Delinquents	1,404	285	1,689
	11.3	2.3	6.8
One-time	1,033	255	1,288
	8.3	2.1	5.2
Recidivists	371	30	401
(2 or more offenses)	3.0	.25	1.6
Non-chronic recidivists	211	20	231
(2 offenses)	1.7	.16	.94
Chronic recidivists	160	10	170
(3 or more offenses)	1.3	.08	.69

Percentages are of total cases.

Table 2.5 first shows that for both sexes the one-time offender category is predominant, with 74 percent of males and 90 percent of females being classified as having had only one official delinquent act. Most crucial, however, is that male delinquents are about twice as likely to be two-time recidivists (15 percent vs. 7 percent) and, while 11 percent of the male delinquents are chronic recidivists who have at least three crimes, females show only ten chronic delinquents, or 3.5 percent of all the delinquent females. Thus, even when females recidivate, they are less likely to reach the important stage of the very frequent violations of the law associated with the habitual offender.

TABLE 2.5 Number and Percentage (of Specific Delinquent Group) of Delinquents by Frequency Category and Sex

	SEX		
Delinquency Category	Male	Female	Both
Delinquents	1,404	285	1,689
One-time	1,033	255	1,288
	73.6	89.5	76.3
Two-time	211	20	231
	15.0	7.0	13.7
Three or more	160	10	170
	11.4	3.5	10.0
Recidivists	371	30	401
Two-time	211	20	231
	56.9	66.7	57.6
Three or more	160	10	170
	43.1	33.3	42.4

Percentages are column percents of the number of delinquents or recidivists.

Delinquency in Puerto Rico

In Table 2.6 we turn to a color breakdown of delinquency categories. These data once again show that the vast majority of delinquents commit only one offense regardless of color. Seventy-two percent of nonwhite and trigueño delinquents were one-time offenders, while slightly more, 79 percent of white delinquents committed just one offense. There is a slight color effect, however, for chronic delinquency, where nonwhites (16 percent) are more likely to be chronic recidivists than are either trigueños (11 percent) or whites (9 percent). This nonwhite effect is also evident among recidivists as a group, where about 55 percent are chronic compared to about 40 percent for trigueños and whites.

TABLE 2.6 Number and Percentage (of Specific Delinquent Group) of Delinquents by Frequency Category and Color

Delinquency Category	COLOR OF OFFENDER			
	Nonwhite	Trigueño	White	All
<u>Delinquents</u>	135	635	919	1,689
	---	---	---	---
One-time	97	462	729	1,288
	72.0	72.8	79.3	76.3
Two-time	17	103	111	231
	12.6	16.2	12.1	13.7
Three or more	21	70	79	170
	15.6	11.0	8.6	10.1
<u>Recidivists</u>	38	173	190	401
	--	---	---	--
Two-time	17	103	111	231
	44.7	59.5	58.4	57.6
Three or more	21	70	79	170
	55.3	40.5	41.6	42.4

Percentages are column percents of the number of delinquents or recidivists.

In order to ensure that the color and sex effects in the data are genuine, we have reported the color data

Prevalence

separately by sex categories. These results are displayed in Tables 2.7 and 2.8.

The data for males in Table 2.7 confirm that recidivist delinquency is more prevalent among nonwhites. This group is more likely to be chronic delinquent recidivists (17 percent) than are either trigueños (13 percent) or whites (10 percent). It is especially noteworthy that even when looking at the recidivist subset separately, nonwhites (56 percent) are much more likely to be the chronic offender type than are trigueños (42 percent) or whites (42 percent).

TABLE 2.7 Number and Percentage (of Specific Delinquent Group) of Male Delinquents by Frequency Category and Color

MALES

Delinquency Category	Color of Offender			
	Nonwhite	Trigueño	White	All
Delinquents	116	540	748	1,404
	---	---	---	---
One-time	82	376	575	1,033
	70.7	69.6	76.9	74.0
Two-time	15	96	100	211
	12.9	17.8	13.4	15.0
Three or more	19	68	73	160
	16.4	12.6	9.8	11.4
Recidivists	34	164	190	371
	--	---	---	--
Two-time	15	96	100	211
	44.1	58.5	52.6	56.9
Three or more	19	68	73	160
	55.9	41.5	38.4	43.1

Percentages are column percents of the number of delinquents or recidivists.

Delinquency in Puerto Rico

The data for females shown in Table 2.8 are as informative in this context of recidivism because, despite the very small number of female recidivists, nonwhites show a much higher percentage of recidivists. For nonwhites, 21 percent were recidivists (and one-half of these were chronic) compared to about a ten percent recidivism chance for trigueños and whites.

TABLE 2.8 Number and Percentage (of Specific Delinquent Group) of Female Delinquents by Frequency Category and Color

FEMALES

Delinquency Category	Color of Offender			
	Nonwhite	Trigueño	White	All
<u>Delinquents</u>	19	95	171	285
One-time	15	86	154	255
	79.0	90.5	90.1	89.5
Two-time	2	7	11	20
	10.5	7.4	6.4	7.0
Three or more	2	2	6	10
	10.5	2.1	3.5	3.5
<u>Recidivists</u>	4	9	17	30
Two-time	2	7	11	20
	50.0	77.8	64.7	66.7
Three or more	2	2	6	10
	50.0	22.2	35.3	33.3

Percentages are column percents of the number of delinquents or recidivists.

In Table 2.9 we report the delinquency prevalence data by the three areas of Puerto Rico that are included in the study. These results very clearly indicate that there are no significant differences across areas in the delinquency status categories. For example, about three-quarters of the delinquents in all areas are one-time

Prevalence

offenders and about 10 percent are chronic recidivists (three or more offenses).

It is extremely important that the areas are so very much alike in terms of the three delinquency status categories. This means that in our later analyses we will not have to be concerned that differences that we find in our results are due to the particular area in which a delinquent resides.

TABLE 2.9 Number and Percentage (of Specific Delinquent Group) of Delinquents by Frequency Category and Jurisdiction

Delinquency Category	JURISDICTION			
	Bayamon	Carolina	San Juan	All
Delinquents	734	467	488	1,689
	---	---	---	---
One-time	547	361	380	1,288
	74.5	77.3	77.8	76.3
Two-time	114	58	59	231
	15.5	12.4	12.1	13.7
Three or more	73	48	49	170
	9.9	10.3	10.0	10.1
Recidivists	187	106	108	401
	--	---	---	--
Two-time	114	58	59	231
	60.9	54.7	54.6	57.6
Three or more	73	48	49	170
	39.0	45.3	45.4	42.4

Percentages are column percents of the number of delinquents or recidivists.

We had available several offender-based variables relating to residence and schooling. We present these data by sex, color, and delinquency category in Tables 2.10 through 2.24.

For males, Table 2.10 shows that public residence is related to recidivism status. About 21 percent of public delinquents are two-time offenders and about 17 percent

29

are chronic. These proportions are much higher than those for either barrio or private-residence delinquents. Table 2.10 also shows that urban area is related to a higher chance of nonchronic recidivism (15 percent) and chronic recidivism (12 percent) than is rural area (13 percent and 9 percent).

TABLE 2.10 Number and Percentage of Male Delinquents by Frequency Category, Type, and Location of Residence

MALES

Residence	Delinquency Category			
	One-time	Two-time	3 or more	All
Barrio	351	61	36	448
	78.4	13.6	8.0	---
Private	494	84	69	647
	76.3	12.9	10.7	---
Public	149	49	39	237
	62.9	20.7	16.4	---
Rural	291	48	32	371
	78.5	12.9	8.6	---
Urban	703	145	112	960
	73.2	15.1	11.7	---

Percentages are row percents of the total number of delinquents in each row category.

For females, Table 2.11 shows that public residence is again related to two-time recidivism (13 percent), but barrio has the highest percentage of chronic recidivists (6 percent). Urban and rural areas, however, are not especially different in relation to recidivism, as both areas have about the same percentage of two and three-time offenders.

A very similar picture emerges for the color categories as well (see Tables 2.12, 2.13, 2.14). For all three color groups a higher proportion of delinquents are recorded as two-time recidivists if they are public residents as compared to barrio or private. The proportion is highest among nonwhites with 23.7 percent two-time delinquents, followed by trigueño (21.2 percent) and whites (15.3 percent). For chronic recidivists, the

TABLE 2.11 Number and Percentage of Female Delinquents by Frequency Category, Type, and Location of Residence

FEMALES

Residence	Delinquency Category			
	One-time	Two-time	3 or more	All
Barrio	75	9	5	89
	84.3	10.1	5.6	--
Private	119	3	2	124
	95.9	2.4	1.6	--
Public	47	7	2	56
	83.9	12.5	3.6	--
Rural	79	7	3	89
	88.7	7.9	3.4	--
Urban	163	12	6	181
	90.1	6.6	3.3	--

Percentages are row percents of the total number of delinquents in each row category.

TABLE 2.12 Number and Percentage of Nonwhite Delinquents by Frequency Category, Type, and Location of Residence

NONWHITE

Residence	Delinquency Category			
	One-time	Two-time	3 or more	All
Barrio	35	4	7	46
	76.1	8.7	15.2	--
Private	35	3	9	47
	74.5	6.4	19.2	--
Public	26	9	3	38
	68.4	23.7	7.9	--
Rural	26	4	5	35
	74.3	11.4	14.3	--
Urban	70	12	14	96
	72.9	12.5	14.6	--

Percentages are row percents of the total number of delinquents in each row category.

TABLE 2.13 Number and Percentage of Trigueño Delinquents by Frequency Category, Type, and Location of Residence

TRIGUEÑO

Residence	Delinquency Category			
	One-time	Two-time	3 or more	All
Barrio	180	33	22	235
	76.6	14.0	9.4	--
Private	175	36	22	233
	75.1	15.5	9.4	--
Public	89	29	19	137
	64.9	21.2	13.9	--
Rural	157	25	18	200
	78.5	12.5	9.0	--
Urban	286	72	45	403
	70.9	17.9	11.2	--

Percentages are row percents of the total number of delinquents in each row category.

TABLE 2.14 Number and Percentage of White Delinquents by Frequency Category, Type, and Location of Residence

WHITE

Residence	Delinquency Category			
	One-time	Two-time	3 or more	All
Barrio	211	33	12	256
	82.4	12.9	4.7	--
Private	403	48	40	491
	82.1	9.8	8.2	--
Public	81	18	19	118
	68.6	15.3	16.1	--
Rural	187	26	12	225
	83.1	11.6	5.3	--
Urban	510	73	59	642
	79.4	11.4	9.2	--

Percentages are row percents of the total number of delinquents in each row category.

public delinquents, however, are the least likely to have committed three or more offenses (7.9 percent) compared to private (19.2 percent) and barrio (15.2). For trigueño (13.9 percent) and white (16.1 percent), the public category shows the highest percentage of three-time offenders.

Concerning urban area, it appears that only for trigueño delinquents does this variable have an effect on recidivism. For trigueño delinquents, 17.9 percent were two-time recidivists and 11 percent were three-time recidivists compared to smaller proportions for rural offenders. Among nonwhites the percentages are very similar between rural and urban delinquents. For whites there is no difference between rural and urban delinquents for two-time recidivism, but there is a large difference at the chronic level where 9.2 percent of urban delinquents compared to 5.3 percent of rural delinquents were chronic recidivists.

In general, therefore, delinquent recidivists are more likely to occupy public-type residences and live in urban as compared to rural areas. This is the case regardless of sex or color of delinquent.

The school data given in Tables 2.15 to 2.19 reveal some distinct differences. For both males and females, Tables 2.15 and 2.16 report that public school delinquents are much more likely than either type of private school delinquents to be recidivists and especially chronic recidivists. For males the percentages are 15.3 and 11.9, while for females the proportions are 8.1 and 4.1. Neither type of private school delinquent approaches these figures for either males or females. Similarly, the "not in school" delinquents are much more likely to be recidivists than in school offenders. For males, not in school delinquents are about twice as likely to be chronic recidivists than those in school. For females the ratio is over 3 to 1.

Tables 2.17, 2.18, and 2.19 show generally, that these same school effects hold for color categories as well, but not as strongly. For nonwhites (Table 2.17) all but one offender was in public school so school type could not have an effect. Concerning attendance status, the data show that 13 percent of the delinquents were not in school compared to 15 percent in school.

For trigueño delinquents (Table 2.18) public school was once again the most frequent school type by far, and this type contained the highest proportion of chronic recidivists (11 percent). The attendance data show a strong result with about 14 percent of the not in school group being chronic and 22 percent being two-timers

TABLE 2.15 Number and Percentage of Male Delinquents by Frequency Category, Type of School, and Attendance Status

MALES

School	Delinquency Category			
	One-time	Two-time	3 or more	All
Public	855	180	140	1,175
	72.8	15.3	11.9	--
Private Denominational	58	6	3	67
	86.6	8.9	4.5	--
Private Nondenominational	24	3	1	28
	85.7	10.7	3.6	--
Not in school	228	67	60	355
	64.2	18.9	16.9	--
In school	764	126	82	972
	78.6	12.9	8.4	--

Percentages are row percents of the total number of delinquents in each row category.

TABLE 2.16 Number and Percentage of Female Delinquents by Frequency Category, Type of School, and Attendance Status

FEMALES

School	Delinquency Category			
	One-time	Two-time	3 or more	All
Public	196	18	9	223
	87.8	8.1	4.1	--
Private Denominational	21	1	0	22
	95.5	4.5	0.0	--
Private Nondenominational	9	0	0	9
	100.0	0.0	0.0	--
Not in school	56	4	5	65
	86.2	6.2	7.7	--
In school	188	15	4	207
	90.8	7.3	1.9	--

Percentages are row percents of the total number of delinquents in each row category.

TABLE 2.17 Number and Percentage of Nonwhite Delinquents by Frequency Category, Type of School, and Attendance Status

	NONWHITE Delinquency Category			
School	One-time	Two-time	3 or more	All
Public	90 72.0	16 12.8	19 15.2	125 --
Private Denominational	0 0.0	0 0.0	0 0.0	0 --
Private Nondenominational	1 100.0	0 0.0	0 0.0	1 --
Not in School	33 84.6	1 2.6	5 12.8	39 --
In school	62 68.1	15 16.5	14 15.4	91 --

Percentages are row percents of the total number of delinquents in each row category.

TABLE 2.18 Number and Percentage of Trigueño Delinquents by Frequency Category, Type of School, and Attendance Status

	TRIGUEÑO Delinquency Category			
School	One-time	Two-time	3 or more	All
Public	399 72.6	90 16.7	61 11.1	550 --
Private Denominational	14 77.8	3 16.7	1 5.6	18 --
Private Nondenominational	6 75.0	2 25.0	0 0.0	8 --
Not in School	113 64.6	38 21.7	24 13.7	175 --
In school	327 77.3	60 14.2	36 8.5	423 --

Percentages are row percents of the total number of delinquents in each row category.

Delinquency in Puerto Rico

compared to 9 percent chronic and 14 percent two-timers for in school offenders.

The results for whites (Table 2.19) are very indicative of the school effects. Public offenders (9.6 percent) are at least twice as likely as either private denominational (2.8 percent) or private nondenominational (3.6 percent) to be chronic. The same ratio obtains for nonchronic recidivism as well. The effect of being in school is similarly strong. About 18 percent of the not in school group are chronic compared to 5 percent of the in school delinquents, while 16 percent of the former and 10 percent of the latter are two-time offenders.

TABLE 2.19 Number and Percentage of White Delinquents by Frequency Category, Type of School, and Attendance Status

WHITE

School	Delinquency Category			
	One-time	Two-time	3 or more	All
Public	560	92	69	721
	77.7	12.8	9.6	--
Private Denominational	65	4	2	71
	91.6	5.6	2.8	--
Private Nondenominational	26	1	1	28
	92.9	3.6	3.6	--
Not in School	138	32	36	206
	66.9	15.5	17.5	--
In school	563	66	36	665
	84.7	9.9	5.4	--

Percentages are row percents of the total number of delinquents in each row category.

Tables 2.20 to 2.24 report delinquency status categories by highest grade attained. Clearly, these data indicate that as grade attained increases, the percentage of chronic delinquents decreases. For example, among males (Table 2.20) about 39 percent of the offenders with less than a 4th grade education are chronic, but this percentage decreases substantially to 9.1 percent at the twelfth grade level. Similarly, 50 percent of the females (Table 2.21) with the lowest education level are chronic, but chronic offending decreases even more dramatically to 3.3 percent at the

TABLE 2.20 Number and Percentage of Male Delinquents by Frequency Category and Highest Grade Attained

MALES

Grade	Delinquency Category		
	One-time	Two-time	3 or more
1 - 3	32	12	28
	44.4	16.7	38.9
4 - 6	172	95	242
	33.8	18.7	47.5
7	149	74	99
	46.3	22.9	30.7
8	138	83	73
	46.9	28.2	24.8
9	195	69	92
	54.8	19.4	25.8
10	178	40	38
	69.5	15.6	14.8
11	105	15	12
	79.5	11.4	9.1
12	9	5	
	64.3	35.7	

Percentages are row percents of the total number of delinquents in each grade.

TABLE 2.21 Number and Percentage of Female Delinquents by Frequency Category and Highest Grade Attained

FEMALES

Grade	Delinquency Category		
	One-time	Two-time	3 or more
1 - 3	3		3
	50.0		50.0
4 - 6	29	6	2
	78.4	16.2	5.4
7	36	7	7
	72.0	14.0	14.0
8	43	6	6
	78.2	10.9	10.9
9	46	11	7
	71.9	17.2	10.9
10	55	4	2
	90.2	6.6	3.3
11	24	4	
	85.7	14.3	
12	5		
	100.0		

Percentages are row percents of the total number of delinquents in each grade.

tenth grade level, and no female chronics were observed at either the eleventh or twelfth grade levels.

Tables 2.22, 2.23, and 2.24 repeat this general pattern for the three color groups. Chronic delinquency decreases for nonwhites from 60 percent for the grade 1 to 3 category to 9 percent at grade 10 (with no chronics at grades 11 or 12). Among trigueño delinquents the decrease is present but is not as substantial as chronic delinquents decline from 36 percent to about 18 percent (none at grade 12). For whites the pattern is about the same with about 38 percent chronics at the lowest grade level and 3 percent at the highest.

TABLE 2.22 Number and Percentage of Nonwhite Delinquents by Frequency Category and Highest Grade Attained

NONWHITE

Grade	Delinquency Category		
	One-time	Two-time	3 or more
1 - 3	1	3	6
	10.0	30.0	60.0
4 - 6	23	7	43
	31.5	9.6	58.9
7	22	8	12
	52.4	19.0	28.6
8	16	2	3
	76.2	9.5	14.3
9	17	8	13
	44.7	21.1	34.2
10	9	1	1
	81.8	9.1	9.1
11	6	4	
	60.0	40.0	
12	1		
	100.0		

Percentages are row percents of the total number of delinquents in each grade.

In Tables 2.25 to 2.29 we turn to the distribution of offender types by household composition. That is, these data reflect the range of adult persons with whom the delinquents are living, persons that can provide socialization experiences, discipline, and social control in the home environment.

TABLE 2.23 Number and Percentage of Trigueño Delinquents by Frequency Category and Highest Grade Attained

TRIGUEÑO
Delinquency Category

Grade	One-time	Two-time	3 or more
1 - 3	17	6	13
	47.2	16.7	36.1
4 - 6	90	46	98
	38.5	19.7	41.9
7	78	33	44
	50.3	21.3	28.4
8	77	42	33
	50.7	27.6	21.7
9	75	44	45
	45.7	26.8	27.4
10	59	17	11
	67.8	19.5	12.6
11	38	4	9
	74.5	7.8	17.6
12	1	2	
	33.3	66.7	

Percentages are row percents of the total number of delinquents in each grade.

TABLE 2.24 Number and Percentage of White Delinquents by Frequency Category and Highest Grade Attained

White
Delinquency Category

Grade	One-time	Two-time	3 or more
1 - 3	17	3	12
	53.1	9.4	37.5
4 - 6	88	48	103
	36.8	20.1	43.1
7	85	40	50
	48.6	22.9	28.6
8	88	45	43
	50.0	25.6	24.4
9	149	28	41
	68.3	12.8	18.8
10	165	26	28
	75.3	11.9	12.8
11	85	11	3
	85.9	11.1	3.0
12	12	3	
	80.0	20.0	

Percentages are row percents of the total number of delinquents in each grade.

Delinquency in Puerto Rico

Table 2.25 indicates that chronic male delinquents are much less likely (26 percent) than either one-time (49 percent) or two-time (36 percent) delinquents to be living with their fathers. Similarly, they are less likely to be living in a household in which their mothers are present. Not surprisingly, about 7 percent of chronic male delinquents were in institutions compared to none of the one-time offenders and less than 1 percent of two-time offenders.

TABLE 2.25 Number and Percentage of Male Delinquents by Household Members

MALES

Members	Delinquency Category		
	One-time	Two-time	3 or more
Father	510	153	185
	49.4	36.3	26.2
Mother	874	344	495
	84.6	81.5	70.1
Stepfather	120	64	114
	11.6	15.2	16.1
Stepmother	18	2	10
	1.7	.5	1.4
Other Relative	56	41	76
	5.4	9.7	10.8
Guardian	4		1
	.4		.1
Foster Parents	3		5
	.3		.7
Spouse	5	5	10
	.5	1.2	1.4
Institution		4	51
		.9	7.2

Percentages are column percents of delinquents in each family member category.

Table 2.26 shows similar data for females. Female delinquents are very likely to be living with their mothers regardless of their offender status. Chronic delinquents are less likely to be living with their fathers (27.3%) and are slightly more likely to be living with stepfathers (30.3%). Few females are living with other relatives or in a situation away from home.

Prevalence

TABLE 2.26 Number and Percentage of Female Delinquents by Household Members

FEMALES
Delinquency Category

Members	One-time	Two-time	3 or more
Father	92	14	9
	36.1	35.0	27.3
Mother	208	37	28
	81.6	92.5	84.8
Stepfather	30	6	10
	11.8	15.0	30.3
Stepmother			
Other Relative	13	2	2
	5.1	5.0	6.1
Guardian	1		
	.4		
Foster Parents			
Spouse	14	1	
	5.5	2.5	
Institution	4		2
	1.6		6.1

Percentages are column percents of delinquents in each family member category.

Tables 2.27, 2.28, and 2.29 report household data by color. These results show color differences. For nonwhites, chronic offenders are the most likely to be living with their father and the least likely to be living with their mother. For both trigueño and white delinquents, the more familiar pattern emerges with the chronic delinquent being less likely to be living with their mother than either the one-time or two-time offender. For all three colors the chronic delinquent as expected is very much more likely to be in an institution.

PREVALENCE SUMMARY

The results concerning the prevalence of delinquency in the 1970 cohort reveal several findings that emerged repeatedly by sex and color.

First, males are five times more likely than females to be delinquent, and males are 12 times more likely than females to be recidivist offenders. On the other hand,

Delinquency in Puerto Rico

females have a very high percentage of one-time offenders, 90 percent, compared to males (74 percent), thus indicating that even when females commit delinquent acts, they are very likely to do so only once. The results by color show that nonwhites and trigueños are about equally likely to be recidivists but nonwhites show a higher proportion of chronic recidivists.

Second, there are a few social context variables that were related to prevalence regardless of sex or color. Delinquents from public type residences were more likely to be recidivists. Urban area was also significantly related to recidivism for males. Concerning the school factors, the public school and the "not in school" groups were more highly recidivist compared to private school and "in school" delinquents. This was true for sex and color groups. Also, highest grade achieved varied inversely with offender status, that is, the more offenses then the fewer the number of years of school completed.

TABLE 2.27 Number and Percentage of Nonwhite Delinquents by Household Members

NONWHITE

Members	Delinquency Category		
	One-time	Two-time	3 or more
Father	33	10	34
	34.0	29.4	36.9
Mother	85	31	67
	87.6	91.2	72.8
Stepfather	19	5	12
	19.6	14.7	13.0
Stepmother	1		
	1.0		
Other Relative	7	1	6
	7.2	2.9	6.5
Guardian	1		
	1.0		
Foster Parents			
Spouse	2		4
	2.1		4.3
Institution		1	9
		2.9	9.8

Percentages are column percents of delinquents in each family member category.

TABLE 2.28 Number and Percentage of Trigueño Delinquents by Household Members

TRIGUEÑO Delinquency Category

Members	One-time	Two-time	3 or more
Father	202	67	72
	43.7	32.5	22.2
Mother	379	174	218
	82.0	84.5	67.1
Stepfather	64	35	39
	13.9	16.9	12.0
Stepmother	4	2	4
	.9	.9	1.2
Other Relative	21	21	40
	4.5	10.2	12.3
Guardian	3		
	.6		
Foster Parents	2		2
	.4		.6
Spouse	8		2
	1.7		.6
Institution	2	2	24
	.4	.9	7.4

Percentages are column percents of delinquents in each family member category.

TABLE 2.29 Number and Percentage of White Delinquents by Household Members

WHITE Delinquency Category

Members	One-time	Two-time	3 or more
Father	367	90	88
	50.3	40.5	27.3
Mother	618	176	238
	84.8	79.3	73.9
Stepfather	67	30	73
	9.2	13.5	22.7
Stepmother	13		6
	1.8		1.9
Other Relative	41	21	32
	5.6	9.5	9.9
Guardian	1		1
	.1		.3
Foster Parents	1		3
	.1		.9
Spouse	9	6	4
	1.2	2.7	1.2
Institution	2	1	20
	.3	.5	6.2

Percentages are column percents of delinquents in each family member category.

3
Incidence

After considering the issue of the proportion of persons in a population that are delinquents and the demographic differences that can be uncovered, the next basic issue in a cohort study of delinquency concerns the extent and character of the delinquency offenses. This issue focusing on offense characteristics rather than offenders has two parts: a) the incidence or frequency of delinquency, and b) the severity or seriousness (the character) of the delinquent acts themselves. Thus, we report below analyses that concern the incidence of delinquency in the 1970 cohort, the severity of these crimes, and special issues surrounding delinquent behaviors such as violence, weapons, and drugs.

INCIDENCE AND SEVERITY

Table 3.1 presents, by sex category, the frequency, percent, and offense rate (per one thousand subjects) of select offenses in the Puerto Rican crime code. These data reflect very distinct sex differences in the kinds of delinquency committed in our 1970 cohort.
Males predominate in the most serious acts of delinquency, especially the violent crimes. The first seven offense types listed are known as Federal Bureau of Investigation (FBI) Uniform Crime Report (UCR) index crimes, and for males these offenses constitute about 39 percent of all the offenses, while for females these very serious crimes comprise about 24 percent of the total offenses. The only two serious offenses for which females are at all close to or exceed males are simple assault (female = 24.1 percent vs. male = 7.8 percent)

TABLE 3.1 Number, Percent, and Rate (per thousand) of Select Offenses by Sex

Offense	Male N	Male %	Male Rate	Females N	Females %	Females Rate	Both N	Both %	Both Rate
Homicide, Mansl., Att. Homicide	36	1.7	2.9	3	.91	.24	39	1.6	1.6
Rape	5	.23	.40	-	---	---	5	.20	.20
Robbery	170	7.9	13.6	9	2.7	.74	179	7.2	7.2
Agg. Assault	94	4.3	7.5	19	5.8	1.5	113	4.5	4.5
Burglary	263	12.2	21.1	12	3.7	.98	275	11.0	11.1
Larceny	213	9.8	17.1	36	10.9	2.9	249	10.0	10.1
Auto Theft	51	2.4	4.1	--	----	---	51	2.0	2.1
Assault	170	7.8	13.6	79	24.1	6.3	249	10.0	10.1
R. S. P.	113	5.1	9.1	2	.61	.16	113	4.5	4.6
Mischief	144	6.7	11.6	8	2.4	.65	152	6.1	6.2
Weapons	63	2.9	5.0	7	2.1	.57	70	2.8	2.8
Narcotics	154	7.1	12.3	12	3.7	.98	166	6.7	6.7
Traffic	316	14.6	23.4	54	16.4	4.4	370	14.9	14.9
Breach of Peace	95	4.4	7.6	48	14.6	3.9	143	5.7	5.7
Total Above	1,887	87.3	151.5	289	88.1	23.6	2,176	87.4	88.2
Other crimes	274	12.7	22.0	39	11.9	3.2	313	12.6	12.7
Grand Total	2,161	----	173.5	328	---	26.8	2,489	---	100.9

Percentages are column percents.

TABLE 3.2 Number and Percent of Select Offenses by Color

Offense	Nonwhite N	Nonwhite %	Trigueño N	Trigueño %	White N	White %
Homicide, Mansl., & Att. Homicide	6	2.7	14	1.4	19	1.5
Rape	0	0.0	3	0.3	2	.16
Robbery	23	10.3	84	8.5	72	5.7
Agg. Assault	11	4.9	41	4.1	61	4.8
Burglary	34	15.3	116	11.7	125	9.8
Larceny	22	9.9	101	10.2	126	9.9
Auto Theft	2	.90	15	1.5	34	2.7
Assault	25	11.2	90	9.1	124	9.7
Receive Stolen Prop.	10	4.5	50	5.0	53	4.2
Mischief	9	4.0	56	5.6	87	6.8
Weapons	3	1.4	31	3.1	36	2.8
Narcotics	13	5.8	85	8.6	68	5.3
Traffic	16	7.2	118	11.9	236	18.5
Breach of Peace	12	5.4	56	5.6	75	5.9
Total Above	186	83.4	860	86.7	1,118	87.8
Other crimes	37	16.6	133	13.3	155	12.2
Grand Total	223	----	993	----	1,273	----

and larceny (female = 10.9 percent vs. male = 9.8 percent).

Table 3.1 also shows extensive sex differences for other crimes as well. For example, males as opposed to females are 8 times more likely to commit the offense of receiving stolen property (5.1% vs, .61%), are close to three times more likely to commit mischief (6.76% vs. 2.4%), and are about twice as likely to commit a drug offense (7.1% vs. 3.7%). Males are only slightly more likely to use weapons and to breach the peace.

Table 3.2 reports crime code data by frequency, percent, and color. These results show that 44 percent of nonwhite offenses are serious UCR index crimes as compared to 36 percent for trigueños and 32 percent for whites. Beyond these serious offense differences, the offense data are not very dissimilar by color. Nonwhites are most likely to commit burglary, assault and robbery; whites are most likely to commit mischief; and trigueños are slightly more likely to receive stolen property and commit drug offenses.

In Table 3.3 we report data concerning the number of offenders and offenses, and the mean number by sex for select offense groupings that represent meaningful categories. These data add to our understanding gained above that males are not only more likely to be delinquent but they are more likely to repeat the serious offenses. With only a few exceptions, the average number of offenses committed by males is higher than that for females regardless of offense type. Males predominate the most among the serious offenses.

Tables 3.4 and 3.5 repeat this analysis for color categories. These data again confirm our earlier finding that nonwhites are slightly more delinquent than are trigueños or whites. The mean number of offenses are usually slightly higher for nonwhites than for the other two color groups. But, the mean scores are not very divergent thus indicating the similar extent of delinquency across the color groups.

One of the components of delinquency that will concern us in our severity scoring classification of the crimes in the 1970 cohort involves the extent of property value stolen or damaged in theft, robbery, or burglary crimes, for example. Our procedure for scoring a crime will add seriousness weights as the dollar value increases. In Tables 3.6 to 3.9 we report these dollar values by sex and color.

Table 3.6 indicates that male theft offenses consistently involve greater dollar values than do those for females. Twice as many female offenses (43 percent) involve thefts of less than $100 compared to males (22 percent). On the other hand, 30 percent of male offenses

TABLE 3.3 Number of Offenders and Offenses and Mean Number of Offenses for Select Crimes by Sex

	Males			Females		
	Offender	Offenses	Mean	Offender	Offenses	Mean
All Offenses	1,404	2,161	1.5	285	328	1.2
UCR Index	564	832	1.5	73	79	1.1
UCR Nonindex	1,033	1,329	1.3	222	249	1.1
Homicide, Rape, Agg. Assault	128	135	1.1	21	22	1.0
Robbery	128	170	1.3	8	9	1.1
Burglary	193	263	1.4	11	12	1.1
Theft and Auto theft	224	264	1.2	36	36	1.0
Injury	286	305	1.1	105	111	1.1
Theft	343	457	1.3	38	40	1.1
Damage	263	284	1.1	30	30	1.0
Combination	205	253	1.2	21	22	1.0
Nonindex	678	862	1.3	111	125	1.1

TABLE 3.4 Number of Offenders and Offenses and Mean Number of Offenses for Select Crimes by Color

	Nonwhite			Trigueño		
	Offender	Offenses	Mean	Offender	Offenses	Mean
All Offenses	135	223	1.7	635	993	1.6
UCR Index	62	98	1.6	247	374	1.5
UCR Nonindex	96	125	1.3	470	619	1.3
Homicide, Rape, Agg. Assault	15	17	1.1	55	58	1.1
Robbery	16	23	1.4	57	84	1.5
Burglary	22	34	1.5	78	116	1.5
Theft and Auto theft	22	24	1.1	100	116	1.2
Injury	40	45	1.1	138	145	1.1
Theft	34	44	1.3	156	216	1.4
Damage	20	21	1.1	95	104	1.1
Combination	28	42	1.5	89	112	1.3
Nonindex	56	71	1.3	317	416	1.3

Incidence

TABLE 3.5   Number of Offenders and Offenses and Mean
            Number of Offenses for Select Crimes by Color

	White		
	Offender	Offenses	Mean
All Offenses	919	1273	1.4
UCR Index	328	439	1.3
UCR Nonindex	689	834	1.2
Murder, Rape, Agg. Assault	79	82	1.1
Robbery	63	72	1.1
Burglary	104	125	1.2
Theft and Auto theft	138	160	1.2
Injury	213	226	1.1
Theft	191	237	1.2
Damage	178	189	1.1
Combination	109	121	1.1
Nonindex	416	500	1.2

show dollar theft losses of $1,000 or above compared to about 21 percent of female thefts. The median dollar value stolen for males ($320) is more than twice that for females ($153), while the mean values indicate about the same ($1,944 vs. $786). Table 3.7 shows that whites ($350) commit theft offenses with the highest median dollar loss value compared to trigueños ($300) and nonwhites ($210).

TABLE 3.6   Dollar Loss Value of Theft Offenses by Sex

Value	Males		Females		Both	
	N	%	N	%	N	%
L.T. 100	134	21.6	22	42.3	156	23.2
100 - 250	149	23.9	11	21.2	160	23.8
251 - 499	83	13.4	4	7.7	87	12.9
500 - 999	69	11.1	4	7.7	73	10.9
1,000 - 4,999	111	17.9	8	15.4	119	17.7
5,000 - 9,999	41	6.6	3	5.8	44	6.5
10,000 +	34	5.5	0	0.0	34	5.0
Total	621	---	52	---	673	--
Median value	$320		$153		$300	
Mean value	$1,944.2		$768.2		$1,853.4	

Percentages are column percents.

Delinquency in Puerto Rico

TABLE 3.7 Dollar Loss Value of Theft Offenses by Color

Value	Nonwhite N	%	Trigueño N	%	White N	%
L.T. 100	22	27.5	70	23.6	64	21.5
100 - 250	21	26.3	76	25.7	63	21.2
251 - 499	9	11.3	36	12.2	42	14.1
500 - 999	8	10.0	28	9.5	37	12.5
1,000 - 4,999	11	13.8	53	17.9	55	18.5
5,000 - 9,999	2	2.5	20	6.8	22	7.4
10,000 +	7	8.8	13	4.4	14	4.7
Total	80	---	296	---	297	--
Median value	$210		$300		$350	
Mean value	$2,325.8		$1,779.5		$1,799.7	

Percentages are column percents.

Table 3.8 turns to the dollar loss that is caused in damage offenses. Here we see, surprisingly, that females damage a higher dollar value than do males. This result is obtained whether the comparison is mean value ($937.7 vs. $444.8) or medians ($350 vs. $100). Damage offenses are much less frequent among females, but it is significant that females have the higher value nonetheless.

Table 3.9 again shows the more serious dollar losses inflicted by whites. As they were for theft, white damage offenses have a higher median dollar value ($150) than do the offenses of trigueños ($100) or nonwhites

TABLE 3.8 Dollar Loss Value of Damage Offenses by Sex

Value	Males N	%	Females N	%	Both N	%
L.T. 100	195	40.5	9	19.1	204	38.6
100 - 250	150	31.1	10	21.3	160	30.3
251 - 499	52	10.8	10	21.3	62	11.7
500 - 999	31	6.4	6	12.8	37	6.9
1,000 - 4,999	49	10.2	10	21.3	59	11.1
5,000 +	5	1.0	2	4.2	7	1.3
Total	482	---	47	---	529	---
Median value	$100		$350		$100	
Mean value	$444.8		$937.7		$488.6	

Percentages are column percents.

Incidence

($100). The mean scores similarly indicate that whites ($636.2) commit damage offenses that on average are more serious than those for nonwhites ($386.6) or trigueños ($296.7).

TABLE 3.9 Dollar Loss Value of Damage Offenses by Color

Value	Nonwhite		Trigueño		White	
	N	%	N	%	N	%
L.T. 100	20	44.4	86	43.7	98	34.1
100 - 250	15	33.3	56	28.4	89	31.1
251 - 499	5	11.1	18	9.1	39	13.6
500 - 999	1	2.2	19	9.6	17	5.9
1,000 - 4,999	4	8.9	18	9.1	37	12.9
5,000 or more	0	0.0	0	0.0	7	2.4
Total	45	---	197	---	287	---
Median value	$100		$100		$150	
Mean value	$386.6		$296.7		$636.2	

Percentages are column percents.

In addition to dollar value, our system for scoring the seriousness of offenses primarily involves injury components that are displayed in Table 3.10. These data indicate that few offenses involve multiple victims at the various injury levels, most offenses have only one injury victim. Minor-harm offenses involve 11 percent with one victim and about 1.5 percent with more than one victim. For offenses where treatment by a doctor is involved, about seven percent have one victim and about 1 percent have more than one. As we move to the most serious injury levels, about 1.6 percent have hospitalization and only one-half of one percent have the death of one victim. Also, all rape offenses have only one victim.

VIOLENT OFFENSES

In Tables 3.11 to 3.15 we focus on the most violent offenses in the study, the homicides, manslaughters, and attempted homicides. Our interest here concerns the demographic, delinquency status, and weapon use differences that the violent offenses exhibit.

Delinquency in Puerto Rico

TABLE 3.10   Components of Offense Seriousness

		Frequency Category			
Component	0	1	2	3	4
Number of Victims of Minor Harm	2,183 87.7	273 11.0	22 0.9	7 0.3	4 0.2
Number of Victims Treated & Discharged	2,296 92.2	167 6.7	19 0.8	5 0.2	2 0.1
Number of Victims Hospitalized	2,448 98.4	39 1.6	2 0.1		
Number of Victims Killed	2,475 99.4	13 0.5	1 0.1		
Number of Victims Raped	2,463 99.0	1 1.0			
Number of Vehicles Stolen	2,451 98.5	38 1.5			

Percentages are row percents.

   Table 3.11 gives the data on the three violent offenses by various demographic group offense counts. Males committed all the homicides, three out of the four manslaughters, and 23 of the 25 attempted homicides. Considering the size of the nonwhite offender group, it is noteworthy that they committed 40 percent of the 10 homicides. Whites committed the most homicides (5) and all of the manslaughters, while trigueños were responsible for the most attempts (13).
   The residence data show the public type has the most homicides (5), but it is the barrio-type residences that had the higher violence, generally, with 4 homicides, 10 attempted homicides, and 1 manslaughter. By area, the data quite clearly indicate the predominance of the urban category. The urban area was involved in 8, or 80 percent, of the homicides, 3, or 75 percent of the manslaughters, and 76 percent of the attempted homicides (19).
   Table 3.12 reports data concerning offender status and violent offenses. We can see that chronic offenders were responsible for the majority of homicides (60 percent) and 40 percent of the attempted homicides. One-time offenders were surprisingly involved in these serious offenses as they committed 75 percent of the manslaughters and 40 percent of the attempted homicides.

TABLE 3.11 Homicide, Manslaughter, and Attempted
            Homicide Offenses by Sex, Color, and
            Type and Location of Residence

| | Homicide | | Manslaughter | | Attempted Homicide | |
Value	No	Yes	No	Yes	No	Yes
Male	2,151	10	2,158	3	2,138	23
	99.5	.5	99.9	.1	98.9	1.1
Female	328		327	1	326	2
	100.0		99.7	.3	99.4	.6
Nonwhite	219	4	223		221	2
	98.2	1.8	100.0		99.1	.9
Trigueño	992	1	993		980	13
	99.9	.1	100.0		98.7	1.3
White	1,268	5	1,269	4	1,263	10
	99.6	.4	99.7	.3	99.2	.8
Barrio	748	4	751	1	742	10
	99.5	.5	99.9	.1	98.7	1.3
Private	1,079	1	1,077	3	1,072	8
	99.9	.1	99.7	.3	99.3	.7
Public	464	5	469		463	
	98.9	1.1	100.0		98.7	1.3
Rural	631	2	632	1	627	6
	99.7	.3	99.8	.2	99.1	.9
Urban	1,663	8	1,668	3	1,652	19
	99.5	.5	99.8	.2	98.9	1.1

Percentages are row percents.

Delinquency in Puerto Rico

TABLE 3.12 Homicide, Manslaughter, and Attempted Homicide Offenses by Delinquency Status, Single/Multiple Offender, and Number of Co-offenders

Value	Homicide #	Homicide %	Manslaughter #	Manslaughter %	Attempted Homicide #	Attempted Homicide %
One-time	1	10.0	3	75.0	10	40.0
Two-time	3	30.0	1	25.0	5	20.0
Three or more	6	60.0			10	40.0
Single Offender	5	50.0	4	100.0	13	52.0
Multiple Offender	5	50.0			12	48.0
Number of Co-offenders						
1	3	60.0			7	58.3
2	2	40.0				
3					1	8.3
4					2	16.7
5					2	16.7

Percentages are column percents.

Table 3.12 also indicates that single offender crimes are the most usual for manslaughter, as 100 percent of the manslaughters were committed by single offenders. Concerning homicides and attempts, one-half were committed by single offenders and one-half were multiple offender crimes. Of the events with multiple offenders the usual occurrence is that one additional offender was involved. However, the attempted homicides do show that some of these crimes involved four or five cooffenders.

Table 3.13 reports the data concerning the age of the very violent offenders. For homicide and manslaughter, the youngest offender was age 15 and the majority were age 16. For attempted homicide, the youngest offender was age 13, but again the modal age was 16.

In Table 3.14 we report the type of weapon used in the three very violent offenses. All of the homicides were committed by handgun. Handguns also predominate among the attempts, with 72 percent being committed with this weapon. The next most frequent weapon used was a sharp instrument. These violent offenses reveal a much more frequent use of weapons than offenses generally. Weapons were used in 90 percent of these very violent offenses compared to 18 percent of the other offenses in the cohort.

TABLE 3.13 Homicide, Manslaughter, Attempted Homicide, and General Offenses by Offender Age

Age	Homicide #	Homicide %	Manslaughter #	Manslaughter %	Attempted Homicide #	Attempted Homicide %	All Others #	All Others %
LT 10							52	2.1
11							32	1.3
12							78	3.2
13					2	8.0	141	5.8
14					4	16.0	325	13.3
15	3	30.0	1	25.0	4	16.0	577	23.6
16	6	60.0	2	50.0	11	44.0	824	33.7
17	1	10.0	1	25.0	4	16.0	417	17.0
Total	10		4		25		2,446	

Percentages are column percents.

TABLE 3.14 Homicide, Manslaughter, Attempted Homicide, and General Offenses by Weapon Use

Weapon	Homicide #	Homicide %	Manslaughter #	Manslaughter %	Attempted Homicide #	Attempted Homicide %	All Others #	All Others %
Handgun	10	100.0	1	25.0	18	72.0	206	8.4
Other Gun					1	4.0	22	.9
Sharp Instrument					4	16.0	108	4.4
Blunt Instrument					1	4.0	53	2.2
Other Weapon							57	2.3
Weapon Total	10	100.0	1	25.0	24	96.0	446	18.0
Offense Total	10		4		25		2,450	

Percentages are column percents.

Delinquency in Puerto Rico

In Table 3.15 we turn to the question of drugs and violent offenses. The top half of the table shows that none of the very violent offenses were committed by offenders who were in possession of drugs at the time of the offense.

The bottom half of Table 3.15, however, shows that significant proportions of the very violent offenses were committed by delinquents with suspected drug use at the time of the offense or with a history of drug involvement. One-half of the homicides were committed by drug involved offenders who had used either marijuana (50 percent) or cocaine (40 percent). Similarly, a majority of the attempted homicides (64 percent) were drug-related. Marijuana users predominate with 60 percent, followed by cocaine use (32 percent).

TABLE 3.15 Homicide, Manslaughter, and Attempted Homicide Offenses by Drug Possession and Type and Drug Usage and Type

Drug Variable	Homicide #	%	Manslaughter #	%	Attempted Homicide #	%
Possession:						
Any type						
Marijuana						
Heroin						
Cocaine						
Other						
Use/Influence:						
Any type	5	50.0	1	25.0	16	64.0
Marijuana	5	50.0	1	25.0	15	60.0
Heroin	3	30.0			2	8.0
Cocaine	4	40.0			8	32.0
Alcohol					3	12.0
Other	4	40.0			5	20.0
Total Offenses	10		4		25	

Percentages are column percents.

Because weapons and drug use are such important contemporary issues in the study of delinquency, the next two sets of tables will present data pertaining to weapons use and drug possessions or drug use/involvement for all offenses in the cohort.

Incidence

WEAPON OFFENSES

Tables 3.16, 3.17, and 3.18 present weapon-use data. Table 3.16 indicates that handguns are the most prevalent weapon used in any offense, with a frequency of 225 occurrences, or 9 percent of the offenses. The next most likely weapon is sharp instruments which were used 112 times, or 4.5 percent. Handguns and sharp weapons are followed by other weapons (2.3 percent), blunt weapons (2.2 percent), and other guns (.9 percent). All together, weapons were used 471 times, or 18.9 percent of the total offenses.

TABLE 3.16   Frequency and Percent of Weapon Use

Component	No	Yes
Handgun present	2,264	225
	91.0	9.0
Other gun present	2,466	23
	99.1	0.9
Sharp instrument present	2,377	112
	95.5	4.5
Blunt instrument present	2,435	54
	97.8	2.2
Other weapon present	2,432	57
	97.7	2.3

Percentages are row percents.

Table 3.17 reports weapon use for males by crime code. For serious offenses, handguns were used in 100 percent of the homicides, 78 percent of the attempted homicides, 64 percent of the attempted robberies, and 48 percent of the robberies. Other guns are used only rarely--about 5 percent of robberies and aggravated assaults. Sharp instruments are not used as frequently as handguns, but they are used in a variety of crimes--about 13 percent of attempted homicides and robberies, and about 25 percent of rapes, attempted robberies, and aggravated assaults. The only other offense in which a sharp instrument was used more than 10 percent of the time was threats, with 11.8 percent. Blunt instruments are also less frequent and show only two offenses (aggravated

TABLE 3.17 Number and Percent of Weapons Used by Crime Code for Males

MALES

Offense	Handgun N	Handgun %	Other Gun N	Other Gun %	Sharp N	Sharp %	Blunt N	Blunt %	Other N	Other %
Homicide	10	100.0								
Att. Homicide	18	78.3			3	13.1	1	4.3		
Rape					1	25.0				
Robbery	76	47.8	8	5.0	21	13.2	5	3.1	4	2.5
Att. Robbery	7	63.6			3	27.3				
Agg. Assault	2	2.2	5	5.4	24	26.1	17	18.5	6	6.5
Burglary	5	1.9			3	1.1	6	2.3	1	.4
Larceny	8	4.7			2	1.2		.6		
Att. Larceny							1	2.3	1	2.3
Auto Theft	6	15.8								
Assault	2	1.3	1	.6	9	5.6	6	3.7	22	13.8
Mayhem							1	33.3		
R.S.P.	17	15.3	2	1.8						
Mischief	1	.7	1	.7	7	4.9	8	5.6	13	9.0
Sodomy									1	5.6
Narcotics	3	1.9								
Civil Rights	2	66.7								
Kidnapping	5	100.0								
Public Order	1	33.3								
School Tres.	1	1.4								
Escape					1	1.5			1	1.5
Breach Peace	3	3.2	1	1.1	1	1.1	1	1.1	1	1.1
Threats	3	8.8			4	11.8	1	2.9		

Percentages are row percents.

TABLE 3.18 Number and Percent of Weapons Used by Crime Code for Females

FEMALES

Offense	Handgun N	%	Other Gun N	%	Sharp N	%	Blunt N	%	Other N	%
Manslaughter			1	100.0						
Att. Homicide			1	50.0	1	50.0				
Robbery	2	25.0			4	50.0				
Att. Robbery					1	100.0				
Agg. Assault					6	31.6	1	5.3		
Burglary					1	8.3	1	8.3		
Assault					2	2.5	1	1.3	1	1.3
Mayhem					3	7.5				
Mischief							2	25.0		
Narcotics	1	8.3								
Kidnapping					1	100.0				
Breach Peace					1	2.1				
Threats					2	28.6				

Percentages are row percents.

TABLE 3.19 Number and Percent of Weapons Used by Crime Code for Nonwhites

NONWHITE

Offense	Handgun N	%	Other Gun N	%	Sharp N	%	Blunt N	%	Other N	%
Homicide	4	100.0								
Att. Homicide	2	100.0								
Robbery	7	35.0	2	10.0	3	15.0	1	5.0		
Att. Robbery					2	66.7				
Agg. Assault					4	36.4				
Burglary							2	5.9		
Assault					1	4.0			1	4.0
R.S.P.	2	20.0								
Mischief							1	11.1	1	11.1
Civil Rights	2	100.0								
Kidnapping	3	100.0								
Escape									1	12.5

Percentages are row percents.

assault, 18.5 percent, and mayhem 33.3 percent) with more than ten percent use.

Table 3.18 shows that weapon use is very infrequent among female offenders. Only three offenses (2 robberies and 1 drug offense) involved handguns and only two involved other guns (1 manslaughter and 1 attempted homicide). Similarly, only five offenses were committed with blunt instruments. Clearly, the weapon of choice among female delinquents is sharp instruments. These were used in the two attempted robberies and kidnappings and in one-half of the robberies and attempted homicides. Sharp instruments were also used frequently in aggravated assaults (31.6 percent) and threats (28.6 percent).

Table 3.19 shows that nonwhites almost always use handguns and sharp instruments when they use weapons. Handguns were used in 100 percent of the homicides, attempted homicides, civil rights offenses, and kidnappings. Sharp instruments were substantially used in attempted robberies (66.7 percent) and aggravated assaults (36.4 percent). Other guns and blunt instruments are rarely used by nonwhites.

Table 3.20 indicates that trigueño delinquents most often use handguns followed by sharp instruments. Trigueños committed their only homicide with a handgun. They also used handguns frequently in attempted homicide (62 percent), robbery (51 percent), and attempted robbery (67 percent). Sharp instruments were used less often, but mostly involved serious offenses--attempted homicide (31 percent), attempted robbery (33 percent), and aggravated assault (28 percent).

Whites (Table 3.21) show this same general pattern of handgun use in serious offenses--80 percent of attempted homicides, 45 percent of robberies, and 100 percent of attempted robberies. Sharp instruments are used most often in aggravated assault (26 percent), kidnapping (33 percent) and mayhem (20 percent). Whites make by far the greatest use of blunt instruments--25 percent of

TABLE 3.20 Number and Percent of Weapons Used by Crime Code for Trigueños

TRIGUEÑO

Offense	Handgun N	%	Other Gun N	%	Sharp N	%	Blunt N	%	Other N	%
Homicide	1	100.0								
Att. Homicide	8	61.5			4	30.8	1	7.7		
Robbery	40	51.3	4	5.1	12	15.4	2	2.6	1	1.2
Att. Robbery	4	66.7			2	33.3				
Agg. Assault	3	7.7	4	10.3	11	28.2	3	7.7	5	12.8
Burglary	2	1.8			1	.8	2	1.8		
Larceny	5	5.9			1	1.2				
Att. Larceny									1	5.9
Auto Theft	2	18.1								
Assault	1	1.1			4	4.4	3	3.3	14	15.6
Mayhem					2	100.0				
R.S.P.	6	1.2	2	16.7						
Mischief	1	1.8			2	3.6	1	1.8	8	14.3
Sodomy									1	20.0
Narcotics	2	2.4								
Public Order	1	20.0								
School Tres.	1	2.9								
Escape					1	2.9				
Breach Peace	2	3.6			1	1.8				
Threats	1	5.9								

Percentages are row percents.

TABLE 3.21 Number and Percent of Weapons Used by Crime Code for Whites

WHITE

Offense	Handgun N	Handgun %	Other Gun N	Other Gun %	Sharp N	Sharp %	Blunt N	Blunt %	Other N	Other %
Homicide	5	100.0								
Manslaughter	1	25.0								
Att. Homicide	8	80.0	1	10.0						
Robbery	31	44.9	2	2.9	10	14.5	2	2.9	3	4.3
Att. Robbery	3	100.0								
Agg. Assault			1	1.6	16	26.2	15	24.6	1	1.6
Burglary	3	2.5			3	2.5	3	2.5		
Larceny	3	3.0			1	1.0	1	1.0		
Auto Theft	4	16.0								
Assault	1	.8	1	.8	6	4.8	4	3.3	8	6.6
Mayhem					1	20.0	1	20.0		
R.S.P.	9	16.9								
Mischief			1	1.1	5	5.7	8	9.2	4	4.6
Narcotics	2	2.9								
Kidnapping	2	66.7			1	33.3				

Percentages are row percents.

aggravated assaults, 20 percent of mayhem, and 9 percent of mischief. Altogether, whites used a blunt instrument 34 times compared to four times for nonwhites and fourteen times for trigueños.

NARCOTICS OFFENSES

In Tables 3.22 to 3.32 we investigate the relationship between drug use or involvement and delinquent events. Table 3.22 first indicates that about one-quarter of the offenses concern delinquents who have used or were under the influence of marijuana. Cocaine is next most frequent with about 10 percent of the delinquencies. Heroin, alcohol, or other drugs concern only about three to four percent of the offenses.

TABLE 3.22 Frequency and Percent of Prior Drug Use or Under Influence of Drugs/Alcohol

Drug Type	No	Yes
Marijuana	1915	574
	76.9	23.1
Heroin	2400	89
	96.4	3.6
Cocaine	2247	242
	90.3	9.7
Other drug	2395	93
	96.3	3.7
Alcohol	2389	100
	96.0	4.0

Percentages are row percents.

Table 3.23 gives the drug use data for males by residence and school. These results show that drug usage is most prevalent among public-residence offenders. About 40 percent of these offenders have used any drug, 38 percent have used marijuana, and about 20 percent have used cocaine. Concerning school type, public students predominate with 31 percent drug use compared to 21 percent and 9 percent for the two types of private schools. The largest drug effect occurs for school

Incidence

attendance, where 51 percent of the not-in-school delinquents have used drugs compared to just 18 percent of the in school group.

Table 3.24 presents drug use data for female offenses. These results repeat the male findings reported above. Public residence, public school, and not in school are all related to higher percentages of drug use generally, and the specific types of drugs. Generally, females have used marijuana the most, followed by cocaine and alcohol.

The color data do not give a consistent picture of drug use by the designated factors. Table 3.25 shows that the private-residence offenders have used drugs more often among nonwhites. Tables 3.26 and 3.27 show, however, that public residence is related to drugs for trigueños and whites. Public school is related to drugs for nonwhites and trigueños, but this may be due to the great absence of private school for these two color groups. Among whites, drug use is more frequent among the private nondenominational offenses. For all three colors, the offenses committed by not-in-school offenders are much more likely to involve drugs than those committed by in-school delinquents.

In Table 3.28 our attention turns to the issue of the specific offenses that are suspected to have involved a delinquent with a drug experience among male members of the cohort. These data indicate the connection between drugs and crime. For example, of the very serious UCR

TABLE 3.23 Number and Percent of Male Drug Users by Location and Type of Residence, School Type, and Enrollment

MALES

USER OR UNDER INFLUENCE OF

Category	Any Drug N	%	Marijuana N	%	Heroin N	%	Cocaine N	%	Alcohol N	%	Other Drug N	%
Rural	140	28.3	129	26.1	13	2.6	48	9.7	25	5.1	11	2.2
Urban	423	30.3	390	27.9	62	4.4	162	11.6	57	4.1	74	5.3
Barrio	161	26.7	142	23.5	17	2.8	51	8.5	22	3.6	23	3.8
Private	252	28.8	235	25.9	21	2.3	81	8.9	44	4.8	26	2.9
Public	151	39.6	143	37.5	37	9.7	78	20.5	16	4.2	36	9.4
Public	550	30.8	506	28.3	71	3.9	205	11.5	79	4.4	85	4.8
Private Denomin.	7	9.3	7	9.3	3	4.0	4	5.3	-	---	-	---
Private Nondenom.	7	21.2	7	21.2	1	3.0	1	3.0	3	9.1	-	---
Not in school	347	51.3	317	46.8	59	8.7	140	20.7	65	9.6	58	8.6
In school	217	17.8	203	16.7	16	1.3	70	5.8	17	1.4	27	2.2

Percentages are row percents.

TABLE 3.24 Number and Percent of Female Drug Users by Location and Type of Residence, School Type, and Enrollment

FEMALES

USER OR UNDER INFLUENCE OF

Category	Any Drug N	%	Marijuana N	%	Heroin N	%	Cocaine N	%	Alcohol N	%	Other Drug N	%
Rural	9	9.6	1	1.1	1	1.1	6	6.4	4	4.3	—	—
Urban	24	12.2	15	7.7	7	3.6	7	3.6	9	4.6	2	1.0
Barrio	12	12.4	12	12.4	3	3.1	8	8.2	4	4.1	2	2.1
Private	9	7.1	4	3.2	1	.8	2	1.6	5	3.9	—	---
Public	12	17.8	8	11.8	4	5.9	3	4.5	5	5.9	—	---
Public	32	12.5	23	8.9	7	2.7	12	4.7	13	5.1	2	.8
Private Denomin.	—	---	—	---	—	---	—	---	—	---	—	---
Private Nondenom.	1	10.0	1	10.0	1	10.0	1	10.0	—	---	—	---
Not in school	14	21.2	9	13.6	6	9.1	7	10.6	6	9.1	—	---
In school	19	8.5	15	6.3	2	.9	6	2.7	7	3.1	2	.9

Percentages are row percents.

69

TABLE 3.25 Number and Percent of Nonwhite Drug Users by Location and Type of Residence, School Type, and Enrollment

NONWHITE

USER OR UNDER INFLUENCE OF

Category	Any Drug N	%	Marijuana N	%	Heroin N	%	Cocaine N	%	Alcohol N	%	Other Drug N	%
Rural	18	34.6	18	34.6	5	9.6	6	11.5	3	5.8	—	—
Urban	59	38.6	53	34.6	14	9.2	28	18.3	4	2.6	10	6.5
Barrio	25	32.1	23	29.5	7	8.9	9	11.5	—	—	2	2.6
Private	36	49.3	32	43.8	3	4.1	16	21.9	6	8.2	1	1.4
Public	16	29.6	16	29.6	9	16.7	9	16.7	1	1.9	7	12.9
Public	77	37.7	71	34.8	19	9.3	34	16.7	7	3.4	10	4.9
Private Denomin.	—	—	—	—	—	—	—	—	—	—	—	—
Private Nondenom.	—	—	—	—	—	—	—	—	—	—	—	—
Not in school	42	52.5	40	50.0	11	13.8	25	31.3	1	1.3	4	5.0
In school	35	28.0	31	24.8	8	6.4	9	7.2	6	4.8	6	4.8

Percentages are row percents.

TABLE 3.26 Number and Percent of Trigueño Drug Users by Location and Type of Residence, School Type, and Enrollment

TRIGUEÑO

USER OR UNDER INFLUENCE OF

Category	Any Drug N	%	Marijuana N	%	Heroin N	%	Cocaine N	%	Alcohol N	%	Other Drug N	%
Rural	82	30.5	77	28.6	7	2.6	33	12.3	18	6.7	9	3.3
Urban	206	34.4	193	32.2	32	5.3	79	13.2	27	4.5	33	5.5
Barrio	105	32.4	95	29.3	11	3.4	40	12.3	19	5.9	13	4.0
Private	98	29.5	96	28.9	10	3.0	24	7.2	15	4.5	8	2.4
Public	86	40.8	80	37.9	18	8.5	48	22.7	11	5.2	21	9.9
Public Private	288	34.6	270	32.4	39	4.7	112	13.4	45	5.4	42	5.0
Denomin. Private	1	4.8	1	4.8	—	---	—	---	—	---	—	---
Nondenom.	—	---	—	---	—	---	—	---	—	---	—	---
Not in school	177	52.9	165	49.4	30	8.9	72	21.6	34	10.2	30	8.9
In school	112	21.0	106	19.9	9	1.7	40	7.5	11	2.1	12	2.3

Percentages are row percents.

TABLE 3.27 Number and Percent of White Drug Users by Location and Type of Residence, School Type, and Enrollment

WHITE

USER OR UNDER INFLUENCE OF

Category	Any Drug N	%	Marijuana N	%	Heroin N	%	Cocaine N	%	Alcohol N	%	Other Drug N	%
Rural	49	18.3	43	16.0	2	.7	15	5.6	8	2.9	2	.7
Urban	182	21.6	159	18.9	23	2.7	62	7.4	35	4.2	33	3.9
Barrio	43	14.4	36	12.1	2	.7	10	3.4	7	2.3	10	3.3
Private	127	20.2	111	17.6	9	1.4	43	6.8	28	4.4	17	2.7
Public	61	33.3	55	30.1	14	7.6	24	13.1	8	4.4	8	4.4
Public Private	217	21.6	188	18.7	20	1.9	71	7.1	40	3.9	35	3.5
Denomin. Private	6	7.7	6	7.7	3	3.9	4	5.2	—	---	—	---
Nondenom.	8	27.6	8	27.6	2	6.9	2	6.9	3	10.3	—	---
Not in school	142	43.2	121	36.8	24	7.3	50	15.2	36	10.9	24	7.3
In school	89	11.4	81	10.4	1	.1	27	3.5	7	.9	11	1.4

Percentages are row percents.

Incidence

index offenses, from 20 percent to 65 percent concern drug involvement. As expected, drugs were involved in substantial proportions of property offenses--robbery (54 percent), attempted robbery (36 percent), burglary and larceny (33 percent), auto theft (36 percent), and receiving stolen property (47 percent).

Table 3.28 also indicates that marijuana is most likely the drug that is involved, but there are a few offenses that do involve cocaine. For example, 40 percent of homicides, 30 percent of attempted homicides, and 25 percent of robberies involved cocaine. Heroin and alcohol are not indicated in many offenses, and few that were committed frequently, have more than a ten percent involvement--heroin: (homicide 30 percent, robbery 11 percent, other property 13 percent); alcohol: (attempted homicide 13 percent).

The bottom panel of Table 3.28 indicates the relation between chronic offending and drugs. The data show that over one-half of the offenses by three-time offenders (52.5 percent) involve drugs compared to 26 percent for two-timers and 11 percent for one-timers. According to these results, it is apparent that drug involvement is one of the prime facilitators of repeat delinquency in this cohort.

Like the case for weapons reported earlier, Table 3.29 indicates that females do not have extensive drug involvements. Because the frequency of female offenses is so small, it is unwise to give much importance to the percentages shown in the table (that is to say, the small numbers render the data unreliable compared to males). Bearing in mind these small offense frequencies, drugs were involved in 50 percent of attempted homicides, receiving stolen property, and disrespect; and 25 percent of robberies and burglaries. Drugs were also involved in 100 percent of the single attempted robbery and the civil rights and other status offenses.

Like the male offenses, the female data show that drug involvement is related to delinquency status. That is, 42 percent of the offenses by chronics involved drugs compared to 28 percent for two-time offenders and 4 percent for one-time offenses.

Tables 3.30 through 3.32 report the drug and crime code data by color. In Table 3.30 we see that large proportions of nonwhite offenses involve drug use. The drug that is usually involved is marijuana, but there are more than a few instances in which cocaine or heroin is involved. For nonwhites the delinquency status data indicate that the three-time-recidivist offenses are very substantially drug related (66 percent) as compared to two-time (12 percent) and one-time (13 percent).

TABLE 3.28

Number and Percent of Male Drug Users by Crime Code and Delinquency Status

MALES

USER OR UNDER INFLUENCE OF

Offense	Any Drug N	%	Marijuana N	%	Heroin N	%	Cocaine N	%	Alcohol N	%	Other Drug N	%
Homicide	5	50.0	5	50.0	3	30.0	4	40.0	-	---	4	40.0
Manslaughter	1	33.0	1	33.0	-	---	-	---	-	---	-	--
Att Homicide	15	65.2	14	60.9	2	8.7	7	30.4	3	13.0	5	21.7
Robbery	85	53.5	83	52.2	17	10.7	39	24.5	9	5.7	6	3.8
Att. Robbery	4	36.4	4	36.4	1	9.1	-	---	-	---	-	--
Agg. Assault	19	20.7	17	18.5	2	2.2	4	4.3	6	6.5	3	3.3
Burglary	87	33.7	82	31.8	10	3.9	36	13.9	13	5.0	14	5.4
Larceny	57	33.7	54	31.9	5	2.9	19	11.2	10	5.9	9	5.3
Att. Larceny	7	15.9	6	13.6	2	4.5	2	4.5	-	---	-	--
Auto Theft	14	36.8	13	34.2	2	5.2	3	7.9	3	7.9	4	10.5
Assault	17	10.6	14	8.7	1	.6	7	4.1	2	1.2	1	.6
R.S.P.	52	46.8	47	42.3	6	5.4	16	14.4	10	9.0	7	6.3
Mischief	14	9.7	12	8.3	1	.7	7	4.9	4	2.8	7	4.9
Weapons	19	9.7	19	30.6	3	4.8	8	12.7	1	1.6	2	3.2
Sodomy	2	11.1	2	11.1	-	---	1	5.6	1	5.6	1	5.6
Narcotics	110	71.4	97	62.9	18	11.7	46	29.8	10	6.5	16	10.4
Traffic	16	5.1	13	4.1	2	.6	4	1.3	6	1.9	1	.3
Civil Rights	3	100.0	3	100.0	-	---	2	66.7	1	33.3	-	--
Kidnapping	2	40.0	2	40.0	-	---	2	40.0	-	---	-	--
Other Prop.	4	50.0	3	37.5	1	12.5	1	12.5	1	12.5	1	12.5
Public Auth.	2	66.7	2	66.7	-	---	1	33.3	-	---	-	--
School Tres.	10	14.5	10	14.5	-	---	3	4.3	1	1.4	1	1.4
Escape	13	19.1	12	17.6	1	1.5	6	8.8	-	---	4	5.9
Other Status	3	100.0	3	100.0	-	---	-	---	-	---	-	--
Breach Peace	14	14.7	12	12.6	1	1.1	2	2.1	3	3.2	2	2.1
Threats	7	20.6	7	20.6	1	2.9	3	8.8	-	---	1	2.9
Delinquency Status												
One-time	112	10.8	96	9.3	15	1.5	28	2.7	11	1.1	10	.9
Two-time	111	26.3	104	24.6	10	2.4	47	11.1	25	5.9	18	4.3
Three or more	371	52.5	347	49.2	56	7.9	151	21.4	51	7.2	63	8.9

Percentages are row percents.

TABLE 3.29 Number and Percent of Female Drug Users by Crime Code and Delinquency Status

FEMALES

USER OR UNDER INFLUENCE OF

Offense	Any Drug N	%	Marijuana N	%	Heroin N	%	Cocaine N	%	Alcohol N	%	Other Drug N	%
Att Homicide	1	50.0	1	50.0	-	---	1	50.0	-	---	-	---
Robbery	2	25.0	1	12.5	1	12.5	1	12.5	-	---	-	---
Att. Robbery	1	100.0	-	---	1	100.0	1	100.0	-	---	-	---
Agg. Assault	2	10.5	1	5.3	-	---	-	---	-	---	1	5.3
Burglary	3	25.0	1	8.3	2	16.7	-	---	2	16.7	-	---
Larceny	5	15.6	5	15.6	1	3.1	2	6.3	1	3.1	-	---
Assault	2	2.5	-	---	-	---	-	---	-	---	-	---
R.S.P.	1	50.0	1	50.0	-	---	1	50.0	-	---	-	---
Weapons	3	42.9	3	42.9	1	14.3	2	28.6	-	---	1	14.3
Narcotics	6	50.0	6	50.0	1	8.3	3	25.0	1	8.3	1	8.3
Civil Rights	1	100.0	1	100.0	-	---	1	100.0	-	---	-	---
Disrespect	1	50.0	1	50.0	-	---	-	---	1	50.0	-	---
Other Status	2	100.0	2	100.0	-	---	1	50.0	2	100.0	-	---
Breach Peace	5	10.4	3	6.3	1	2.1	2	4.2	2	4.2	-	---
Delinquency Status												
One-time	11	4.3	10	3.9	2	.8	5	1.9	2	.8	-	---
Two-time	11	27.5	9	22.5	4	10.0	6	15.0	1	2.5	2	5.0
Three or more	14	42.4	8	24.2	2	6.1	5	15.2	10	30.3	-	---

Percentages are row percents.

TABLE 3.30 Number and Percent of Nonwhite Drug Users by Crime Code and Delinquency Status

| | \multicolumn{10}{c}{NONWHITE USER OR UNDER INFLUENCE OF} | | | | | | | | | |
Offense	Any Drug N	%	Marijuana N	%	Heroin N	%	Cocaine N	%	Alcohol N	%	Other Drug N	%
Homicide	2	50.0	2	50.0	2	50.0	2	50.0	—	---	2	50.0
Att Homicide	1	50.0	1	50.0	—	---	—	---	—	---	—	---
Robbery	12	60.0	12	60.0	3	15.0	9	45.0	—	---	2	10.0
Agg. Assault	2	18.2	2	18.2	1	9.1	1	9.1	—	---	1	9.1
Burglary	12	35.3	11	32.4	5	14.7	7	20.6	1	2.9	2	5.9
Larceny	6	33.3	6	33.3	1	5.6	1	11.2	—	---	—	---
Att. Larceny	1	25.0	—	---	1	25.0	1	5.6	—	---	—	---
Assault	5	20.0	3	12.0	—	---	1	25.0	2	8.0	—	---
R.S.P.	4	40.0	4	40.0	2	20.0	1	4.0	1	10.0	—	---
Mischief	3	22.2	2	22.2	—	---	—	---	—	---	—	---
Weapons	3	100.0	3	100.0	1	33.3	1	33.3	—	---	1	33.3
Narcotics	12	92.3	12	92.3	—	---	3	23.1	—	---	1	7.7
Traffic	2	12.5	2	12.5	1	6.3	1	6.3	—	---	—	---
Civil Rights	2	100.0	2	100.0	—	---	2	100.0	—	---	—	---
Kidnapping	2	66.7	2	66.7	—	---	2	66.7	—	---	—	---
Other Prop.	1	100.0	1	100.0	1	100.0	—	---	1	100.0	—	---
School Tres.	1	14.3	1	14.3	—	---	—	---	—	---	—	---
Escape	1	12.5	1	12.5	1	12.5	1	12.5	—	---	1	12.5
Breach Peace	5	41.7	3	25.0	1	8.3	1	8.3	2	16.7	1	8.3
Threats	1	33.3	1	33.3	—	---	1	33.3	—	---	—	---

Delinquency Status

	N	%	N	%	N	%	N	%	N	%	N	%
One-time	13	13.4	13	13.4	1	1.0	4	4.1	—	---	1	1.0
Two-time	4	11.8	4	11.8	—	---	—	---	—	---	—	---
Three or more	61	66.3	55	59.8	19	20.6	31	33.7	7	7.6	10	10.9

Percentages are row percents.

Table 3.31 also shows substantial offenses that are drug related for trigueño delinquents. Among the most frequent offenses that are drug related are robbery (64 percent), burglary (36 percent), larceny (40 percent), and receiving stolen property (50%). As with other groups, the most usual drug that trigueños use is marijuana, but there are a few offenses in which cocaine is used frequently--attempted homicide (54 percent), robbery (27 percent), burglary (15 percent), and larceny (18 percent). The difference for trigueños concerning delinquency status is not nearly as great as for nonwhites, but it is clear that three-time offenses (55 percent) are more drug related than those for the other two groups--34 percent for two-time and 13 percent for one-time.

Table 3.32 displays the data for white delinquents. As before, there is a range of offenses that involve drug use. UCR index offenses generally show at least a twenty-five percent to a 50 percent drug share. The drug used most often is again marijuana, while heroin and cocaine are used in many offense types, but these drugs are not used in very high proportions of the offenses. Among whites, the offenses of three-timers are twice as likely to involve drugs as those of the two-timers, and these in turn are about three times more likely to involve drugs than those of one-timers.

In the next set of tables, 3.33 to 3.42, we turn to the issue of drug possession during the delinquent events in the cohort. Unlike the previous data, these results pertain to the presence of drugs during the crime regardless of whether the drug was consumed or whether the delinquent was known to be a drug user. We can expect, therefore, that fewer drug possessions will be evident than was the case for drug usage which referred to the drug using reputation of the offender historically.

Table 3.33 presents drug possessions for males by residence and school variables. We note, that neither type of area nor type of residence is strongly associated with drug possession. For type of school, only the public type is very noteworthy because of the almost complete absence of drug possessions for the two types of private school. As we observed earlier, the not-in-school offenders are more likely to possess drugs, but the percentage differences are not very great.

In Table 3.34 we observe that very few female offenses involve drug possession. The few small effects that are evident consist of urban area, public residence, public school, and not in school. The observed percentages are not very great however.

TABLE 3.31 Number and Percent of Trigueño Drug Users by Crime Code and Delinquency Status

						TRIGUEÑO USER OR UNDER INFLUENCE OF						
	Any Drug		Marijuana		Heroin		Cocaine		Alcohol		Other Drug	
Offense	N	%	N	%	N	%	N	%	N	%	N	%
Homicide	1	100.0	1	100.0	—	—	—	—	—	—	—	—
Att Homicide	10	76.9	9	69.2	2	15.4	7	53.8	3	23.1	5	38.5
Robbery	50	64.1	48	61.5	10	12.8	21	26.9	6	7.7	3	3.8
Att. Robbery	4	66.7	3	50.0	2	33.3	1	16.7	—	—	—	—
Agg. Assault	10	25.6	10	25.6	—	—	—	—	3	7.7	—	—
Burglary	41	35.9	40	35.1	2	1.8	17	14.9	7	6.1	9	7.9
Larceny	33	39.3	32	38.1	3	3.6	15	17.9	7	8.3	7	8.3
Att. Larceny	3	17.6	3	17.6	—	—	—	—	2	11.8	1	5.9
Auto Theft	1	9.1	1	9.1	—	—	—	—	1	1.1	—	—
Assault	8	8.9	7	7.8	—	—	3	3.3	1	1.1	—	—
Mayhem	1	50.0	1	50.0	—	—	1	50.0	1	50.0	—	—
R.S.P.	25	50.0	24	48.0	1	2.0	9	18.0	2	1.7	3	6.0
Mischief	4	7.1	4	7.1	—	—	2	4.0	—	—	2	4.0
Weapons	11	35.5	11	35.5	3	9.7	5	16.1	1	3.2	2	6.5
Sodomy	1	20.0	1	20.0	—	—	—	—	—	—	—	—
Narcotics	63	74.1	54	63.5	16	18.8	32	37.6	7	8.2	10	11.8
Traffic	4	3.4	3	2.5	—	—	1	.8	2	1.7	—	—
Civil Rights	2	100.0	2	100.0	—	—	1	50.0	1	50.0	—	—
Pub. Author.	2	40.0	2	40.0	—	—	1	20.0	—	—	—	—
School Tres.	5	14.7	5	14.7	—	—	2	5.9	1	2.9	—	—
Escape	5	14.3	5	14.3	—	—	2	5.7	—	—	1	2.9
Breach Peace	8	14.3	7	12.5	—	—	1	1.8	1	1.8	—	—
Threats	3	17.6	3	17.6	1	5.9	1	5.9	—	—	—	—
Delinquency Status												
One-time	60	12.9	50	10.8	9	1.9	17	3.7	8	1.7	5	1.1
Two-time	70	33.9	66	32.0	14	6.8	36	17.5	16	7.8	12	5.8
Three +	173	54.9	168	53.3	17	5.4	70	22.2	24	7.6	27	8.5

TABLE 3.32 Number and Percent of White Drug Users by Crime Code and Delinquency Status

WHITE
USER OR UNDER INFLUENCE OF

Offense	Any Drug N	%	Marijuana N	%	Heroin N	%	Cocaine N	%	Alcohol N	%	Other Drug N	%
Homicide	2	40.0	2	40.0	1	20.0	2	40.0	-	--	2	40.0
Manslaughter	1	25.0	1	25.0	-	--	-	--	-	--	-	--
Att Homicide	5	50.0	5	50.0	-	--	1	10.0	-	--	-	--
Robbery	25	36.2	24	34.8	5	7.2	10	14.5	3	4.3	1	1.4
Att. Robbery	1	33.0	1	33.0	-	--	-	--	-	--	-	--
Agg. Assault	9	14.8	6	9.8	1	1.6	3	4.9	4	6.6	-	--
Burglary	37	30.3	32	26.2	5	4.1	12	9.8	7	5.7	3	2.5
Larceny	23	23.2	21	21.2	2	2.0	5	5.1	4	4.0	2	2.0
Att. Larceny	3	11.1	3	11.1	1	3.7	1	3.7	-	--	-	--
Auto Theft	11	44.0	10	41.7	2	8.3	3	12.5	3	12.5	4	16.7
Assault	6	4.8	4	3.2	1	.8	3	2.4	1	.8	1	.8
R.S.P.	24	44.4	20	37.0	3	5.6	7	12.9	7	12.9	4	7.4
Mischief	8	9.2	6	6.9	1	1.1	5	5.7	4	4.6	5	5.7
Weapons	8	22.2	8	22.2	-	--	4	11.1	-	--	-	--
Sodomy	1	9.1	1	9.1	-	--	1	9.1	1	9.1	1	9.1
Narcotics	41	60.2	37	54.4	3	4.4	14	20.6	4	5.9	6	8.8
Traffic	10	4.2	8	3.4	1	.4	2	.8	4	1.7	1	.4
Other Prop.	3	50.0	2	33.3	-	--	1	16.7	-	--	1	16.7
School Tres.	4	12.5	4	12.5	-	--	1	3.1	-	--	1	3.1
Escape	7	20.6	6	17.6	-	--	3	8.8	-	--	2	5.9
Breach Peace	6	8.0	5	6.7	1	1.3	2	2.6	2	2.6	1	1.3
Threats	3	14.3	3	14.3	-	--	1	4.8	-	--	1	4.8
Delinquency Status												
One-time	50	6.9	43	5.9	7	.1	12	1.6	5	.7	4	.5
Two-time	48	21.6	43	19.4	-	--	17	7.6	10	4.5	8	3.6
Three +	151	46.8	132	40.9	22	6.9	55	17.0	30	9.3	26	8.0

Percentages are row percents.

79

TABLE 3.33 Number and Percent of Drug Possessions by Location and Type of Residence, School Type, and Enrollment for Males

MALES

POSSESSION OF

Category	Any Drug N	%	Marijuana N	%	Heroin N	%	Cocaine N	%	Other N	%
Rural	32	6.5	30	6.1	2	.4	4	.8	—	—
Urban	121	8.7	87	6.2	12	8.6	40	2.9	4	.3
Barrio	47	7.8	38	6.3	4	.7	13	2.2	—	—
Private	70	7.7	56	6.2	5	.6	16	4.2	2	.2
Public	38	9.9	24	6.3	5	1.3	16	1.8	2	.5
Public	151	8.5	114	6.4	14	.8	45	2.5	4	.2
Private Denomin.	—	---	—	---	—	---	—	---	—	---
Private Nondenom	4	12.1	4	12.1	—	---	—	---	—	---
Not in school	69	10.2	49	7.2	11	1.6	26	3.8	2	.3
In school	86	6.9	69	5.7	3	.2	19	1.6	2	.2

Percentages are row percents.

TABLE 3.34 Number and Percent of Drug Possessions by Location and Type of Residence, School Type, and Enrollment for Females

FEMALES
POSSESSION OF

Offense	Any Drug N	%	Marijuana N	%	Heroin N	%	Cocaine N	%	Other N	%
Rural	1	1.1	1	1.1	—	—	—	—	—	—
Urban	11	5.6	9	4.6	1	.5	2	1.0	—	—
Barrio	5	5.2	4	4.1	1	1.0	1	1.0	—	—
Private	2	1.6	2	1.6	—	—	—	—	—	—
Public	5	7.5	4	5.9	—	—	1	1.5	—	—
Public	12	4.7	10	3.9	1	.4	2	.8	—	—
Private Denomin.	—	—	—	—	—	—	—	—	—	—
Private Nondenom.	—	—	—	—	—	—	—	—	—	—
Not in school	4	6.0	3	4.5	—	—	—	—	—	—
In school	8	3.6	7	3.1	1	.4	1	.4	—	—

Percentages are row percents.

Delinquency in Puerto Rico

The data given in Tables 3.35, 3.36, and 3.37 present much the same results for the color categories. For all groups, the urban-area category has more drug possessions. By type of residence, the scores are all very close, but public residence has slightly higher percentages of drug possessions. The same is true of public school type. As we observed many times before, offenses committed by not-in-school offenders show the greatest proportions of drug possessions regardless of color category.

The final two sets of tables related to drug possession concern the specific offenses in which drugs were present. As expected, the most substantial percentages of drugs present during an offense concerns the drug violations of the crime code. We include these offenses only to indicate the particular type of drugs that were possessed. Our primary interest concerns what other types of crimes included a drug possession component.

Table 3.38 indicates first, that marijuana (71 percent) comprises the majority of male narcotics offenses, followed by cocaine (32 percent) and then heroin (10 percent). Beyond these, it is clear that drug possession was only incidental to a few other offenses, none of which shows even a ten percent chance of drug presence. By delinquency status it is also clear that the three offender types are very close and the familiar progression of drugs as recidivism increases is not obtained.

Table 3.39 clearly points out the very scarce drug possession among females. Females committed only 12 drug offenses (10 concerning marijuana). Further, drug possession was evident in no more than one of any of the other offenses. As was the case for males, it is two-time offenses (10 percent) that show the highest drug possession compared to three-time (6 percent) and one-time (4 percent). These percentages and the differences are all too small to be noteworthy.

The color data reported in Tables 3.40, 3.41, and 3.42, mirror the results by sex. Nonwhites committed narcotics violations infrequently (13 times) and eleven of these concern marijuana. There are only three other offenses that involve drugs and none of these occurs more than once. Trigueños show the highest frequency of narcotics offenses (82), with 67 percent related to marijuana and 37 percent related to cocaine. A few other offenses show drugs, but most occur only once. Two-time offenses (16 percent) have the highest drug presence compared to one-time (8 percent) and three-time (7 percent). Likewise, most white drug presence concerns narcotics offenses (64). Also, there is infrequent drug possession beyond these. Last, none of the delinquency status groups seems

TABLE 3.35 Number and Percent of Nonwhite Drug Possessions by Location and Type of Residence, School Type and Enrollment

NONWHITE

POSSESSION OF

Offense	Any Drug N	%	Marijuana N	%	Heroin N	%	Cocaine N	%	Other N	%
Rural	3	5.8	3	5.8	1	1.9	1	1.9	—	—
Urban	12	7.8	10	6.5	—	—	3	1.9	1	.7
Barrio	6	7.7	4	5.1	—	—	2	2.6	—	—
Private	5	6.8	5	6.8	—	—	—	—	—	—
Public	4	7.4	4	7.4	1	1.9	2	3.7	1	1.9
Public	15	7.4	13	6.4	1	.5	4	1.9	1	.5
Private Denomin.	—	—	—	—	—	—	—	—	—	—
Private Nondenom.	—	—	—	—	—	—	—	—	—	—
Not in school	8	10.0	7	8.8	1	10.0	3	30.0	1	10.0
In school	7	5.6	6	4.8	—	—	1	.8	—	—

Percentages are row percents.

TABLE 3.36 Number and Percent of Trigueño Drug Possessions by Location and Type of Residence, School Type and Enrollment

TRIGUEÑO

POSSESSION OF

Category	Any Drug N	%	Marijuana N	%	Heroin N	%	Cocaine N	%	Other N	%
Rural	16	5.9	15	5.6	1	.4	2	.7	--	--
Urban	71	11.9	46	7.7	10	1.7	28	4.7	3	.5
Barrio	28	8.6	22	6.8	4	1.2	9	2.8	--	--
Private	35	10.5	23	6.9	4	1.2	13	3.9	2	.6
Public	25	11.8	16	7.6	3	1.4	9	4.3	1	.5
Public	88	10.6	61	7.3	11	1.3	31	3.7	3	.4
Private Denomin.	--	--	--	--	--	--	--	--	--	--
Private Nondenom.	--	--	--	--	--	--	--	--	--	--
Not in school	45	13.5	30	8.9	9	2.7	18	5.4	1	.3
In school	43	8.1	31	5.8	2	.4	13	2.4	2	.4

Percentages are row percents.

TABLE 3.37 Number and Percent of White Drug Possessions by Location and Type of Residence, School Type and Enrollment

WHITE

POSSESSION OF

Category	Any Drug N	%	Marijuana N	%	Heroin N	%	Cocaine N	%	Other N	%
Rural	14	5.2	13	4.9	—	——	1	.4	—	——
Urban	49	5.8	40	4.8	3	.4	11	1.3	—	——
Barrio	18	6.0	16	5.4	1	.3	3	1.0	—	——
Private	32	5.1	30	4.8	1	.2	3	.5	—	——
Public	14	7.7	8	4.4	1	.5	6	3.3	—	——
Public	60	5.9	50	4.9	3	.3	12	1.2	—	——
Private Denomin.	—	——	—	——	—	——	—	——	—	——
Private Nondenom.	4	13.8	4	13.8	—	——	—	——	—	——
Not in school	20	6.1	15	4.6	1	.3	6	1.8	—	——
In school	44	5.6	39	4.9	2	.3	6	.8	—	——

Percentages are row percents.

TABLE 3.38 Number and Percent of Male Drug Possessions by Crime Code and Delinquency Status

MALES
POSSESSION OF

Offense	Any Drug N	%	Marijuana N	%	Heroin N	%	Cocaine N	%	Other N	%
Robbery	2	1.3	2	1.3	—	---	—	---	—	---
Larceny	5	2.9	5	2.9	—	---	1	.6	—	---
Auto Theft	1	2.6	1	2.6	—	---	—	---	—	---
Weapons	2	3.2	1	1.6	—	---	1	1.6	—	---
Narcotics	148	96.1	109	70.8	16	10.4	49	31.8	4	2.6
Traffic	1	.3	1	.3	—	---	—	---	1	.3
Public Authority	1	33.3	1	33.3	—	---	—	---	—	---
Threats	2	5.9	2	5.9	—	---	—	---	—	---
Delinquency Status										
One-time	77	7.5	59	5.7	7	.7	20	1.9	2	.2
Two-time	42	9.9	31	7.3	5	1.2	19	4.5	3	.7
Three +	44	6.2	32	4.5	4	.6	12	1.7	—	---

Percentages are row percents.

TABLE 3.39 Number and Percent of Drug Possessions by Crime Code and Delinquency Status

FEMALES

POSSESSION OF

Offense	Any Drug N	%	Marijuana N	%	Heroin N	%	Cocaine N	%	Other N	%
Larceny	1	3.1	1	3.1	-	---	-	---	-	---
Weapons	1	14.3	-	---	-	---	1	14.3	-	---
Narcotics	12	100.0	10	83.3	1	8.3	3	25.0	-	---
Public Authority	1	33.3	-	---	-	---	1	33.3	-	---
Breach of Peace	1	2.1	1	2.1	-	---	-	---	-	---
Delinquency Status										
One-time	9	3.5	7	2.7	1	.4	3	1.2	-	---
Two-time	4	10.0	3	7.5	-	---	2	5.0	-	---
Three +	2	6.1	2	6.0	-	---	-	---	-	---

Percentages are row percents.

TABLE 3.40 Number and Percent of Nonwhite Drug Possessions by Crime Code and Delinquency Status

NONWHITE

POSSESSION OF

Offense	Any Drug N	%	Marijuana N	%	Heroin N	%	Cocaine N	%	Other N	%
Robbery	1	5.0	1	5.0	-	---	-	---	-	---
Larceny	1	5.5	1	5.5	-	---	-	---	-	---
Narcotics	13	100.0	11	84.6	1	7.7	4	30.8	1	7.7
Traffic	1	6.3	1	6.3	-	---	-	---	-	---
Delinquency Status										
One-time	11	11.3	9	9.3	1	1.0	4	4.1	1	1.0
Two-time	-	---	-	---	-	---	-	---	-	---
Three +	5	5.4	5	5.4	-	---	-	---	-	---

Percentages are row percents.

TABLE 3.41 Number and Percent of Trigueño Drug Possessions by Crime Code and Delinquency Status

TRIGUEÑO
POSSESSION OF

Offense	Any Drug N	%	Marijuana N	%	Heroin N	%	Cocaine N	%	Other N	%
Robbery	1	1.3	1	1.3	-	---	-	---	-	---
Larceny	2	2.4	2	2.4	-	---	1	1.2	-	---
Weapons	1	3.2	-	---	-	---	1	3.2	-	---
Narcotics	82	96.5	57	67.1	11	12.9	31	36.5	3	3.5
Public Authority	2	40.0	1	20.0	-	---	1	20.0	-	---
Breach of Peace	1	1.8	1	1.8	-	---	-	---	1	1.8
Threats	1	5.9	1	5.9	-	---	-	---	-	---
Delinquency Status										
One-time	35	7.6	24	5.2	3	.6	11	2.4	1	.2
Two-time	33	16.0	22	10.7	5	2.4	17	8.3	3	1.5
Three +	23	7.1	17	5.2	3	9.2	6	1.8	-	---

Percentages are row percents.

TABLE 3.42 Number and Percent of Drug Possessions by Crime Code and Delinquency Status

WHITE
POSSESSION OF

Offense	Any Drug N	%	Marijuana N	%	Heroin N	%	Cocaine N	%	Other N	%
Larceny	3	3.0	3	3.0	—	—	—	—	—	—
Auto Theft	1	4.0	1	4.0	—	—	—	—	—	—
Weapons	2	5.5	1	2.8	—	—	1	2.8	—	—
Narcotics	64	94.1	51	75.0	5	7.4	17	25.0	—	—
Threats	1	4.8	1	4.8	—	—	—	—	—	—
Delinquency Status										
One-time	40	5.5	33	4.5	4	.5	8	1.1	—	—
Two-time	13	5.7	12	5.3	—	—	4	1.8	—	—
Three +	18	5.5	12	3.7	1	.3	6	1.8	—	—

Percentages are row percents.

related to drug possession as about five percent of the offenses of each group concerns drug possession.

INCIDENCE SUMMARY

The incidence data, like the case for prevalence, show several distinct results that are very noteworthy.

First, males predominate in serious offenses, with 39 percent UCR index crimes compared to 24 percent for females. Nonwhites (44 percent) also have the greater share of UCR index crimes compared to trigueños (36 percent) and whites (32 percent).

Second, concerning the set of the most serious UCR index crimes--homicide, manslaughter, and attempted homicide offenses--the sex effect is very pronounced. Males committed all of the homicides, three-quarters of the manslaughters, and 92 percent of the attempted homicides. These violent offenses were also more prevalent in barrio residences and the urban area. Further, handguns and drug-involved delinquents were significantly involved in these most serious acts of violence.

Third, there was a distinct relationship between drugs and delinquency. Twenty five percent of all the offenses were committed by delinquents who were users of drugs. These offenders were also very highly involved in the property offenses and the violent crimes. Most significant, drug use was very strongly related to chronic recidivism status. Thus, delinquents with a drug history were much more delinquent, especially in the more serious acts of delinquency, and they were responsible for one quarter of all the crime and much higher proportions of the serious crime in the cohort.

4
Age and Delinquency

In this chapter we present analyses of the relationship between delinquency and two measures of age. The first, age-at-onset, concerns the specific age at which an offender begins his or her delinquency career. Because this age-at-onset measure marks the boundaries of the juvenile's period at risk of being delinquent, we will be investigating the extent to which: a) the age distribution of the onset of delinquency differs across sex and color groups, and b) the extent to which a delinquency career begun early leads to the accumulation of more offenses than a delinquency career that was begun at a later age.

The second set of analyses, age-at-offense, concern the specific ages at which offenses were committed. Here we will be concerned with whether the frequency or character of delinquency varies as juveniles move toward adulthood--age eighteen in Puerto Rico.

AGE-AT-ONSET

Table 4.1 depicts for males and females the delinquency onset years from age five through age seventeen and the number, percent, and cumulative percent of delinquents. These data indicate a very close similarity between males and females in terms of the age at which delinquency was started. In general, delinquency increases from the lowest onset year through age sixteen and then declines at age seventeen for both males and females. Very few delinquents begin their careers before age thirteen, cumulatively, 8 percent for males and 7.4 percent for females. The biggest percentage increase (about 100 percent) occurs between ages 13 and 14. At this

93

Delinquency in Puerto Rico

juncture, males increase from 6.4 percent to 13.7 percent and females increase from 7.7 percent to 14.4 percent.

TABLE 4.1 Number, Percent, and Cumulative Percent of Offenders by Age-At-Onset and Sex

Age	MALES			FEMALES		
	Number	%	Cum. %	Number	%	Cum. %
5	2	.14	.14	–	–	---
6	1	.07	.21	–	–	---
7	1	.07	.28	1	.35	.35
8	4	.28	.56	–	–	.35
9	11	.78	1.3	1	.35	.70
10	21	1.5	2.8	2	.70	1.4
11	22	1.6	4.4	7	2.5	3.9
12	50	3.6	8.0	10	3.5	7.4
13	90	6.4	14.4	22	7.7	15.1
14	193	13.7	28.1	41	14.4	29.5
15	340	24.2	52.3	56	19.6	49.1
16	449	31.9	84.2	85	29.8	78.9
17	218	15.5	99.7	60	21.1	100.0

Percentages do not sum to 100.0% due to a few missing ages.

The age-at-onset distributions further indicate that about one-half of the delinquents begin between the lowest age and age 15--specifically, 52 percent for males and 49 percent for females. The modal year of starting a delinquency career is age sixteen for both sexes. About 32 percent of males begin at age sixteen with an accumulation of 85 percent up to and including this age, while about 30 percent of females begin at age sixteen with an accumulation of 79 percent by this age.

Age and Delinquency

Age data, with its continuous increments, is especially well suited to graphical presentations. Thus, we have graphed the age and delinquency data in line charts in order to depict the relationship between the age-at-onset of delinquency and the cumulative percentages by sex and color. The cumulative percentage allows us to examine the points at which each sex group attained a particular accumulation of delinquents--25 percent, 50 percent, and so on.

Figure 4.1 displays the age-at-onset and delinquency percentages by sex. This chart clearly indicates that for both males and females, the curve of the percentage of delinquents is very flat between age five and age eleven, where the percentage of delinquents accounted for is less than ten percent for both sexes. At age eleven the percentage starts to increase and sharply rises, with about 50 percent of the offenders known by age fifteen. This upward trend continues until all the delinquents have been accounted for by age seventeen. The chart also depicts quite well the fact that males and females follow the same basic trend, regardless of age.

Table 4.2 shows the relationship between age-at-onset and two measures of career offenses--the offense frequency and the mean number of offenses. The data are somewhat different by sex category. For males, there is a tendency for those offenders who began from age 10 through age 13, to have committed more offenses on average in their careers than those delinquents who began at ages five through 9 and after age 13. That is, there is no linear relationship between age-at-onset and the frequency of delinquency. This means that it is not the earliest starters who commit the greatest number of offenses, rather, it is the offenders who begin in the middle of the age range that accumulate the highest mean number of offenses.

For females, this group of middle starters is observed for ages 12 and 13. These two groups commit a higher average number of delinquencies than any other age-at-onset groups. The mean number of offenses before age 12 and after age 13 are lower and are consistently in the 1.0 to 1.1 range.

Figure 4.2 presents a line chart of the mean number of career offenses by age-at-onset and sex. The curves clearly reflect the different tabular results by sex. For males, there is a definite spike in mean number of offenses for ages 10 through 13, while for females, only ages 12 and 13 show a higher mean number of offenses.

Table 4.3 turns to age-at-onset percentages for the three color categories. These data portray much the same picture as did the data by sex. Regardless of color, few delinquents begin before age thirteen, less than 8

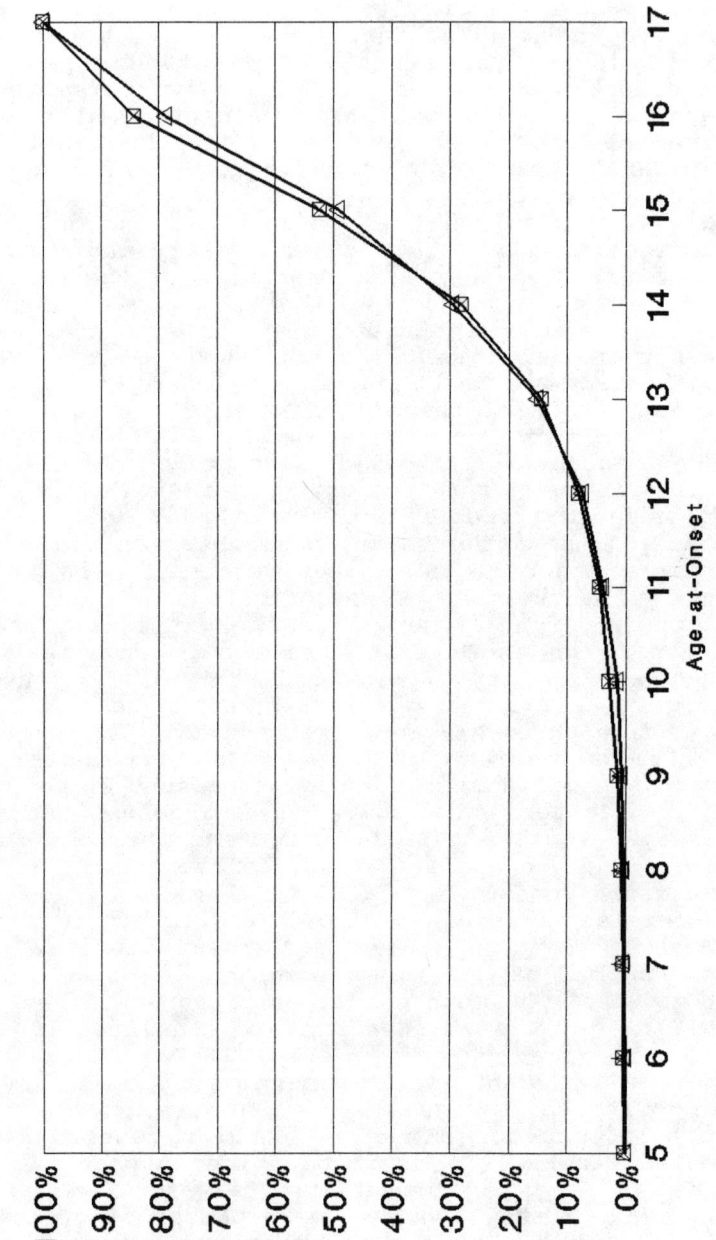

TABLE 4.2 Offenders, Offenses, and Mean Number of Offenses by Age-At-Onset and Sex

Age	ALL Offend.	ALL Offense	ALL Mean	MALES Offend.	MALES Offense	MALES Mean	FEMALES Offend.	FEMALES Offense	FEMALES Mean
5	2	5	2.5	2	5	2.5	–	–	–
6	1	1	1.0	1	1	1.0	–	–	–
7	2	2	1.0	1	1	1.0	1	1	1.0
8	4	6	1.5	4	6	1.5	–	–	–
9	12	17	1.4	11	16	1.5	1	1	1.0
10	23	59	2.6	21	57	2.7	2	2	1.0
11	29	81	2.8	22	74	3.4	7	7	1.0
12	60	119	1.9	50	105	2.1	10	14	1.4
13	112	231	2.1	90	201	2.2	22	30	1.5
14	234	385	1.6	193	337	1.7	41	48	1.2
15	396	607	1.5	340	540	1.6	56	67	1.2
16	534	668	1.3	449	573	1.3	85	95	1.1
17	278	300	1.1	218	237	1.1	60	63	1.1

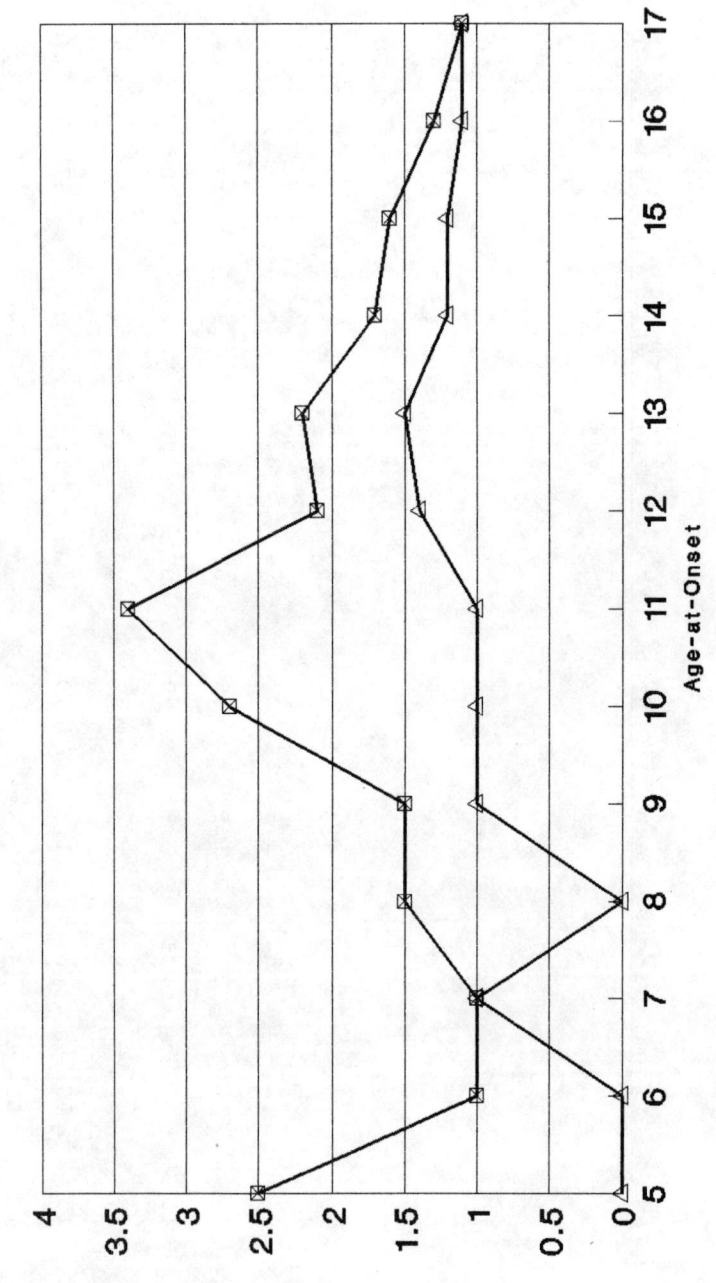

Figure 4.2
Mean Number of Offenses
by Age-at-Onset and Sex

TABLE 4.3 Number, Percent, and Cumulative Percent of Offenders by Age-At-Onset and Color

Age	Nonwhite			Trigueño			White		
	Number	%	Cum. %	Number	%	Cum. %	Number	%	Cum. %
5	—	—	—	1	.16	.16	1	.10	.10
6	—	—	—	1	.16	.32	—	—	.10
7	—	—	—	—	—	.32	2	.22	.32
8	1	.74	.74	2	.31	.63	1	.10	.42
9	—	—	.74	4	.63	1.3	8	.87	1.4
10	1	.74	1.5	11	1.7	3.0	11	1.2	2.6
11	3	2.2	3.7	8	1.3	4.3	18	1.9	4.5
12	4	2.9	6.6	23	3.6	7.9	31	3.4	7.9
13	9	6.7	13.3	47	7.4	15.3	56	6.1	14.0
14	21	15.6	28.9	88	13.9	29.2	125	13.6	27.6
15	37	27.4	56.3	143	22.5	51.7	216	23.5	51.1
16	33	24.4	80.7	212	33.4	85.1	289	31.4	82.4
17	23	17.0	99.7	94	14.8	99.9	161	17.5	99.9

Percentages do not sum to 100.0% due to a few missing ages.

percent for all three color groups. Nonwhites exhibit a slightly higher tendency to begin early. That is, the modal year of onset is age 15 (27 percent) and 56 percent of the delinquents are accounted for by this age for nonwhites. The modal year of onset is one year later for trigueños (33 percent) and whites (31 percent), and both of these groups have about 51 percent of the offenders starting by this age.

Figure 4.3, like Figure 4.1, depicts the cumulative delinquency data by age-at-onset. This chart reflects the very close similarity of the percentages by color. For all three color categories, a substantial upward trend is not evident until age fourteen.

Table 4.4 presents the career data by age-at-onset and color. The middle group of years, ages 10 through 13, once again show the strongest relationship to average career offenses. It is strongest for trigueños who average 3.4 and 3.9 offenses for onset years 10 and 11 respectively. These are followed by nonwhites who show a high average at age 13 (3.3) and by whites who have lower averages but ones that are still high at ages 10, 11, and 12. These results are given graphically in Figure 4.4.

Table 4.5 depicts the relationship between particular offense-specific offender groups and age-at-onset and sex. These data first indicate that males begin their careers earlier for the three main categories, chronic delinquents, injury offenders, and UCR index offenders. The data further reveal the important finding that compared to overall delinquency, there is a definite trend for males--early onset leads to a higher number of serious offenses. Male chronics who begin before age 14 show a higher average number of offenses than chronic recidivists who begin after this age. Similarly, male injury offenders who begin before age 14 accumulate a higher average number of offenses that resulted in personal injury to a victim than injury offenders who start this type of offense at age 14 or later. This result is also found for the general category of UCR index offenses, although the differences are not as strong as for injury offenses.

For females, there does not appear to be a very strong relationship between an early start of serious offending and the accumulation of a high number of offenses. For chronics only age 13 has a mean, 3.7, that is very different from the other ages which mostly show an average of 3.0. Similarly, only one age-at-onset of injury offenses, age 12, is appreciably higher than the usual average of 1.2. For UCR index offenses, the male pattern discussed above does emerge. That is, females who begin committing this serious category of crimes at

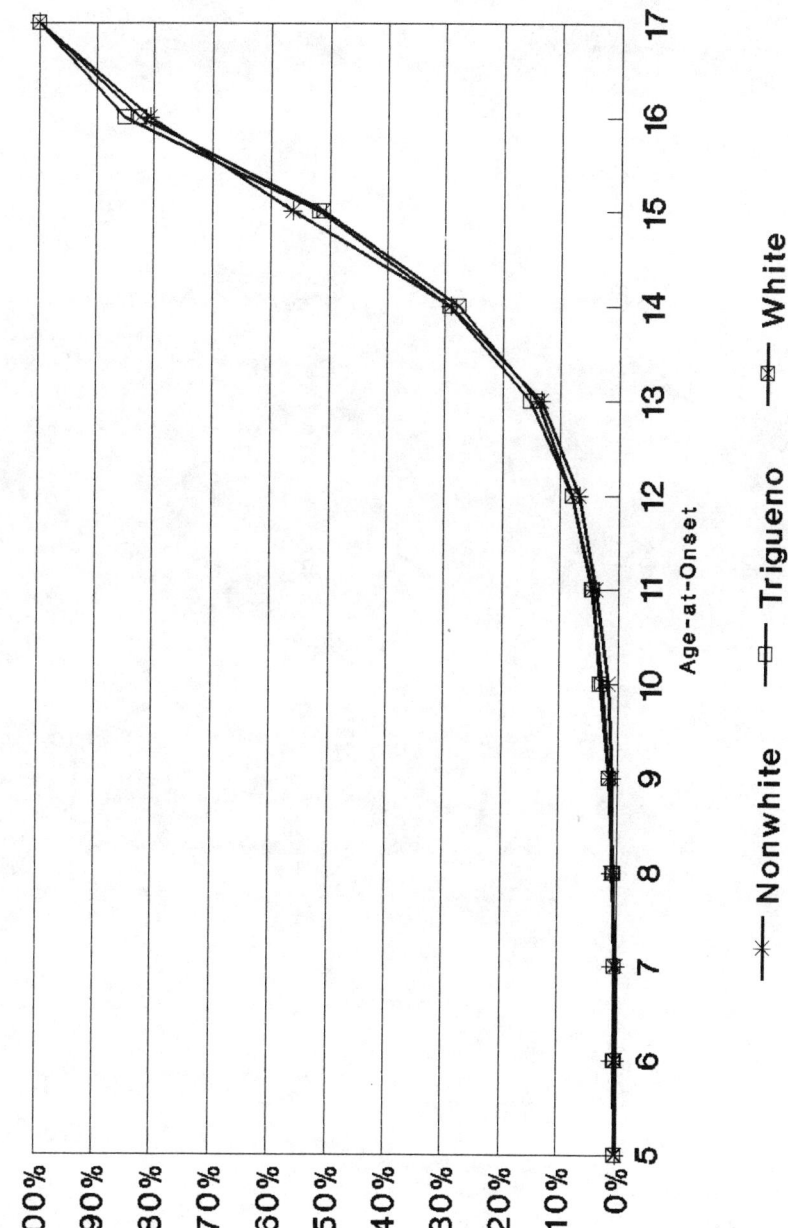

Figure 4.3
Cumulative Percentage of Offenders
by Age-at-Onset and Color

TABLE 4.4 Offenders, Offenses, and Mean Number of Offenses by Age-At-Onset and Color

Age	NONWHITE Offend.	Offense Mean	Trigueño Offend.	Offense Mean	WHITE Offend.	Offense Mean
5	–	–	1	4.0	1	1.0
6	–	–	1	1.0	–	–
7	–	–	–	–	2	1.0
8	1	1.0	2	3	1	2.0
9	–	–	4	6	1.5	1.4
9	–	–	4	6	1.5	
10	1	2.0	11	37	3.4	8	11	1.8
11	3	2.3	8	31	3.9	18	20	2.4
12	4	1.5	23	47	2.0	31	44	2.0
13	9	3.3	47	98	2.1	56	62	1.9
14	21	2.3	88	146	1.7	125	106	1.6
15	37	1.8	143	230	1.6	216	195	1.5
16	33	2.9	212	281	1.3	289	315	1.2
17	23	2.7	94	103	1.1	161	342	1.1

Percentages do not sum to 100.0% due to a few missing ages.

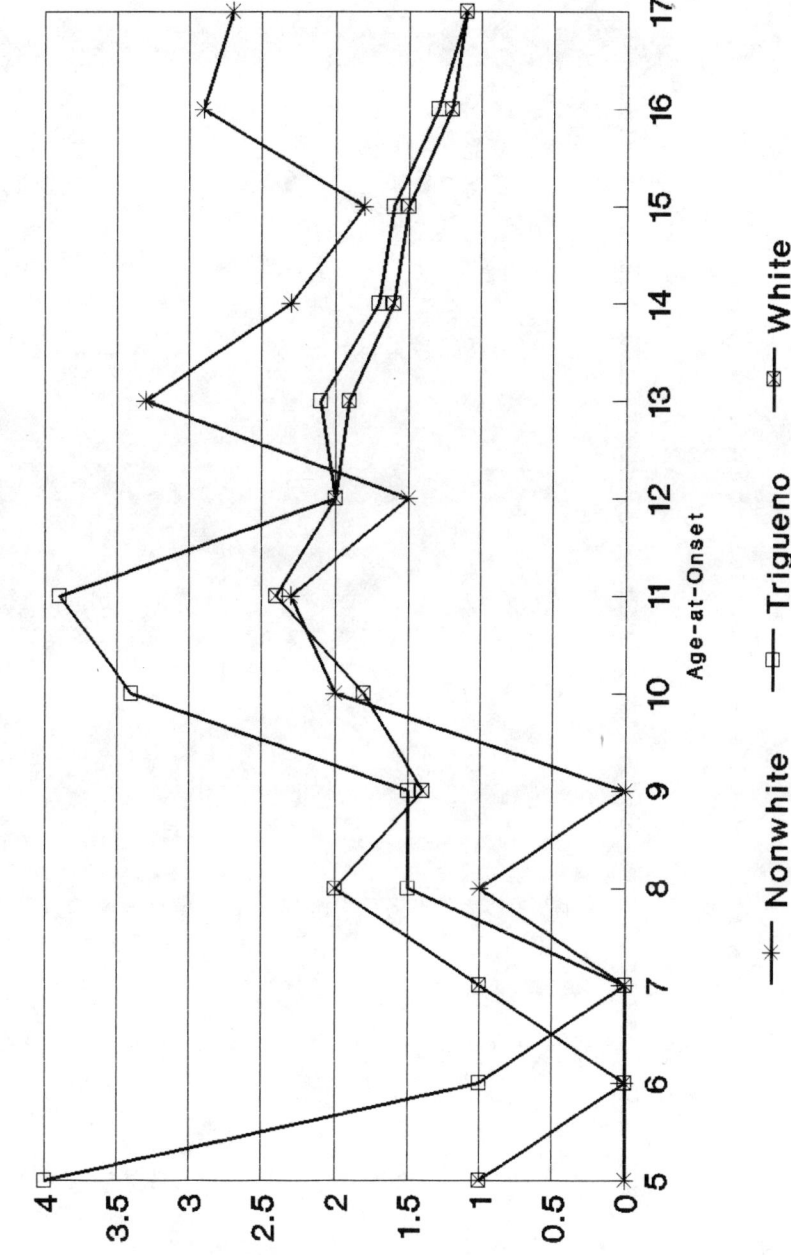

Figure 4.4
Mean Number of Offenses by
Age-at-Onset and Color

—✱— Nonwhite   —□— Trigueno   —⊠— White

TABLE 4.5 Mean Number of Offenses for Select Offense Groups by Age-At-Onset and Sex

Age	ALL Offenders	Mean	CHRONIC Offenders	Mean	INJURY Offenders	Mean	UCR INDEX Offenders	Mean
Male								
<10	19	1.5	2	3.5	2	2.5	7	2.3
10	21	2.7	8	5.0	6	4.0	14	3.2
11	22	3.4	9	6.2	6	4.7	14	4.5
12	50	2.1	11	5.3	10	3.0	24	3.0
13	90	2.2	24	4.9	32	2.7	51	2.8
14	193	1.8	35	4.1	52	2.1	97	2.2
15	340	1.6	44	4.2	104	1.9	156	2.1
16	449	1.3	23	3.6	113	1.3	147	1.6
17	218	1.1	3	3.0	168	1.1	53	1.3
All	1404	1.5	160	4.4	375	1.8	564	2.1
Female								
<10	2	1.0	—	—	—	—	—	—
10	2	1.0	—	—	—	—	—	—
11	7	1.0	—	—	3	1.0	4	1.0
12	10	1.4	1	3.0	4	1.8	3	1.0
13	22	1.4	3	3.7	11	1.0	6	1.7
14	41	1.2	2	3.0	21	1.2	13	1.5
15	56	1.2	3	3.3	23	1.4	12	1.4
16	85	1.1	1	3.0	33	1.2	23	1.2
17	60	1.1	—	—	24	1.1	12	1.1
All	285	1.2	10	3.3	119	1.2	73	1.3

ages 13, 14, or 15 have a higher career average than other index offenders.

Table 4.6 repeats this offense-group analysis by color categories. These data show that particular years (or sets of years) of starting the various kinds of offenses are related to career accumulation. Nonwhites do not have a distinct effect for chronic offending, as most chronic delinquents average about 4.4 offenses regardless of age-at-onset. But, nonwhites who begin injury offending at 14 or 15 do show higher means, 2.6 and 2.4 respectively, than other ages. For index offending, the age effect starts a little earlier, age 12, and continues to age 15.

Among the trigueño delinquents there is not a particular set of years that carry a much higher average, there is one year, age 12, that shows a very high mean number of offenses. This age-at-onset group was responsible for a mean of 8.3 offenses by chronics, a mean of 6.3 injury offenses, and a mean of 5.4 index offenses. These values are all higher than for any other age-at-onset group.

For the white offenders, the sets of years that show the most delinquency are ages 11 (5.6) and 12 (5.8) for chronics, ages 10 (5.0) and 12 (2.7) for injury offenses, and ages 10 (3.4) and 11 (2.9) for UCR index offenses. These data thus indicate a somewhat strong linear relationship by age—the younger the age-at-onset, the greater the number of serious offenses that a delinquent will accumulate in his or her career.

Despite this age-at-onset effect for whites, the data overall do not demonstrate the expected inverse age effect. Rather, it appears to be the middle period of juvenile years, around ages 12 to 14, that seem to be related to career delinquency. Regardless of sex or color, delinquents who begin committing offenses in these middle years generally, or the serious variety of delinquent acts, seem to exhibit the highest average rates of offending.

This result is not what would have been expected. On the contrary, a priori expectations would be that the earlier the start point, the higher the number of total offenses, given the fact of a greater exposure period.

AGE-AT-OFFENSE

In Tables 4.7 to 4.16 we turn to the analyses of the ages at which various offense types were committed, regardless of when the offender started his or her delinquency career.

TABLE 4.6

Mean Number of Offenses for Select Offense Groups by Age-At-Onset and Color

Age	ALL Offenders	Mean	CHRONIC Offenders	Mean	INJURY Offenders	Mean	UCR INDEX Offenders	Mean
Nonwhite								
<10	1	1.0	-	-	-	-	-	-
10	1	2.0	-	-	-	-	1	2.0
11	3	2.0	1	3.0	1	1.0	3	2.0
12	6	1.7	1	5.0	4	2.0	2	3.0
13	9	3.0	5	4.6	2	2.0	7	3.0
14	21	2.1	5	4.6	11	2.6	17	2.3
15	37	1.7	6	4.5	15	2.4	16	2.3
16	33	1.4	3	3.7	15	1.5	12	1.7
17	23	1.0	-	-	3	1.3	3	1.0
All	135	1.7	21	4.4	51	2.0	62	2.2
Trigueño								
<10	8	1.8	1	4.0	-	-	4	2.5
10	11	3.4	5	5.8	5	3.8	7	4.3
11	8	3.9	3	8.3	3	6.3	5	5.4
12	23	2.0	6	4.5	4	3.3	11	2.6
13	47	2.1	10	5.6	20	2.6	23	3.1
14	88	1.7	15	3.8	23	1.8	42	2.2
15	143	1.6	17	4.5	45	1.9	70	1.9
16	212	1.3	10	3.9	49	1.2	67	1.6
17	94	1.1	2	3.0	25	1.0	18	1.2
All	635	1.6	70	4.6	174	1.8	247	2.1
White								
<10	12	1.3	1	3.0	2	2.5	3	2.0
10	11	1.8	3	3.7	1	5.0	6	2.2
11	18	2.4	5	5.6	5	2.2	10	3.4
12	31	2.0	5	5.8	6	2.7	14	2.9
13	56	1.9	12	4.3	21	2.1	27	2.3
14	125	1.6	17	4.0	39	1.7	51	2.0
15	216	1.5	24	3.9	67	1.6	82	2.0
16	289	1.2	11	3.3	82	1.2	91	1.4
17	161	1.1	1	3.0	46	1.1	44	1.2
All	919	1.4	79	4.1	269	1.5	328	1.0

Age and Delinquency

Table 4.7 presents the number and percent of offenders by age and sex. Like the age-at-onset data reported above, the age-at-offense data are very similar by sex. The greatest number of offenders is observed committing crimes at age 16 (34 percent for males; 31 percent for females). The number of offenders increases with age to a peak at the modal year of 16, and then declines at age seventeen.[8] The average number of offenses committed across the various ages does not differ very much, thus indicating that there is no age effect.

TABLE 4.7 Number and Percent of Offenders and Mean Number of Offenses by Age and Sex

Age	MALES			FEMALES		
	Number	%	Mean	Number	%	Mean
Up to 10	43	2.4	1.1	4	1.3	1.0
11	22	1.2	1.1	7	2.3	1.0
12	62	3.5	1.1	10	3.3	1.0
13	104	5.9	1.2	22	7.2	1.0
14	224	12.6	1.3	42	13.7	1.1
15	415	23.4	1.3	60	19.6	1.1
16	594	33.5	1.2	94	30.7	1.1
17	304	17.2	1.2	67	21.9	1.0
Total	1,772	----	1.2	306	----	1.1

Percentages do not sum to 100.0% due to missing ages.

Table 4.8 presents the number of offenses by age and sex. These data are practically identical to the previous table. Offenses increase steadily with age. The peak occurs at age 16 with 34 percent of the male offenses and 32 percent of the female delinquencies occurring at this age.

TABLE 4.8 Number and Percent of Offenses by Age and Sex

Age	MALES		FEMALES	
	Number	%	Number	%
Up to 10	48	2.2	4	1.2
11	25	1.2	7	2.1
12	68	3.2	10	3.1
13	121	5.6	22	6.7
14	284	13.2	45	13.7
15	519	24.1	66	20.1
16	739	34.3	104	31.7
17	353	16.4	70	21.3
Total	2,157	----	328	----

Percentages do not sum to 100.0% due to a few missing ages.

TABLE 4.9 Number and Percent of Offenders and Mean Number of Offenses by Age and Color

	NONWHITE			TRIGUEÑO			WHITE		
Age	Number	%	Mean	Number	%	Mean	Number	%	Mean
Up to 10	2	1.1	1.0	20	2.5	1.0	25	2.3	1.2
11	3	1.7	1.0	8	.98	1.1	18	1.6	1.2
12	7	4.0	1.0	29	3.6	1.0	36	3.3	1.1
13	10	5.7	1.0	53	6.6	1.1	63	5.8	1.1
14	23	13.1	1.1	103	12.7	1.2	140	12.8	1.2
15	47	26.9	1.5	176	21.7	1.3	252	23.0	1.2
16	50	28.6	1.3	274	33.9	1.3	364	33.3	1.2
17	32	18.3	1.1	144	17.8	1.2	195	17.8	1.1
Total	175	----	1.3	809	----	1.2	1,094	----	1.2

Percentages do not sum to 100.0% due to a few missing ages.

Table 4.9 presents offender data by age and color. We see from these data that the number of offenders increases with age as it did for the two sex groups. The only discernable differences exhibited by the table are for nonwhites. Nonwhites have a higher percentage of offenses occurring at each of the ages of 14 (13 percent), 15 (27 percent), and 16 (29 percent) than is the case for trigueños and whites. The mean number of offenses across the ages from 10 to 17 do not show any notable pattern with the exception of age 15 for nonwhites. This group of offenders (n=47) had a mean of 1.5 offenses which is the highest average shown in the table.

Table 4.10 gives offense data by age and color. These data confirm the general finding that offenses increase throughout the age range and peak at the end of the age period--age 16 for trigueños and whites, but at age 15 for nonwhites. Also noteworthy is the fact that for trigueños and whites, almost every age shows approximately the exact same percentages of offenses.

TABLE 4.10   Number and Percent of Offenses by Age and Color

Age	NONWHITE Number	%	TRIGUEÑO Number	%	WHITE Number	%
Up to 10	2	.9	21	2.1	29	2.3
11	3	1.4	8	.8	21	1.7
12	7	3.2	31	3.1	40	3.1
13	10	4.5	64	6.5	69	5.4
14	26	11.7	135	13.6	168	13.2
15	72	32.4	220	22.2	293	23.0
16	66	29.7	342	34.5	435	34.2
17	36	16.2	170	17.2	217	17.1
Total	222	----	991	----	1,272	--

Percentages do not sum to 100.0% due to missing ages.

Table 4.11 displays the number and percent of UCR index and nonindex offenses by age and sex. For index offenses the peak age is earlier for males, age 15 (27 percent), than for females, age 16 (37 percent). Concerning the nonindex category, the data show that males and female distributions are very similar by age.

Figure 4.5 presents a histogram of the index offense percentages by age-at-offense by sex. This chart shows the interesting finding that females have a higher percentage than males of their index offenses at later ages. For females, about 37 percent of index offenses

TABLE 4.11 Index and Nonindex Offenses (UCR) by Age and Sex

	UCR INDEX MALE		UCR INDEX FEMALE		UCR NONINDEX MALE		UCR NONINDEX FEMALE	
Age	Number	%	Number	%	Number	%	Number	%
Up to 10	20	2.4	0	---	28	2.1	4	1.6
11	16	1.9	4	5.1	9	.68	3	1.2
12	33	3.9	3	3.8	35	2.6	7	2.8
13	53	6.4	5	6.3	68	5.1	17	6.8
14	130	15.6	13	16.5	154	11.6	32	12.9
15	221	26.6	13	16.5	298	22.5	53	21.3
16	263	31.7	29	36.7	476	35.9	75	30.1
17	95	11.4	12	15.2	258	19.5	58	23.3

Figure 4.5
Percentage of Index Offenses
by Age-at-Offense and Sex

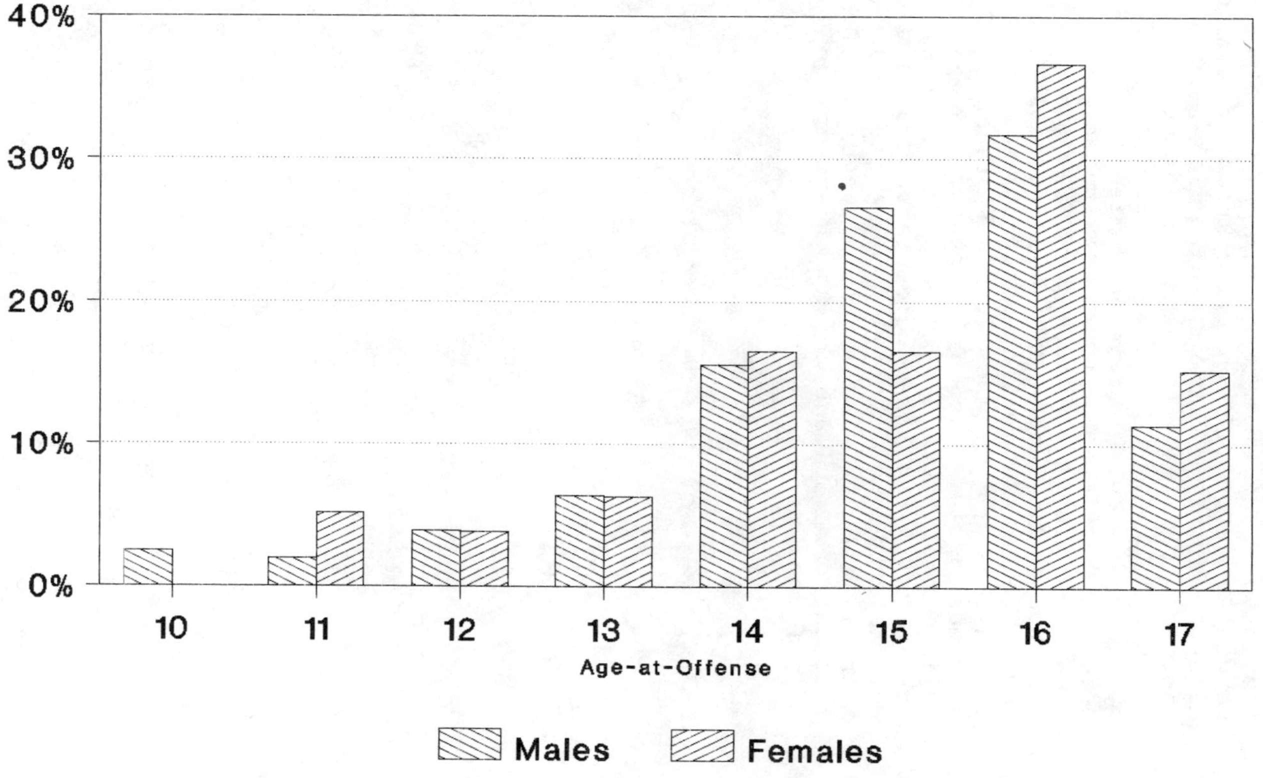

Delinquency in Puerto Rico

were committed at age sixteen and 15 percent were committed at age seventeen compared to 32 percent and 11 percent at ages fifteen and sixteen, respectively, for males. Thus, index offending is generally a late emerging phenomenon for female delinquents.

Table 4.12 shows the type of index offenses committed by age and sex. The male data are all consistent. The percent of offenses increases with age up to 16. The modal year is age sixteen for all four types of index offenses. The female data are inconsistent. That is, for violence, the percentages increases to age 13, stays the same at 14, declines at 15, increases at 16 and then declines again. Robbery offenses are only committed during three ages 15, 16, and 17, and thus, we cannot make much of the three percentages that are available. For the property category of index crime, the increasing trend with age is found, however. Despite the fluctuations with age the modal age is age 16 like the case for males.

TABLE 4.12 Type of UCR Index Offenses by Age and Sex

Age	Violence Number	%	Robbery Number	%	Property Number	%	Vehicle Number	%
Male Up to								
10	1	.74	-	---	19	4.0	-	-
11	2	1.5	-	---	14	2.9	-	-
12	4	2.9	-	---	27	5.7	2	3.9
13	9	6.7	5	2.9	35	7.4	4	7.8
14	19	14.1	16	9.4	88	18.5	7	13.7
15	34	25.2	51	30.0	125	26.3	11	21.6
16	47	34.8	67	39.4	130	27.4	19	37.3
17	19	14.1	31	18.2	37	7.8	8	15.7
All	135	----	170	----	475	----	51	-
Female Up to								
10	-	---	-	---	-	---	-	-
11	2	9.0	-	---	2	4.2	-	-
12	-	---	-	---	3	6.3	-	-
13	4	18.2	-	---	1	2.1	-	-
14	4	18.2	-	---	9	18.8	-	-
15	2	9.0	1	11.1	10	20.8	-	-
16	6	27.3	6	66.7	17	35.4	-	-
17	4	18.2	2	22.2	6	12.5	-	-
All	22	----	9	----	48	----	-	-

Age and Delinquency

Table 4.13 reports the number and percentage of index and nonindex offenses by age and color. The index data repeat the color finding we observed earlier that nonwhites peak earlier, age 15 (37 percent) than trigueños, age 16 (31 percent), and whites, age 16 (35 percent). The nonindex offenses follow the general pattern of increasing offenses with age up to a peak at age 16. Figure 4.6 shows that nonwhites and trigueños generally have higher percentages of index offenses from age 10 through age 15, but at ages 16 and 17, whites predominate.

Table 4.14 gives the type of index offenses by age and color. Few violent offenses are committed at the early ages for any color category. Nonwhites seem to have a higher percentage earlier, age 14 (29.4 percent) compared to trigueños (14 percent) and whites (12 percent) at this age. All three color categories peak at age 16 for violent offenses. Nonwhites also commit robbery offenses earlier. The peak year is age 15, with 57 percent of the robberies compared to age 16 for trigueños (44 percent) and whites (43 percent). For all three color categories, the property offense data generally follow the increasing trend with age, but the peak age is different. Nonwhites peak at age 15 (31 percent); trigueños also peak at age 15 (27 percent) but age 16 is very close (26 percent); and whites clearly peak at age 16 (31 percent). Motor vehicle thefts are almost nonexistent for nonwhites--2 at age 15. For trigueños, these offenses start at age 13 and peak at age 16 (27 percent), while for whites, these offenses begin at age 12 and peak at age 16 (44 percent).

Tables 4.15 and 4.16 present data on the alternate offense classification system--the Sellin-Wolfgang index system. Table 4.15 indicates that, for both males and females, injury offenses increase with age up to the peak year, age 16. Even though males commit more than three times the number of injury offenses, the percentages by age are very similar.

When we turn to the theft/damage category, we note that the first year for which more than ten percent of the offenses to have occurred is age 14 for both males (15 percent) and females (16 percent). Once again, the peak is at age 16 showing 34 percent of the offenses for both sexes. The trend is increasing up to this peak and then declines. It is once again important that, even though males committed more than ten times the number of theft/damage offenses as did females, the age distributions were remarkably alike.

In terms of nonindex offenses, those that did not involve any injury, theft, or damage, we again see that

TABLE 4.13 Index and Nonindex Offenses (UCR) by Age and Color

	UCR INDEX						UCR NONINDEX					
	NONWHITE		TRIGUEÑO		WHITE		NONWHITE		TRIGUEÑO		WHITE	
Age	N	%	N	%	N	%	N	%	N	%	N	%
Up to 10	1	1.0	8	2.1	11	2.5	1	.8	13	2.1	18	2.2
11	3	3.1	5	1.3	12	2.7	0	---	3	.5	9	1.1
12	3	3.1	13	3.5	20	4.6	4	3.2	18	2.9	20	2.4
13	6	6.2	25	6.7	27	6.2	4	3.2	39	6.3	42	5.0
14	17	17.5	65	17.4	61	13.9	9	7.2	70	11.4	107	12.9
15	36	37.1	104	27.8	94	21.4	36	28.8	116	18.8	199	23.9
16	24	24.7	116	31.0	152	34.6	42	33.6	226	36.6	283	33.9
17	7	7.2	38	10.2	62	14.1	29	23.2	132	21.4	155	18.6

TABLE 4.14 Type of UCR Index Offenses by Age and Color

Age	Violence #	%	Robbery #	%	Property #	%	Vehicle #	%
Nonwhite								
Up to								
10					1	1.8		
11	1	5.9			2	3.6		
12					3	5.5		
13	1	5.9			5	9.1		
14	5	29.4	2	8.7	10	18.2		
15	4	23.5	13	56.5	17	30.9	2	100.0
16	6	35.3	5	21.7	13	23.6		
17			3	13.0	4	7.3		
All	17		23		55		2	
Trigueño								
Up to								
10	1	1.7			7	3.2		
11	1	1.7			4	1.8		
12	1	1.7			12	5.5		
13	3	5.2	2	2.4	19	8.8	1	6.7
14	8	13.8	7	8.3	48	22.1	2	13.3
15	18	31.0	22	26.2	59	27.2	5	33.3
16	19	32.8	37	44.0	56	25.8	4	26.7
17	7	12.2	16	19.0	12	5.5	3	20.0
All	58		84		217		15	
White								
Up to								
10					11	4.4		
11	2	2.4			10	3.9		
12	3	3.7			15	5.9	2	5.9
13	9	10.9	3	4.2	12	4.8	3	8.8
14	10	12.2	7	9.7	39	15.5	5	14.7
15	14	17.1	17	23.6	59	23.5	4	11.8
16	28	34.1	31	43.0	78	31.1	15	44.1
17	16	19.5	14	20.0	27	10.8	5	14.7
All	82		72		251		34	

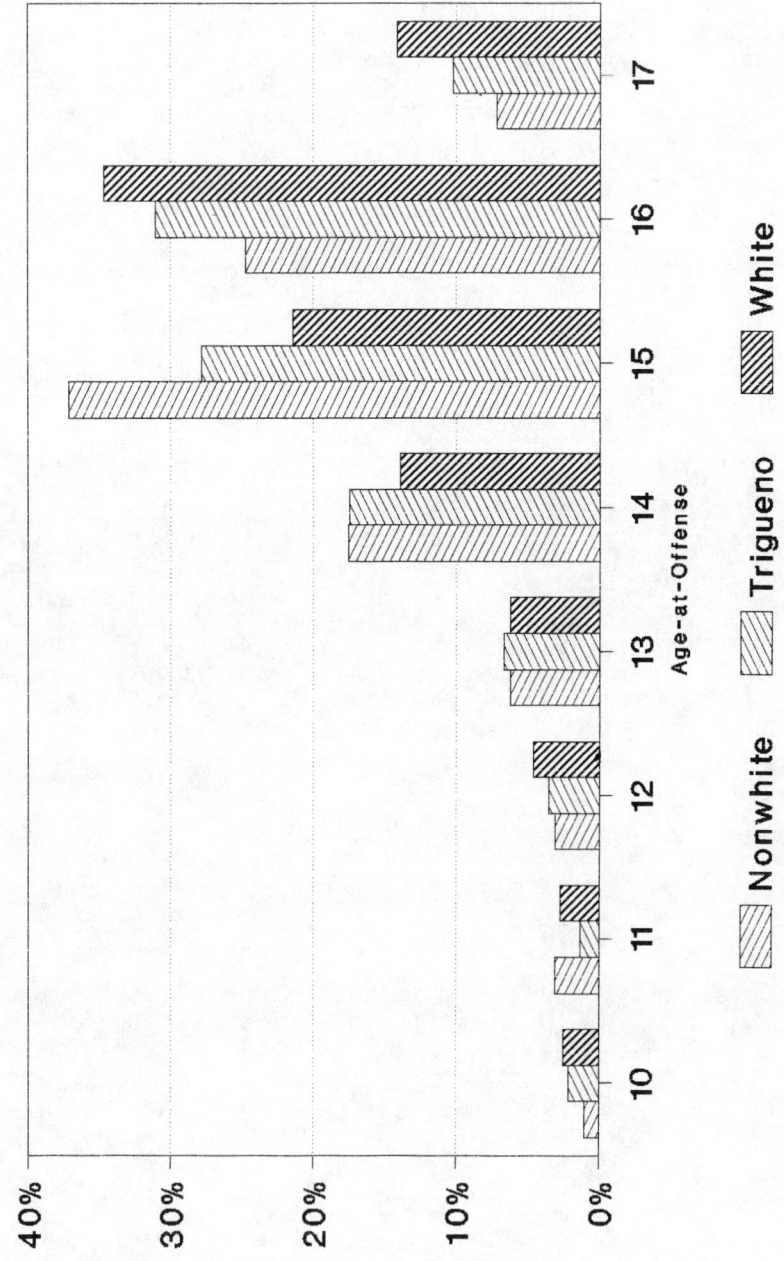

Figure 4.6
Percentage of Index Offenses
by Age-at-Offense and Color

TABLE 4.15 Sellin-Wolfgang Index Offenses by Age and Sex

	Injury		Theft/Damage		Nonindex	
Age	Number	Percent	Number	Percent	Number	Percent
Male						
Up to						
10	8	1.9	10	1.1	30	3.5
11	4	.96	12	1.4	9	1.0
12	7	1.7	29	3.3	32	3.7
13	28	6.7	43	4.9	50	5.8
14	49	11.7	135	15.3	100	11.7
15	102	24.4	235	26.7	182	21.2
16	148	35.4	296	33.6	295	34.4
17	72	17.2	121	13.7	160	18.6
All	418		881		858	
Female						
Up to						
10					9	7.2
11	3	2.4	2	2.6	2	1.6
12	3	2.4	2	2.6	5	4.0
13	11	8.7	1	1.3	10	8.0
14	20	15.9	12	15.6	13	10.4
15	24	19.1	15	19.5	27	21.6
16	39	30.9	26	33.8	39	31.2
17	26	20.6	19	24.7	20	16.0
All	126		77		125	

TABLE 4.16 Sellin-Wolfgang Index Offenses by
            Age and Color

	Injury		Theft/Damage		Nonindex	
Age	Number	Percent	Number	Percent	Number	Percent
Nonwhite						
Up to						
10			1	1.2	1	1.4
11	1	1.5	2	2.4		
12	3	4.5	3	3.5	1	1.4
13	2	3.0	5	5.9	3	4.3
14	11	16.4	11	12.9	4	5.7
15	24	35.8	27	31.8	21	30.0
16	20	29.9	21	24.7	25	35.7
17	6	8.9	15	17.7	15	21.4
All	67		85		70	
Trigueño						
Up to						
10	5	2.7	5	1.3	11	2.7
11	2	1.1	4	1.0	2	.48
12	2	1.1	11	2.8	18	4.4
13	20	10.6	19	4.9	25	6.0
14	23	12.2	64	16.5	48	11.6
15	41	21.8	110	28.3	69	16.7
16	60	31.9	123	31.6	159	38.4
17	35	18.6	53	13.6	82	19.8
All	188		389		414	
White						
Up to						
10	3	1.0	4	.83	22	4.4
11	4	1.4	8	1.7	9	1.8
12	5	1.7	17	3.5	18	3.6
13	17	5.9	20	4.1	32	6.4
14	35	12.1	72	14.9	61	12.2
15	61	21.1	113	23.4	119	23.9
16	107	37.0	178	36.8	150	30.1
17	57	19.7	72	14.9	88	17.6
All	289		484		499	

the increasing frequency with age is present with a mode at age 16 for both males and females.

The final age-related table depicts the Sellin-Wolfgang offense data for color categories. Table 4.16 clearly indicates that nonwhites have an earlier involvement in injury offenses. For this group, 52 percent of the injury offenses were committed at ages 14 and 15 with a cumulative total of 61 percent by the peak age of 15. For trigueños, the cumulative percent is 49 percent by age 15, while for whites the cumulative percent is 43 percent. Both these color groups show a later peak age, age 16. The theft/damage data repeats this pattern. Nonwhites have a peak year of age 15, while trigueños and whites peak at age 16.

For the generic category of nonindex offenses, all three color groups exhibit the same trend. Offenses increase with age to a peak at age 16. Nonwhites show the greatest concentration of nonindex offenses at the end of the age period, showing 87 percent of the offenses at the age of 15 or later. Trigueños are next with a concentration of 75 percent, followed by whites with 72 percent.

AGE AND DELINQUENCY SUMMARY

The preceding sets of tables, one for age-at-onset and the other for age-at-offense, present data that indicate a relatively consistent pattern of results across the various sex and color categories.

With respect to age-at-onset, the data show the following results. First, the data are very similar by sex and color. Few offenders begin before age 13, and all groups except nonwhites (age 15) have a peak at age 16.

Second, the expected relationship between beginning early and using this longer period at risk to commit more offenses was generally not found. Males did exhibit this trend for certain types of serious offenders, but not for general delinquency. Similarly, there were particular onset years by color which produced a greater career average, but it was not necessarily the early starters.

Third, the most active offenders appeared to be those who began their careers in the middle age period--ages 13 to 15.

Concerning the other age effect, age-at-offense, we found the following. First, regardless of very different volumes of offenses, males and females show a very close age distribution. Offenses increase with age to a peak at age 16. This is generally true for delinquency overall and for serious offenses as well.

Delinquency in Puerto Rico

Second, there are a few notable differences by color. Nonwhites generally show an earlier peak year, age 15, compared to trigueños and whites (age 16). Other than this aberrant year for nonwhites, the data concerning age and delinquency followed the trend of increasing offenses to age 16, followed by a decline at age 17.

5
Delinquent Recidivism

From the point of view of both theory and of public policy, perhaps the most informative delinquency analyses concern delinquent recidivism. It is, of course, undesirable for young people to be delinquent, but it is not surprising that some youth will break the law once or even twice. Deviant behavior is a customary aspect of all societies. But, when youths continue to break the law three, four, or more times, then delinquency becomes more significant because it then begins to represent the initiation of a pattern of deviance that can continue into adulthood. Thus, our analyses in this section will be concerned with a number of topics and emphases surrounding delinquent recidivism. Data given above indicate that recidivism does not involve a very substantial proportion of the 1970 cohort, especially for females. It is especially important, therefore, to examine closely those offenders who do recidivate frequently.

CHRONIC OFFENDERS

Table 5.1 reports data on offenders and offenses by the three delinquency status categories. The group of greatest policy importance is the three-time offender--the chronic recidivist. The data indicate that the 170 chronics comprise about ten percent of the 1,689 delinquents in the 1970 cohort. On the other hand, these chronic delinquents committed 739, or about 30 percent of the delinquency in the cohort. When we focus on just the recidivists we note that 42 percent of the recidivists were chronic, and these chronics were responsible for about 62 percent of the delinquency among the recidivist subset.

TABLE 5.1 Number and Percent of Offenders and Offenses by Delinquency Status and Recidivist Groups

	Offenders No.	%	Offenses No.	%
Delinquents:	1,689	100.0	2,489	100.0
One-time	1,288	76.3	1,288	51.8
Two-time	231	13.7	462	18.6
Three or more	170	10.1	739	29.7
Recidivists:	401	100.0	1,201	100.0
Two-time	231	57.6	462	38.5
Three or more	170	42.4	739	61.5

Percentages are column percents.

Table 5.2 presents the offender/offense data by sex. We note first, that for males there is an observed chronic-offender effect. Among males, the chronic delinquent represents 11 percent of the delinquents. This set of chronic offenders committed 706 offenses which amounts to 33 percent of all the 2,161 male delinquencies. Turning to the recidivist subset we can observe that male chronics are about 43 percent of the recidivists but they committed 63 percent of the recidivist offenses.

The data for females are dissimilar and do not show a chronic offender effect at all. That is, female chronics are a very small proportion of female delinquents--10 offenders or just 3.5 percent of the offenders. This small group of chronics was responsible for 10 percent of the female delinquency. Thus, like males, female chronics are a small proportion of the pool of delinquents, but unlike males, the chronics do not commit a disproportionate share of the delinquency.

The lack of a chronic-offender effect for females is due to the overabundance of one-time offenders. That is, of the total pool of female offenders (n=285), 255 delinquents, or about 90 percent, did not go on to a second offense. Consequently, there were only 30 female recidivists eligible to become chronic. Of these 30 recidivists, 20, or two-thirds stopped at the second

TABLE 5.2 Number and Percent of Offenders and Offenses by Delinquency Status, Recidivist Groups, and Sex

	MALES				FEMALES			
	Offenders No.	%	Offenses No.	%	Offenders No.	%	Offenses No.	%
<u>Delinquents</u>	1,404	100.0	2,161	100.0	285	100.0	328	100.0
One-time	1,033	73.6	1,033	47.8	255	89.5	255	77.7
Two-time	211	15.0	422	19.5	20	7.0	40	12.2
Three or more	160	11.4	706	32.7	10	3.5	33	10.1
<u>Recidivists</u>	371	100.0	1,128	100.0	30	100.0	73	100.0
Two-time	211	56.9	422	37.4	20	66.7	40	54.8
Three or more	160	43.1	706	62.6	10	33.3	33	45.2

Percentages are column percents.

offense. The remaining ten females who were chronic are neither large enough nor offensive enough to skew the rates of offending in their favor as was the case for males.

Table 5.3 reports the same data as above but by color category. With these results we can observe a distinct chronic-offender effect that differs by color. Chronic offending involves the highest proportion for nonwhites, for whom 13 percent of the delinquents were chronic. The nonwhite chronics committed 41 percent of the nonwhite delinquency. Nonwhites are followed by trigueños with 11 percent chronic recidivists who were responsible for 33 percent of the trigueño offenses. Last, we have whites for whom chronic recidivism involves about 9 percent of the delinquents and 25 percent of the offenses. Looking at the recidivist subset in particular we see that for nonwhites the chronic offenders committed almost three-quarters of all the delinquency. The percentage is less, about 60 percent for the other two color categories.

In Table 5.4 we give offense data for a variety of offense groupings by offender categories and sex. For males we can see that generally, the chronics are responsible for the largest share of the most serious offenses as measured by the UCR index system. The 11 percent pool of chronic male delinquents committed 43 percent of the UCR index offenses, 44 percent of the homicides, 55 percent of the robberies.

For females, the opposite is true. Female chronics do not exhibit a disproportionate share of any offense type or grouping, not even the more serious offenses. It is quite clear, therefore, that chronic recidivism is not a female phenomenon in our 1970 cohort.

The results in Table 5.5 confirm the color data we discussed earlier. Nonwhite chronic delinquents predominate in most of the serious forms of delinquency as they did in delinquency generally. The situation for trigueños shows a chronic- recidivism effect, but one that is smaller than for nonwhites. Last, the white group is overrepresented in serious delinquency but their involvement is not nearly as skewed as was the case for nonwhites especially.

OFFENSE PROBABILITIES

Recidivism is not just a categorical variable (that is, 1, 2 or 3 or more offenses) where one chronic should be treated just like any other. Recidivism is also a set of probabilities from a first offense to a second, from a second to a third, and so on. In the next set of

TABLE 5.3 Number and Percent of Offenders and Offenses by Delinquency Status, Recidivist Groups, and Color

	NONWHITE		TRIGUEÑO		WHITE	
	Offenders	Offenses	Offenders	Offenses	Offenders	Offenses
Delinquents	135	223	635	993	919	1,273
	100.0	100.0	100.0	100.0	100.0	100.0
One-time	97	97	462	462	729	729
	71.8	43.5	72.8	46.5	79.3	57.3
Two-time	17	34	103	206	111	222
	12.6	15.3	16.2	20.8	12.1	17.4
Three or more	21	92	70	325	79	322
	15.6	41.3	11.0	32.7	8.6	25.3
Recidivists	38	126	173	531	190	544
	100.0	100.0	100.0	100.0	100.0	100.0
Two-time	17	34	103	206	111	222
	44.7	26.9	59.5	38.8	58.4	40.8
Three or more	21	92	70	325	79	322
	55.3	73.0	40.5	61.2	41.6	59.2

Percentages are column percents.

TABLE 5.4 Number and Percent of Select Offenses by Delinquency Status and Sex

Crime Code	MALES						FEMALES					
	One-time		Two-time		3 or more		One-time		Two-time		3 or more	
	N	%	N	%	N	%	N	%	N	%	N	%
All Offenses	1033	47.8	422	19.5	706	32.7	255	77.7	40	12.2	33	10.1
UCR Index	304	36.5	169	20.3	359	43.2	60	75.9	10	12.6	9	11.4
UCR Nonindex	729	54.9	253	19.0	347	26.1	195	78.3	30	12.1	24	9.6
Homicide	11	30.6	19	25.0	16	44.4	3	100.0				
Rape	2	40.0	2	40.0	1	20.0						
Robbery	36	21.2	40	23.5	94	55.3	5	55.6	4	44.4		
Agg. Assault	55	58.5	15	15.9	24	25.5	15	78.9	2	10.5	2	10.5
Burglary	87	33.1	50	19.0	126	47.9	6	50.0	2	16.7	4	33.3
Larceny	95	44.6	41	19.3	77	36.2	31	86.1	2	5.6	3	8.3
Auto Theft	18	35.3	12	23.5	21	41.2						
UCR Violent	68	50.4	26	19.3	41	30.4	18	81.8	2	9.1	2	9.1
UCR Property	200	37.9	103	19.5	224	42.5	37	77.1	4	8.3	7	14.6
Injury	194	63.6	48	15.7	63	20.7	89	80.2	14	12.6	8	7.2
Theft	152	33.3	103	22.5	202	44.2	29	72.5	6	15.0	5	12.5
Damage	163	57.4	59	20.8	62	21.8	28	93.3	2	6.7		
Nonindex	419	48.6	172	19.9	271	31.4	92	73.6	16	12.8	17	13.6

Percentages are row percents.

TABLE 5.5

Number and Percent of Select Offenses by Delinquency Status and Color

	NONWHITE			TRIGUEÑO			WHITE		
	1	2	3+	1	2	3+	1	2	4+
All Offenses	97	34	92	462	206	325	729	222	322
	43.5	15.3	41.3	46.5	20.8	32.7	57.3	17.4	25.3
UCR Index	33	16	49	133	79	162	198	84	157
	33.7	16.3	50.0	35.6	21.1	43.3	45.1	19.1	35.8
UCR Nonindex	64	18	43	329	127	163	531	138	165
	51.2	14.4	34.4	53.2	20.5	26.3	63.7	16.6	19.8
Homicide	1	-	5	4	4	6	9	5	5
	16.7	---	83.3	28.6	28.6	42.9	47.4	26.3	26.3
Rape	-	-	-	1	1	1	1	1	-
	---	---	---	33.3	33.3	33.3	50.0	50.0	---
Robbery	6	1	16	16	22	46	19	21	32
	26.1	4.4	69.6	19.1	26.2	54.8	26.4	29.2	44.4
Agg. Assault	9	1	1	25	6	10	36	10	15
	81.8	9.1	9.1	60.9	14.6	24.4	59.0	16.4	24.6
Burglary	7	7	20	35	20	61	51	25	49
	20.6	20.6	58.8	30.2	17.2	52.6	40.8	20.0	39.2
Larceny	9	6	7	48	20	33	69	17	40
	40.9	27.3	31.8	47.5	19.8	32.7	54.8	13.5	31.8
Auto Theft	1	1	-	4	6	5	13	5	16
	50.0	50.0	---	26.7	40.0	33.3	38.2	14.7	47.1
UCR Violent	10	1	6	30	11	17	46	16	20
	58.8	5.9	35.3	51.7	18.9	29.3	56.1	19.5	24.4
UCR Property	17	14	27	87	46	99	133	47	105
	29.3	24.1	46.6	37.5	19.8	42.7	46.7	16.5	36.8
Injury	24	10	11	98	19	28	161	33	32
	53.3	22.2	24.4	67.6	13.1	19.3	71.2	14.6	14.2
Theft	15	9	20	74	45	97	92	55	90
	34.1	20.5	45.5	34.3	20.8	44.9	38.8	23.2	39.7
Damage	11	2	8	56	25	23	124	32	33
	52.4	9.5	38.1	53.9	24.0	22.1	65.6	16.9	17.5
Nonindex	33	9	29	193	92	131	285	87	128
	46.5	12.7	40.9	46.4	22.1	31.5	57.0	17.4	25.6

Percentages are row percents.

tables (5.6 to 5.14) we turn to analyses of offense probabilities by sex, color, and offense type.

In Table 5.6 we can see that those male offenders who do recidivate seem to do so with an increasing probability. Overall, males show an eleven percent chance of delinquency, a 26 percent chance of recidivism, and a 43 percent chance of chronic recidivism. Thereafter, we note than the chances increase to more than 50 percent from the fourth out to the tenth offense and beyond. The data for females indicate that there is just a 10 percent chance of recidivism, and although one-third of the recidivists become chronic, only 20 percent (two offenders) go on to a fourth offense, one stops at this point, while the other stops at five offenses. Thus, only ten females committed at least three offenses, and most important, only 2 go on to a fourth and just 1 female delinquent committed five offenses.

TABLE 5.6   Probability of Committing One or More Offenses of Any Type by Sex

Offense Number	Males	Females	Both
1 or more	.113	.023	.068
2 or more	.264	.105	.237
3 or more	.431	.333	.424
4 or more	.550	.200	.529
5 or more	.659	.500	.656
6 or more	.500	----	.500
7 or more	.586	----	.586
8 or more	.647	----	.647
9 or more	.636	----	.636
10 or more	.571	----	.571

Initial probability based on number of subjects at risk.

Table 5.7 reports recidivism probabilities by sex for the UCR index category of crime (that is, homicide, rape, robbery, aggravated assault, burglary, larceny, and auto theft). These data show that about one-quarter (27.5%) of the males are recidivists in this type of crime and of this quarter, over one-third (38.7 percent) go on to a third. Thereafter, the chances increase and fluctuate, but generally stay in the range of a fifty percent chance. The data for females reveals that serious recidivism like that of UCR index crimes is practically nonexistent. Six percent of females commit this type of

Delinquent Recidivism

crime twice and only 20 percent go on to a third and last UCR index crime.

TABLE 5.7 Probability of Committing One or More UCR Index Offenses by Sex

Offense Number	Males	Females	Both
1 or more	.045	.006	.026
2 or more	.275	.068	.251
3 or more	.387	.200	.381
4 or more	.417	----	.409
5 or more	.480	----	.480
6 or more	.500	----	.500
7 or more	.500	----	.500
8 or more	.667	----	.667
9 or more	1.000	----	1.000
10 or more	.500	----	.500

Initial probability based on number of subjects at risk.

TABLE 5.8 Probability of Committing One or More Select UCR Index Offenses by Sex

UCR VIOLENT

Offense Number	Males	Females	Both
1 or more	.010	.002	.006
2 or more	.055	.048	.054

UCR PROPERTY

Offense Number	Males	Females	Both
1 or more	.031	.004	.017
2 or more	.208	.043	.191
3 or more	.400	----	.400
4 or more	.344	----	.344
5 or more	.636	----	.636
6 or more	.571	----	.571
7 or more	.750	----	.750
8 or more	.667	----	.667
9 or more	.500	----	.500
10 or more	1.000	----	1.000

Initial probability based on number of subjects at risk.

Delinquency in Puerto Rico

We next divide the UCR index crimes into two types--violence (homicide, rape, and aggravated assault) and property (burglary and larceny). The data in Table 5.8 for the violent offenses are surprising because the chance of a second violent offense is so similar for males (5.5 percent) and females (4.8 percent). The familiar pattern returns, however, for the property offenses. Here, male recidivism shows a generally increasing probability out to the tenth offense, while female recidivism does not go beyond the second offense.

Table 5.9 presents the recidivism chances for the Sellin-Wolfgang system of classifying offenses. In this system the crime code or legal category basis of what is a serious offense is ignored in favor of a measurement of whether the offense actually involved the components of injury, theft of property or money, or damage of property. The nonindex category consists of offenses that did not have any of these three seriousness components.

TABLE 5.9 Probability of Committing One or More Select Sellin-Wolfgang Offenses by Sex

Offense Number	Males	Females	Both
SELLIN-WOLFGANG INJURY			
1 or more	.023	.009	.016
2 or more	.056	.048	.053
3 or more	.188	.200	.190
SELLIN-WOLFGANG THEFT			
1 or more	.028	.003	.015
2 or more	.207	.053	.192
3 or more	.380	----	.369
4 or more	.259	----	.259
SELLIN-WOLFGANG DAMAGE			
1 or more	.021	.002	.012
2 or more	.065	----	.058
3 or more	.176	----	.176
4 or more	.333	----	.333
SELLIN-WOLFGANG NONINDEX			
1 or more	.054	.009	.032
2 or more	.173	.090	.161
3 or more	.342	.400	.346
4 or more	.350	----	.350
5 or more	.500	----	.500
6 or more	.571	----	.571
7 or more	.500	----	.500

Initial probability based on number of subjects at risk.

Delinquent Recidivism

The injury probabilities, like the UCR violence probabilities, show no sex effect. The maximum number of offenses is three for both sexes, and the probabilities are similar, although the chance of a third injury offense is slightly higher for females (20 percent) than for males (18.8 percent). The theft and damage data show that only male recidivists go on to a third and fourth offense. Females commit a maximum of two theft and one damage offenses.

The nonindex recidivism data are akin to an analysis of general delinquency. These results indicate that males have an increasing chance of recidivating out to a seventh offense and beyond, while females do not commit more than three nonindex type offenses.

In Tables 5.10 to 5.14 we turn to recidivism probabilities among the color groups. Because we do not have population based data on color, we cannot compute the initial chance that a member of a given color will commit a first offense. This does not affect, however, the reliability of the recidivism data from the second offense onward, for which we need only the number of delinquents as the base.

TABLE 5.10 Probability of Committing One or More Offenses of Any Type by Color

Offense Number	Nonwhite	Trigueño	White
1 or more	----	----	----
2 or more	.281	.272	.207
3 or more	.553	.405	.416
4 or more	.571	.586	.468
5 or more	.750	.609	.676
6 or more	.444	.600	.400
7 or more	.400	.667	.500
8 or more	.500	.700	.600
9 or more	1.000	.571	.667
10 or more	1.000	.750	.500

Initial probability is not computable due to the lack of data concerning population at risk by color.

Table 5.10 shows that the three color groups are very close in general recidivism. At least a tenth offense was observed for each color, and usually, the chances of moving up the scale of recidivism increased for each color as well. Table 5.11, however, shows that UCR recidivism is most prevalent for trigueños. The chances

131

Delinquency in Puerto Rico

of recidivism for this group increase and are strong as we move from the second to the tenth offense. Nonwhites do not go beyond a fifth UCR index offense and whites do not go beyond a sixth.

TABLE 5.11 Probability of Committing One or More UCR Index Offenses by Color

Offense Number	Nonwhite	Trigueño	White
1 or more	----	----	----
2 or more	.306	.275	.223
3 or more	.474	.397	.342
4 or more	.667	.407	.320
5 or more	.333	.545	.500
6 or more	----	.833	.250
7 or more	----	.600	----
8 or more	----	.667	----
9 or more	----	1.000	----
10 or more	----	.500	----

Initial probability is not computable due to the lack of data concerning population at risk by color.

Table 5.12 repeats this same basic finding for UCR nonindex offenses. Trigueños are seen committing offenses out to at least an eighth, with about a 50 percent chance. Whites are close behind with seven offenses. Nonwhites do not repeat this offense with much regularity. For nonwhites, the highest offense number is four and this rank involves only twenty percent of those at risk.

TABLE 5.12 Probability of Committing One or More UCR Nonindex Offenses by Color

Offense Number	Nonwhite	Trigueño	White
1 or more	----	----	----
2 or more	.177	.187	.147
3 or more	.588	.375	.277
4 or more	.200	.424	.321
5 or more	----	.500	.444
6 or more	----	.571	.500
7 or more	----	.500	.500
8 or more	----	.500	----

Initial probability is not computable due to the lack of data concerning population at risk by color.

Delinquent Recidivism

Table 5.13 shows the very infrequent commission of violent offenses, which have a maximum of only one repeat. Nonwhites (.13) have the highest chance of this repeat followed by trigueño (.05) and whites (.04). When we look at UCR property offenses the more familiar pattern seen previously emerges. That is, trigueños show the most recidivism (out to at least 10 offenses). Whites commit six of this type of offense, and nonwhites trail with no more than four.

TABLE 5.13 Probability of Committing One or More Select UCR Index Offenses by Color

Offense Number	UCR VIOLENT		
	Nonwhite	Trigueño	White
1 or more	----	----	----
2 or more	.133	.054	.038
	UCR PROPERTY		
1 or more	----	----	----
2 or more	.268	.207	.164
3 or more	.454	.029	.378
4 or more	.200	.385	.357
5 or more	----	.800	.600
6 or more	----	.750	.333
7 or more	----	1.000	----
8 or more	----	.667	----
9 or more	----	.500	----
10 or more	----	1.000	----

Initial probability is not computable due to the lack of data concerning population at risk by color.

Last, we see from Table 5.14 that our previous UCR results are somewhat confirmed with the Sellin-Wolfgang system. For injury crimes, trigueños (.40) have the highest probability of repeating to a third offense. This group is followed by nonwhites (.25) and whites (.08). For theft offenses, trigueños again predominate with higher chances of a third, fourth, and fifth offense, but for damage offenses, whites predominate with a much higher chance of a third (.25) and the only group who commits a fourth. The nonindex offense probabilities return to the usual pattern--higher trigueño recidivism, followed by whites, and then by nonwhites.

TABLE 5.14 Probability of Committing One or More
            Select Sellin-Wolfgang Offenses by Color

Offense Number	Nonwhite	Trigueño	White
SELLIN-WOLFGANG INJURY			
1 or more	----	----	----
2 or more	.100	.036	.056
3 or more	.250	.400	.083
SELLIN-WOLFGANG THEFT			
1 or more	----	----	----
2 or more	.235	.205	.173
3 or more	.250	.469	.369
4 or more	----	.333	.259
5 or more	----	1.000	.500
SELLIN-WOLFGANG DAMAGE			
1 or more	----	----	----
2 or more	.050	.084	.045
3 or more	----	.125	.250
4 or more	----	----	.500
SELLIN-WOLFGANG NONINDEX			
1 or more	----	----	----
2 or more	.179	.196	.132
3 or more	.400	.323	.364
4 or more	.250	.400	.250
5 or more	----	.500	.600
6 or more	----	.750	.333
7 or more	----	.667	----

Initial probability based on number of subjects at risk.

OFFENSE TRANSITIONS

In addition to analyzing the probability of repeat offenses, the topic of recidivism concerns another issue of great importance. This issue concerns the extent to which delinquents exhibit offense specialization. Offense specialization refers to the possibility that recidivists might be more likely to repeat the type of offense that they have just committed. On the other hand, recidivists may be more likely to engage in general recidivism with no particular pattern of repeating certain offense types. One principal reason why offense specialization is important is that, if offenders specialize they may show increased tendencies to keep repeating certain offenses which in turn may increase their chance of very frequent recidivism--a situation of reciprocal reinforcement.

The technique of investigating offense specialization using offense transition matrices was pioneered in the 1945 Philadelphia birth cohort study (Wolfgang et al., 1972). We repeat here for the Puerto Rico 1970 cohort this type of analysis, in which the type of previous offense (usually called the kth-1 offense) is compared to the current offense (called the kth offense) type across a series of offense ranks or transitions. Offense specialization exists to the extent that like offense repeats occur with about a fifty percent probability. These transition analyses are given in Tables 5.15 to 5.21.

Table 5.15 reports the male offense transitions from the first through the sixth offense, or five transitions. The most notable finding concerns desistance. At the first transition, we can see that overall 74 percent of the offenders desist or stop committing delinquent acts. Delinquents who had an injury offense as their first offense show the highest chance of desisting (82.7 percent) followed by nonindex (75 percent), and then theft/damage (67 percent). These data thus show that only about one-quarter of the delinquents move on to a second offense.

When males do commit this second offense it is most likely to be a theft/damage offense (11.9 percent), regardless of the type of offense they committed as their first offense. Theft/damage offenders at offense number one do have the highest chance (16.7 percent) of committing this type at offense number two, but this chance is not nearly high enough to show specialization. Similarly, injury (3.9 percent) and nonindex offenses (11.7 percent) are not repeated with high enough percentages to be considered specialization either.

As males move to a second, third, etc. transition, the most likely transition is to the state of desistance for the kth offense, regardless of the type of the kth-1 offense. The only evidence that an offense type is repeated sufficiently often to be noteworthy concerns the theft/damage category. From a first transition of 16.7 percent, this offense type shows percentages of 26.9, 36.6, 35.0, and 41.7 for the second through the fifth transition. These scores do suggest a moderate tendency for theft damage offenders to specialize as the delinquency career progresses. None of the other two offense types are repeated to this extent.

TABLE 5.15 Offense Transitions for Males

MALES: 1st Transition

K-1 / K	Injury		Theft/ Damage		Non-Index		Desist	
Injury	12	3.9	26	8.5	15	4.9	254	82.7
Theft/Damage	24	4.4	90	16.7	66	12.2	360	66.6
Nonindex	22	3.9	51	9.2	65	11.7	419	75.2
Total	58	4.1	167	11.9	146	10.4	1033	73.6

MALES: 2nd Transition

K-1 / K	Injury		Theft/ Damage		Non-Index		Desist	
Injury	9	15.5	5	8.6	10	17.2	34	58.6
Theft/Damage	8	4.8	45	26.9	26	15.6	88	52.7
Nonindex	4	2.7	21	14.4	32	21.9	89	60.9
Total	21	5.7	71	19.1	68	18.3	211	56.9

MALES: 3rd Transition

K-1 / K	Injury		Theft/ Damage		Non-Index		Desist	
Injury	6	28.6	3	14.3	2	9.5	10	47.6
Theft/Damage	3	4.2	26	36.6	13	18.3	29	40.9
Nonindex	6	8.8	11	16.2	18	26.5	33	48.5
Total	15	9.4	40	25.0	33	20.6	72	45.0

MALES: 4th Transition

K-1 / K	Injury		Theft/ Damage		Non-Index		Desist	
Injury	4	26.7	4	26.7	5	33.3	2	13.3
Theft/Damage	2	5.0	14	35.0	11	27.5	13	32.5
Nonindex	5	15.2	6	18.2	7	21.2	15	45.5
Total	11	12.5	24	27.3	23	26.1	30	34.1

MALES: 5th Transition

K-1 / K	Injury		Theft/ Damage		Non-Index		Desist	
Injury	1	9.1	1	9.1	4	36.4	5	45.5
Theft/Damage			10	41.7	4	16.7	10	41.7
Nonindex	1	4.4	4	17.4	4	17.4	14	60.9
Total	2	3.5	15	25.9	12	20.7	29	50.0

Delinquent Recidivism

Table 5.16 reports the offense transitions for females. For females, only three transitions are needed to account for all but two of the 285 female offenders. The situation concerning desistance is stronger than that for males. For females, there is about a 90 percent chance that a delinquent will stop after the first offense. By type the desistance rate is 92.7 percent for injury, 89.7 percent for theft/damage, and 85.9 percent for nonindex.

TABLE 5.16   Offense Transitions for Females

K-1 / K	Injury		FEMALES: Theft/ Damage		1st Transition Non-Index		Desist	
Injury	6	5.5	1	.9	1	.9	102	92.7
Theft/Damage	6	4.4	2	2.9	2	2.9	61	89.7
Nonindex	4	3.7	2	1.9	9	8.4	92	85.9
Total	13	4.6	5	1.8	12	4.2	255	89.5

K-1 / K	Injury		FEMALES: Theft/ Damage		2nd Transition Non-Index		Desist	
Injury			2	15.4	1	7.7	10	76.9
Theft/Damage	1	20.0	2	40.0			2	40.0
Nonindex	1	8.3	0		3	25.0	8	66.7
Total	2	6.7	4	13.3	4	13.3	20	66.7

K-1 / K	Injury		FEMALES: Theft/ Damage		3rd Transition Non-Index		Desist	
Injury							2	100.0
Theft/Damage					1	25.0	3	75.0
Nonindex	1	25.0					3	75.0
Total	1	10.0			1	10.0	8	80.0

As we have discussed above surrounding both recidivism prevalence and the recidivism probabilities, only 30 females moved on to a second offense, of these 30 repeaters, only ten moved on to a third offense, and of these ten, eight desisted at the third transition, thus leaving only two fourth offenses among females. These data thus do not provide very great potential for specialization to occur and Table 5.16 shows this lack of specialization for females.

In addition to a rank by rank analysis, we have included a summary matrix which expresses the kind of transitions that were made in the delinquency career, regardless of which particular offense rank they pertain to. These summary data are shown in Table 5.17.

These summary data clearly indicate that males do not specialize in their repeat offenses. If the offender does not desist, then he is likely to commit a theft/damage offense (15.8 percent), and if he has committed a theft/damage offense, he is likely to repeat this type about 23 percent of the time. This is not sufficient evidence to suggest the presence of offense specialization. For females the data simply show that no offense type is repeated overall more than about ten percent of the time. Most females desist, and most important, most females desist in the early offense ranks.

TABLE 5.17 Summary Offense Transitions by Sex

MALES: Summary Matrix

K-1 / K	Injury		Theft Damage		Non-Index		Desist	
Injury	33	7.9	39	9.3	38	9.1	308	73.7
Theft/Damage	38	4.3	199	22.6	132	14.9	512	58.1
Nonindex	40	4.6	103	11.9	135	15.7	584	67.8
Total	111	5.1	341	15.8	305	14.1	1,404	64.9

FEMALES: Summary Matrix

K-1 / K	Injury		Theft/ Damage		Non-Index		Desist	
Injury	6	4.8	3	2.4	2	1.6	115	91.3
Theft/Damage	4	5.2	4	5.2	3	3.9	66	85.7
Nonindex	6	4.8	2	1.6	13	10.4	105	83.2
Total	16	4.8	9	2.7	18	5.5	285	86.9

Tables 5.18, 5.19, and 5.20 present the offense transitions by color. Across ranks, nonwhite delinquents do not show very high repeat-offense chances for any offense type. Trigueños, however, exhibit a strong tendency to repeat theft/damage offenses. The chances start at 18.3 percent at the first transition and increase to 33.3 percent, 43.8 percent, 35.0 percent, and 87.5 percent from the 2nd to the fifth transition. These data strongly suggest that trigueños do develop a specialized tendency in this offense type. White

TABLE 5.18   Offense Transitions for Nonwhites

NONWHITE: 1st Transition

K-1 / K	Injury	Theft/Damage	Non-Index	Desist
Injury	5 11.6	4 9.3	3 6.9	31 72.1
Theft/Damage	4 8.3	9 18.8	2 4.2	33 68.8
Nonindex	2 4.6	4 9.1	5 11.4	33 75.0
Total	11 8.2	17 12.6	10 7.4	97 71.9

NONWHITE: 2nd Transition

K-1 / K	Injury	Theft/Damage	Non-Index	Desist
Injury	2 18.2	1 9.1	2 18.2	6 54.6
Theft/Damage	1 5.9	5 29.4	4 23.5	7 41.2
Nonindex		2 20.0	4 40.0	4 40.0
Total	3 7.9	8 21.1	10 26.3	17 44.7

NONWHITE: 3rd Transition

K-1 / K	Injury	Theft/Damage	Non-Index	Desist
Injury	1 4.8	2 66.7		
Theft/Damage	2 25.0		2 25.0	4 50.0
Nonindex	3 30.0	2 20.0		5 50.0
Total	6 28.6	4 19.1	2 9.5	9 42.9

NONWHITE: 4th Transition

K-1 / K	Injury	Theft/Damage	Non-Index	Desist
Injury	2 33.3	2 33.3	1 16.7	1 16.7
Theft/Damage		2 50.0	1 25.0	1 25.0
Nonindex		1 50.0		1 50.0
Total	2 16.7	5 41.7	2 16.7	3 25.0

NONWHITE: 5th Transition

K-1 / K	Injury	Theft/Damage	Non-Index	Desist
Injury	1 50.0		1 50.0	
Theft/Damage			2 40.0	3 60.0
Nonindex				2 100.0
Total	1 11.1		3 33.3	5 55.6

TABLE 5.19 Offense Transitions for Trigueños

TRIGUEÑO: 1st Transition

K-1 / K	Injury	Theft/Damage	Non-Index	Desist
Injury	4 2.7	9 6.2	10 6.9	123 84.3
Theft/Damage	12 5.2	42 18.3	29 12.7	146 63.8
Nonindex	8 3.1	21 8.1	38 14.6	193 74.2
Total	24 3.8	72 11.3	77 12.1	462 72.8

TRIGUEÑO: 2nd Transition

K-1 / K	Injury	Theft/Damage	Non-Index	Desist
Injury	2 8.3	2 8.3	5 20.8	15 62.5
Theft/Damage	1 1.4	24 33.3	10 13.9	37 51.4
Nonindex	2 2.6	6 7.8	18 23.4	51 66.2
Total	5 2.9	32 18.5	33 19.1	103 59.5

TRIGUEÑO: 3rd Transition

K-1 / K	Injury	Theft/Damage	Non-Index	Desist
Injury	2 40.0		1 20.0	2 40.0
Theft/Damage	1 3.1	14 43.8	5 15.6	12 37.5
Nonindex	2 6.1	6 18.2	10 30.3	15 45.5
Total	5 7.1	20 28.6	16 22.9	29 41.4

TRIGUEÑO: 4th Transition

K-1 / K	Injury	Theft/Damage	Non-Index	Desist
Injury	2 40.0		1 20.0	2 40.0
Theft/Damage		7 35.0	6 30.0	7 35.0
Nonindex	3 18.8	1 6.3	5 31.3	7 43.8
Total	5 12.2	8 19.5	12 29.3	16 39.0

TRIGUEÑO: 5th Transition

K-1 / K	Injury	Theft/Damage	Non-Index	Desist
Injury		1 20.0	1 20.0	3 60.0
Theft/Damage		7 87.5		1 12.5
Nonindex		3 25.0	3 25.0	6 50.0
Total	-	11 44.0	4 16.0	10 40.0

TABLE 5.20 Offense Transitions for Whites

WHITE: 1st Transition

K-1 / K	Injury	Theft/ Damage	Non-Index	Desist
Injury	9 3.9	14 6.1	3 1.3	202 88.6
Theft/Damage	11 3.3	41 12.4	37 11.2	242 73.1
Nonindex	16 4.4	28 7.8	31 8.6	285 79.2
Total	36 3.9	83 9.0	71 7.7	729 79.3

WHITE: 2nd Transition

K-1 / K	Injury	Theft/ Damage	Non-Index	Desist
Injury	5 13.9	4 11.1	4 11.1	23 63.9
Theft/Damage	7 8.4	18 21.7	12 14.5	46 55.4
Nonindex	3 4.2	13 18.3	13 18.3	42 59.2
Total	15 7.9	35 18.4	29 15.3	111 58.4

WHITE: 3rd Transition

K-1 / K	Injury	Theft/ Damage	Non-Index	Desist
Injury	3 20.0	1 6.7	1 6.7	10 66.7
Theft/Damage		12 34.3	7 20.0	16 45.7
Nonindex	2 6.9	3 10.3	8 27.6	16 55.2
Total	5 6.3	16 20.3	16 20.3	42 53.2

WHITE: 4th Transition

K-1 / K	Injury	Theft/ Damage	Non-Index	Desist
Injury		2 40.0	3 60.0	
Theft/Damage	2 12.5	5 31.3	4 25.0	5 31.3
Nonindex	2 12.5	4 25.0	3 18.8	7 43.8
Total	4 10.8	11 29.7	10 27.0	12 32.4

WHITE: 5th Transition

K-1 / K	Injury	Theft/ Damage	Non-Index	Desist
Injury			2 50.0	2 50.0
Theft/Damage		3 27.3	2 18.2	6 54.6
Nonindex	1 10.0	1 10.0	1 10.0	7 70.0
Total	1 4.0	4 16.0	5 20.0	15 60.0

TABLE 5.21 Summary Offense Transitions by Color

NONWHITE: Summary Matrix

K-1 / K	Injury	Theft/Damage	Non-Index	Desist
Injury	12 17.9	9 13.4	7 10.5	39 58.2
Theft/Damage	7 8.2	18 21.2	11 12.9	49 57.7
Nonindex	5 7.0	10 14.1	9 12.7	47 66.2
Total	24 10.0	37 16.6	27 12.1	135 60.5

TRIGUEÑO: Summary Matrix

K-1 / K	Injury	Theft/Damage	Non-Index	Desist
Injury	10 5.3	12 6.4	19 10.1	147 78.2
Theft/Damage	15 3.9	104 26.7	59 15.2	211 54.2
Nonindex	17 4.1	44 10.6	78 18.8	277 66.6
Total	42 4.2	160 16.1	156 15.7	635 63.9

WHITE: Summary Matrix

K-1 / K	Injury	Theft/Damage	Non-Index	Desist
Injury	17 5.9	21 7.3	14 4.8	237 82.0
Theft/Damage	20 4.1	81 16.7	65 13.4	318 65.7
Nonindex	24 4.8	51 10.2	61 12.2	364 72.8
Total	61 4.8	153 12.0	140 11.0	919 72.2

Delinquent Recidivism

delinquents are like nonwhites, they commit a variety of offenses and do not repeat offense types very often.

The summary matrices reported in Table 5.21 confirm these results. Nonwhites do not show any substantial repeat offense chances and the same is true for whites. Regardless of offense rank, only Trigueños exhibit a moderate tendency to repeat an offense type--theft/damage (26.7 percent).

RECIDIVISM SUMMARY

The recidivism data elaborate on the findings reported earlier concerning the various delinquency status categories. As expected, males show a chronic offender effect as these delinquents committed 33 percent of the male offenses. Females, because of the predominance of one-time delinquents, do not show a highly active group of chronic recidivists--this group was responsible for only 10 percent of female crime in the cohort.

The color data show a distinct pattern. Nonwhites have the greatest recidivism effect, with chronics having committed 41 percent of the delinquency. Trigueños are next with 33 percent and then whites with 25 percent.

As noted above, males have very much higher recidivism and the chance of this recidivism increases as offense number increases. By color, the data show various color effects. Nonwhites have the highest recidivism probabilities for UCR violent crimes and Sellin-Wolfgang injury offenses, Trigueños recidivate the most for UCR index crimes, nonindex crimes, UCR property crimes, and Sellin-Wolfgang theft offenses. White delinquents only predominate for the Sellin-Wolfgang damage category.

The analysis of offense transitions does not generally reveal any significant tendency for the delinquents to specialize in the type of offense that they repeat. Only trigueños show a moderate tendency to repeat theft/damage offenses. But, because of the few delinquents that move from rank to rank repeating this offense, the data can not be considered strong evidence of delinquency career specialization.

6
Police and Court Dispositions

The response of the criminal justice system to delinquents can have a siginificant effect on recidivism. This is especially so very early on in the delinquent career. With effective intervention, the chance of recidivism can be reduced if not prevented altogether. We will be concerned in this chapter with describing the nature and appropriateness of the dispositions given to the offenders in the 1970 cohort. We have included a series of tables that first describe the police and court handling of the delinquents in the cohort. These tables include listings of the dispositions according to the type of offense committed. Last, we present data concerning the type of treatments ordered by the court.

POLICE DISPOSITIONS

Table 6.1 shows that males are more likely to be referred to court for their offenses than are females. Males are referred to court about 65 percent of the time compared to 59 percent for females. Overall, about two-thirds of the offenses are referred to court for adjudication rather than informal handling by the police.

TABLE 6.1 Police Disposition by Sex

Disposition	Males N	%	Females N	%	Both N	%
Administrative	703	32.5	129	39.3	832	33.4
Referred to Court	1,414	65.4	192	58.5	1,606	64.5
Unknown	44	2.1	7	2.1	51	2.1
Total	2,161		328		2,489	

TABLE 6.2 Police Disposition By Crime Code and Sex

Disposition	Males Administrative Resolution		Court		Females Administrative Resolution		Court	
	N	%	N	%	N	%	N	%
UCR Index	187	22.5	636	76.4	7	8.9	71	89.9
UCR Nonindex	516	39.9	778	60.1	122	48.9	121	48.6
Homicide	2	.06	34	94.0			3	100.0
Rape	2	40.0	3	60.0				
Robbery	18	10.6	150	88.2	1	11.1	8	88.9
Aggravated Assault	28	29.8	66	70.2	3	15.8	16	84.2
Burglary	43	16.3	215	81.7			11	91.7
Larceny	85	39.9	128	60.1	3	8.3	33	91.7
Vehicle theft	9	17.6	40	78.4				
Assault	88	55.0	72	45.0	44	55.7	35	44.3
R.S.P.	10	9.2	99	90.8			2	100.0
Mischief	78	54.5	65	45.5	3	37.5	5	62.5
Weapons	5	7.9	58	92.1	7	10.0	63	90.0
Narcotics	21	13.7	132	86.3	3	25.0	9	75.0
Breach of Peace	38	40.4	56	59.6	26	54.2	22	45.8
Threats	24	48.0	16	32.0	4	57.1	3	42.9
Other	272	47.9	266	46.8	42	48.8	38	44.2
Sellin-Wolfgang Index	379	29.2	907	69.8	65	32.0	137	67.5
Sellin-Wolfgang Nonindex	324	36.6	507	58.8	64	51.2	55	44.0
Sellin-Wolfgang Injury	148	35.7	267	64.3	49	38.9	77	61.1

Percents do not sum to 100.0% due to a few missing dispositions.

Police and Court Dispositions

In Table 6.2 we observe two very important results concerning the type of disposition by crime code. First, serious offenses are generally not retained by the police for administrative resolution; these serious offenses are referred to the courts for appropriate action. For example, concerning UCR index offenses males were sent to court 76 percent of the time, while females were referred 90 percent of the time. On the other hand, nonindex offenses reached court 60 percent of the time for males and 49 percent of the time for females. The highest referral rate was observed for homicide, manslaughter, and attempted homicide (males = 94 percent; females = 100 percent), followed by weapons (males = 92 percent; females =90 percent), receiving stolen property (males =91 percent; females =100 percent), robbery (males =88 percent; females = 89 percent), and narcotics (males = 86 percent; females = 75 percent). These percentages clearly indicate that police are not abusing their discretion, and instead, are sending these more serious offenders on to the courts as should be the case.

The second aspect of Table 6.2 that is important concerns the fact that females rather than males generally have the highest court referral rates. This is true for UCR index crimes like homicide, robbery, aggravated assault, burglary, and larceny, and also receiving stolen property and mischief. It appears that the police believe that the courts are the appropriate place to deal with serious offenders, especially if they are female.

TABLE 6.3 Police Disposition by Color

Disposition	Nonwhite N	%	Trigueño N	%	White N	%
Administrative Resolution	59	26.5	297	29.9	476	37.4
Referred for Court Processing	160	71.7	670	67.5	776	60.9
Unknown	4	1.8	26	2.6	21	1.6
Total	223		993		1,273	

Table 6.3 presents police disposition data by color. These data show that nonwhites (72 percent) are the most likely to be referred to court. Trigueños are referred 68 percent of the time, while whites are referred the least, 61 percent of the time.

147

TABLE 6.4 Police Disposition By Crime Code and Color

Disposition	NONWHITE Admin. Resolut. N	NONWHITE Admin. Resolut. %	NONWHITE Court N	NONWHITE Court %	TRIGUEÑO Admin. Resolut. N	TRIGUEÑO Admin. Resolut. %	TRIGUEÑO Court N	TRIGUEÑO Court %	WHITE Admin. Resolut. N	WHITE Admin. Resolut. %	WHITE Court N	WHITE Court %
UCR Index	23	23.5	74	75.5	68	18.2	301	80.5	103	23.5	332	75.6
UCR Nonindex	36	28.8	86	68.8	229	36.9	369	59.6	373	44.7	444	53.2
Homicide, Man.	--	--	6	100	--	--	14	100	2	10.5	17	89.5
Att. Homicide												
Rape	--	--	--	--	1	33.3	2	66.7	1	50.0	1	50.0
Robbery	4	17.4	19	82.6	6	7.1	78	92.9	9	12.7	61	84.7
Aggravated Assault	2	18.2	9	81.8	12	29.3	29	70.7	17	27.9	44	72.1
Burglary	8	23.5	25	73.5	18	15.5	94	81.0	17	13.6	107	85.6
Larceny	9	40.9	13	59.1	29	28.7	72	71.3	50	39.7	76	60.3
Vehicle theft	--	--	2	100	2	13.3	12	80.0	7	20.6	26	76.5
Assault	11	45.8	14	56.0	50	55.6	40	44.4	71	57.3	53	42.7
R.S.P.	--	--	9	90.0	5	10.0	44	88.0	5	9.4	48	90.6
Mischief	4	44.4	5	55.5	30	53.4	25	44.6	47	54.0	40	45.9
Weapons	--	--	3	100	3	9.7	28	90.3	2	5.6	34	94.4
Narcotics	2	15.4	11	94.6	8	9.4	77	90.6	4	20.6	53	77.9
Breach of Peace	4	33.3	8	66.7	22	39.3	33	58.9	38	50.7	37	49.3
Threats	1	33.3	2	66.7	4	23.5	13	76.5	9	42.9	12	57.1
Other	14	28.0	34	68.0	107	45.7	109	46.6	187	50.5	167	45.1
Sellin-Wolfgang Index	37	24.3	114	75.0	152	26.3	417	72.3	255	32.9	513	66.4
Sellin-Wolfgang Nonindex	22	30.9	46	64.8	145	34.9	253	60.8	221	44.2	263	52.6
Sellin-Wolfgang Injury	15	22.4	52	77.6	74	39.4	112	59.6	108	37.4	180	62.3

Percents do not sum to 100.0 due to a few missing dispositions.

Police and Court Dispositions

Table 6.4 reports police dispositions by crime code and color. These results indicate a slight color effect. That is, trigueños (81 percent) are referred to court the most, followed equally by nonwhites (76 percent) and whites (76 percent). However, for nonindex offenses, nonwhites show the highest rate (69 percent) followed by trigueños (60 percent) and whites (53 percent).

Concerning specific serious offenses, the results also vary by color. Nonwhites and trigueños are referred for 100 percent of their homicides, manslaughter, and attempted homicides, while whites are referred for 90 percent of their offenses in this category. Trigueños have the highest rate for robbery (93 percent); nonwhites have the highest rate (82 percent) for aggravated assault; and whites have the highest rate (86 percent) for burglary.

TABLE 6.5 Police Disposition by Sex and Color

| | MALES | | | | | |
| | Nonwhite | | Trigueño | | White | |
Disposition	N	%	N	%	N	%
Administrative Resolution	55	27.9	251	28.3	397	36.9
Referred for Court Processing	139	70.6	612	68.9	663	61.6
Unknown	3	1.5	24	2.7	17	1.6
Total	197		887		1,077	

| | FEMALES | | | | | |
| | Nonwhite | | Trigueño | | White | |
Disposition	N	%	N	%	N	%
Administrative Resolution	4	15.4	46	43.4	79	40.3
Referred for Court Processing	21	80.1	58	54.7	113	57.6
Unknown	1	3.8	2	1.9	4	2.1
Total	26	---	106	---	196	

Table 6.5 presents police disposition data by both color and sex. These results indicate that color and sex do not interact regarding police disposition. That is, among males, nonwhites (71 percent) have the greatest chance of court referral compared to trigueños (69 percent) and whites (62 percent). For females, nonwhites again have the highest chance (80 percent), and this nonwhite percentage is much greater than for the other two colors--trigueño (55 percent) and white (58 percent).

Delinquency in Puerto Rico

In Table 6.6 we turn to the issue of offender status and police disposition. These data present the important finding that recidivists, those delinquents with more than one offense, have a much greater chance (74%) of being referred by the police to court than do the one-time (56 percent) delinquents. These data would seem to suggest that the police are systematically using their discretion in referring cases to court. That is, because of the possibility of desistance, the one-time offender (43.4 percent) is more likely to receive an administrative resolution instead of court referral, but not the recidivist (22.7 percent), whose delinquency needs to be addressed in a court setting.

TABLE 6.6 Police Disposition by Offender Status

Disposition	OFFENDER STATUS					
	One-time		Two or more		Both	
	N	%	N	%	N	%
Administrative Resolution	559	43.4	273	22.7	832	33.4
Referred for Court Processing	721	55.9	885	73.7	1,606	64.5
Unknown	8	0.62	43	3.6	51	2.1
Total	1,288		1,201		2,489	

COURT DISPOSITIONS

Thus far, we have examined the initial handling of a delinquent by the police which can consist of informal handling or court referral. In the next set of tables (6.7 to 6.15) we turn to the type of disposition reached in court. These dispositions range from dismissal to acquittal or to an institutional sentence. Table 6.7 shows that males (40 percent) are more likely than females (27 percent) to receive some kind of court sentence, and males (42 percent) are less likely to have their cases dismissed than females (60 percent). Males and females are about equal concerning the dispositions of diversion, acquittal, and case-pending status, but only males were waived to adult court (1.2 percent of the time).

TABLE 6.7 Type of Court Disposition by Sex

Disposition	Males N	Males %	Females N	Females %	Both N	Both %
Dismissed	537	42.3	109	59.6	646	44.5
Acquitted	41	3.2	6	3.3	47	3.2
Waived	15	1.2			15	1.0
Diversion	107	8.4	14	7.7	121	8.3
Sentenced	532	40.1	50	27.3	582	40.1
Pending/fugitive	37	2.9	4	2.2	41	2.8

In Table 6.8 we see that a sentence disposition varies with the type of crime committed. Males are sentenced the most often for robbery (60 percent). This offense is followed in order by homicide, manslaughter, and attempted homicide (50 percent), UCR index offenses (46 percent), burglary (45 percent), narcotics (44 percent), receiving stolen property (41 percent), vehicle theft (40 percent), larceny (37 percent), and aggravated assault (36 percent). Males are rarely given a diversion disposition, usually less than 10 percent of the time. Similarly, there are very few males waived, usually no more than 2 percent of the time for any offense except for homicide for which 6 males (18 percent) were waived.

The table also indicates that a very high percentage of cases across all the offense types are dismissed. The percentages range from a high of 59 percent for assault to only 18 percent for the homicide, manslaughter, and attempted homicide category. We do not have sufficient information to analyze why these cases were dismissed or whether the observed percentages are high. Thus, these data may be quite usual or they may be aberrant, we just do not know. These issues could warrant further investigation.

Table 6.9 indicates primarily that cases against females will most likely be dismissed when they reach court. For example, 54 percent of the UCR index offenses and 59 percent of the UCR nonindex offenses were dismissed. Concerning specific serious offenses, charges were dismissed or dropped in 33 percent of the homicide, manslaughter, and attempted homicide category, 63 percent of the robberies, 44 percent of the aggravated assaults,

TABLE 6.8 Court Disposition By Crime Code for Males

MALES

Crime Code	Dismis. N	%	Acquitted N	%	Waived N	%	Diversion N	%	Sentenced N	%	Pending N	%
UCR Index	215	33.8	13	2.0	13	2.0	40	6.3	291	45.8	5	.78
UCR Nonindex	322	41.4	28	3.6	2	.25	67	8.6	241	30.9	32	4.1
Homicide, Man.	—	—	—	—	—	—	—	—	—	—	—	—
Att. Homicide.	6	17.6	2	5.9	6	17.6	—	—	17	50.0	1	2.9
Rape	—	—	—	—	—	—	1	33.3	—	—	—	—
Robbery	30	20.0	3	2.0	4	2.7	4	2.7	90	60.0	2	1.3
Aggravated Assault	33	50.0	1	1.5	—	—	5	7.6	24	36.4	—	—
Burglary	81	37.7	2	.93	1	.47	17	7.9	97	45.1	—	—
Larceny	48	37.5	4	3.1	1	.78	13	10.2	47	36.7	2	1.6
Vehicle theft	17	42.5	1	2.5	1	2.5	—	—	16	40.0	—	—
Assault	43	59.7	2	2.8	—	—	5	6.9	7	9.7	—	—
R.S.P.	36	36.4	6	6.1	—	—	9	9.1	41	41.4	3	3.0
Mischief	37	56.9	—	—	—	—	10	15.4	9	13.8	—	—
Weapons	20	34.5	5	8.6	1	1.7	5	8.6	18	31.0	4	6.9
Narcotics	37	28.0	6	4.5	—	—	12	9.1	58	43.9	1	.76
Breach-Peace	28	50.0	3	5.4	—	—	4	7.1	17	30.4	—	—
Threats	7	29.2	1	4.2	—	—	1	4.2	9	37.5	—	—
Other	114	41.9	5	1.8	1	.37	21	7.7	82	30.1	24	8.8
Sellin-Wolfgang Index	355	39.1	24	2.6	11	1.2	73	8.0	373	41.1	11	1.2
Sellin-Wolfgang Nonindex	182	35.6	17	3.4	4	.79	34	6.7	159	31.4	26	5.1
Sellin-Wolfgang Injury	118	35.9	7	1.4	7	1.4	20	3.9	88	17.4	2	.39

Percents do not sum to 100.0% due to a few missing dispositions.

TABLE 6.9 Court Disposition By Crime Code for Females

FEMALES

Crime Code	Dismis. N	%	Acquitted N	%	Waived N	%	Diversion N	%	Sentenced N	%	Pending N	%
UCR Index	38	53.5	1	1.4	—	—	7	9.9	21	29.6	—	—
UCR Nonindex	71	58.7	5	4.1	—	—	7	5.8	29	40.8	4	3.3
Homicide, Man.												
Att. Homicide	1	33.3	—	—	—	—	—	—	1	33.3	—	—
Rape	—	—	—	—	—	—	—	—	—	—	—	—
Robbery	5	62.5	—	—	—	—	—	—	3	37.5	—	—
Aggravated	7	43.8	—	—	—	—	5	31.3	3	18.8	—	—
Assault												
Burglary	9	81.8	—	—	—	—	—	—	2	18.2	—	—
Larceny	16	48.5	1	3.0	—	—	2	6.1	12	36.4	—	—
Vehicle theft	—	—	—	—	—	—	—	—	—	—	—	—
Assault	23	65.7	—	—	—	—	4	11.4	7	20.0	—	—
R.S.P.	1	50.0	1	50.0	—	—	—	—	—	—	—	—
Mischief	4	80.0	1	20.0	—	—	—	—	—	—	—	—
Weapons	3	42.9	—	—	—	—	1	14.3	1	14.3	1	14.3
Narcotics	2	22.2	1	11.1	—	—	1	11.1	3	33.3	—	—
Breach-Peace	13	59.1	1	4.5	—	—	1	4.5	7	31.8	—	—
Threats	2	66.7	—	—	—	—	—	—	1	33.3	—	—
Other	23	60.5	1	2.6	—	—	—	—	10	26.3	3	7.9
Sellin-Wolfgang Index	80	58.4	2	1.5	—	—	11	8.0	38	27.7	—	—
Sellin-Wolfgang Nonindex	29	52.7	4	7.3	—	—	3	5.5	12	21.8	4	7.3
Sellin-Wolfgang Injury	43	55.8	—	—	—	—	9	11.7	20	25.9	—	—

Percents do not sum to 100.0% due to a few missing dispositions.

Delinquency in Puerto Rico

82 percent of the burglaries, 49 percent of the larcenies, and 66 percent of the assaults.

If a case involving a female is not dismissed, then the most likely disposition is a court sentence. Generally, females are sentenced by the court in about 33 percent of the cases. The high is for nonindex offenses (41 percent), while the low occurs for burglary (18 percent).

Table 6.10 presents the court disposition data by color categories. These data show a distinct color effect. That is, nonwhites (32 percent) are the least likely to have their case dismissed compared to trigueños (42 percent) and whites (50 percent). Nonwhites are also the most likely to be waived (3 percent) or convicted (50 percent). Whites have the lowest conviction rate at about 34 percent. Trigueños have the lowest waiver rate at less than one percent (.3 percent).

TABLE 6.10 Type of Court Disposition by Color

Disposition	Nonwhite N	Nonwhite %	Trigueño N	Trigueño %	White N	White %
Dismissed	48	32.0	252	41.5	346	49.8
Acquitted	6	4.0	18	2.9	23	3.3
Waived	4	2.7	2	0.3	9	1.3
Diversion	13	8.7	46	7.6	62	8.9
Sentenced	75	50.0	270	44.5	237	34.1
Pending/fugitive	4	2.7	19	3.1	18	2.6

In Tables 6.11, 6.12, and 6.13 we investigate whether these overall effects differ by crime code categories. Table 6.11 shows that nonwhites are generally more likely to be sentenced than to receive any other disposition. They are sentenced for about 49 percent of their UCR index offenses and for 45 percent of their nonindex offenses. The highest sentence rates are for narcotics (89 percent) and robbery (74 percent). Trigueños (Table 6.12) are sentenced about as often as nonwhites for index offenses (50 percent), but are sentenced less often for nonindex crimes 33 percent vs. 45 percent. The high sentence percentages for trigueños are not as high as for nonwhites and involve the homicide, manslaughter, and attempted homicide category (64 percent) and robbery (60 percent) offenses mostly.

TABLE 6.11 Court Disposition By Crime Code for Nonwhites

NONWHITE

Crime Code	Dismis. N	%	Acquitted N	%	Waived N	%	Diversion N	%	Sentenced N	%	Pending N	%
UCR Index	24	32.4	1	1.4	3	4.1	8	10.8	36	48.7	—	—
UCR Nonindex	24	27.9	5	5.8	1	1.2	5	5.8	39	45.3	4	4.7
Homicide, Man.												
Att. Homicide	2	33.3	—	—	2	33.3	—	—	2	33.3	—	—
Rape	—	—	—	—	—	—	—	—	—	—	—	—
Robbery	3	15.8	1	5.3	1	5.3	—	—	14	73.7	—	—
Aggravated Assault	3	33.3	—	—	—	—	4	44.4	2	22.2	—	—
Burglary	11	44.4	—	—	—	—	3	12.0	9	36.0	—	—
Larceny	4	30.8	—	—	—	—	1	7.7	8	61.5	—	—
Vehicle theft	1	50.0	—	—	—	—	—	—	1	50.0	—	—
Assault	6	42.9	—	—	—	—	3	21.4	1	7.1	—	—
R.S.P.	1	11.1	3	33.3	—	—	—	—	3	33.3	—	—
Mischief	2	40.0	—	—	—	—	1	20.0	2	40.0	—	—
Weapons	—	—	—	—	1	33.3	—	—	2	66.7	—	—
Narcotics	1	9.1	1	9.1	—	—	—	—	8	88.9	—	—
Breach-Peace	5	62.5	—	—	—	—	—	—	3	37.5	—	—
Threats	1	50.0	—	—	—	—	—	—	1	50.0	—	—
Other	8	23.5	1	2.9	—	—	1	2.9	19	55.9	4	11.8
Sellin-Wolfgang Index	37	32.5	4	3.5	2	1.8	12	10.5	54	47.4	1	.87
Sellin-Wolfgang Nonindex	11	23.9	2	4.3	2	4.3	1	2.2	21	45.7	3	6.5
Sellin-Wolfgang Injury	16	30.8	1	1.9	2	3.8	7	13.5	22	42.3	—	—

Percents do not sum to 100.0% due to a few missing dispositions.

TABLE 6.12 Court Disposition by Crime Code for Trigueños

TRIGUEÑO

Crime Code	Dismis. N	%	Acquitted N	%	Waived N	%	Diversion N	%	Sentenced N	%	Pending N	%
UCR Index	98	32.6	5	1.7	1	.33	15	4.9	151	50.2	3	.99
UCR Nonindex	154	41.7	13	3.5	1	.27	31	8.4	119	32.2	16	4.3
Homicide, Man.												
Att. Homicide	2	14.3	1	7.1	—	—	—	—	9	64.3	—	—
Rape	—	—	—	—	—	—	—	—	—	—	—	—
Robbery	16	20.5	2	2.6	—	—	1	1.3	47	60.3	1	1.3
Aggravated Assault	12	41.4	—	—	—	—	3	10.3	13	44.8	—	—
Burglary	36	38.3	—	—	1	1.1	3	3.2	49	52.1	—	—
Larceny	28	38.9	2	2.8	—	—	8	11.1	28	38.9	2	2.8
Vehicle theft	4	33.3	—	—	—	—	—	—	5	41.7	—	—
Assault	24	60.0	1	2.5	—	—	5	12.5	5	12.5	—	—
R.S.P.	18	40.9	1	2.3	—	—	4	9.1	18	40.9	2	4.5
Mischief	14	56.0	1	4.0	—	—	1	4.0	5	20.0	—	—
Weapons	11	39.3	3	10.7	—	—	2	7.1	8	28.6	2	7.1
Narcotics	21	27.3	3	3.9	—	—	9	11.7	33	42.9	1	1.3
Breach-Peace	14	42.4	2	6.1	—	—	4	12.1	11	33.3	—	—
Threats	4	30.8	—	—	—	—	—	—	4	30.8	—	—
Other	48	44.0	2	1.8	1	.92	6	5.5	35	32.1	11	10.1
Sellin-Wolfgang Index	162	38.8	9	2.2	1	.23	26	6.2	184	44.1	6	1.4
Sellin-Wolfgang Nonindex	90	35.6	9	3.6	1	.39	20	7.9	86	33.9	13	5.1
Sellin-Wolfgang Injury	48	42.9	2	1.8	—	—	9	8.0	40	35.7	1	.89

Percents do not sum to 100.0% due to a few missing dispositions.

TABLE 6.13 Court Disposition By Crime Code for Whites

WHITE

Crime Code	Dismis. N	%	Acquitted N	%	Waived N	%	Diversion N	%	Sentenced N	%	Pending N	%
UCR Index	131	39.5	8	2.4	9	2.7	24	7.2	125	37.7	2	.60
UCR Nonindex	215	48.4	15	3.4	—	—	38	8.6	112	25.2	16	3.6
Homicide, Man.												
Att. Homicide	3	17.6	1	5.9	4	23.5	—	—	7	41.2	1	5.9
Rape	—	—	—	—	—	—	—	—	1	100.0	—	—
Robbery	16	26.2	—	—	3	4.9	3	4.9	32	52.5	1	1.6
Aggravated Assault	25	56.8	1	2.3	—	—	3	6.8	12	27.3	—	—
Burglary	43	40.2	2	1.9	—	—	11	10.3	41	38.3	—	—
Larceny	32	42.1	3	3.9	1	1.3	7	7.9	23	30.3	—	—
Vehicle theft	12	46.2	1	3.8	1	3.8	—	—	10	38.5	—	—
Assault	36	67.9	1	1.9	—	—	1	1.9	8	15.1	—	—
R.S.P.	18	37.5	3	6.3	—	—	5	10.4	20	41.7	1	2.1
Mischief	25	62.5	—	—	—	—	8	20.0	2	5.0	—	—
Weapons	12	35.3	2	5.9	—	—	4	11.8	9	26.5	3	8.8
Narcotics	17	32.1	3	5.7	—	—	4	7.5	20	37.7	—	—
Breach-Peace	22	59.5	2	5.4	—	—	1	2.7	10	27.0	—	—
Threats	4	33.3	1	8.3	—	—	1	8.3	5	41.7	—	—
Other	81	48.5	3	1.8	—	—	14	8.4	38	22.8	12	7.2
Sellin-Wolfgang Index	236	46.0	13	2.5	8	1.6	46	8.9	173	33.7	4	.78
Sellin-Wolfgang Nonindex	110	41.8	10	3.8	1	.38	16	6.1	64	24.3	14	5.3
Sellin-Wolfgang Injury	97	53.9	4	2.2	5	2.8	13	7.2	46	25.6	1	.56

Percents do not sum to 100.0% due to a few missing dispositions.

Delinquency in Puerto Rico

Whites are sentenced the least, regardless of offense type. Whites are sentenced for only 38 percent of UCR index offenses and 25 percent of nonindex offenses. These are less than was the case for either nonwhites or trigueños. Similarly, even for the most serious offenses, whites are treated differently. For example, only in the cases of rape, for which the only offender was sentenced, and robbery (52 percent), do the white sentences reach more than 50 percent of the cases. Most white offenses have less than a 40 percent sentence rate.

Table 6.14 presents the court data by both color and sex. These combined data indicate the same color effect regardless of sex. That is, among males, nonwhites are more likely to be sentenced (54 percent) and less likely to be dismissed (30 percent) than are trigueños (46 percent sentenced and 40 percent dismissed) or whites (35 percent sentenced and 47 percent dismissed). The same holds true for females.

TABLE 6.14 Type of Court Disposition by Sex and Color

| | MALES | | | | | |
| | Nonwhite | | Trigueño | | White | |
Disposition	N	%	N	%	N	%
Dismissed	38	29.7	219	39.8	280	47.4
Acquitted	6	4.7	14	2.6	21	3.6
Waived	4	3.1	2	0.4	9	1.5
Diversion	8	6.3	43	7.8	56	9.5
Sentenced	69	53.9	254	46.2	209	35.4
Pending/fugitive	3	2.3	18	3.3	16	2.7

| | FEMALES | | | | | |
| | Nonwhite | | Trigueño | | White | |
Disposition	N	%	N	%	N	%
Dismissed	10	45.5	33	57.9	66	63.5
Acquitted	0	0.0	4	7.0	2	1.9
Waived						
Diversion	5	22.7	3	5.3	6	5.8
Sentenced	6	27.3	16	28.1	28	26.9
Pending/fugitive	1	4.6	1	1.8	2	1.9

Police and Court Dispositions

Table 6.15 indicates a strong difference in type of court disposition by offender status. The courts only dismiss charges in 35 percent of the offenses of recidivists compared to 57 percent of the one-time delinquents. Regarding convictions, the recidivists are convicted about 49 percent of the time compared to just 29 percent for one-time offenders. These results thus indicate the severity with which the courts respond to recidivist offenders.

TABLE 6.15 Type of Court Disposition by Offender Status

	Offender Status					
	One-time		Two or more		Both	
Disposition	N	%	N	%	N	%
Dismissed	357	56.8	289	35.1	646	44.5
Acquitted	23	3.7	24	2.9	47	3.2
Waived	2	0.3	13	1.6	15	1.0
Diversion	59	9.4	62	7.5	121	8.3
Sentenced	180	28.6	402	48.9	582	40.1
Pending/fugitive	8	1.3	33	4.1	41	2.8

COURT SENTENCES

The next set of tables, 6.16 to 6.24 portray the kind of sentences that were given out by the courts. These sentences concern custody of parents or others, probation, restitution, other restrictions on the offender, or institutional placement. Because we coded the data to indicate all the sentences that applied in a given case, the categories are not mutually exclusive, an offender could be given more than one court disposition per offense.

TABLE 6.16 Type of Court Sentence by Sex

	Males		Females		Both	
Sentence	N	%	N	%	N	%
Parents custody	392	18.1	28	8.5	420	16.9
Probation	379	17.5	29	8.8	408	16.4
Restrictions	368	17.0	29	8.8	397	15.6
Restitution	143	6.6	15	4.6	158	6.4
Institution	194	8.9	10	3.1	204	8.2

Delinquency in Puerto Rico

Table 6.16 clearly shows that male delinquents are much more likely to receive each of the five kinds of sentences. Males are generally twice as likely to receive the four sentences that do not involve institutionalization, and are about three times more likely to receive an institution-type sentence.

Table 6.17 presents for males by crime code the various sentences ordered by the courts. Males are more likely to receive an institution sentence for index (42 percent) rather than nonindex offenses (30 percent). With respect to specific serious crimes, males receive an institution sentence for 53 percent of the homicide, manslaughter, and attempted homicide category and 55 percent of robberies. The percentage falls to 44 percent for burglaries and to 34 percent for larcenies. The lowest index percentage occurs for aggravated assault with just 16 percent institutional sentences.

The courts make a much greater use of various probation and restriction sentences. These approach 70 to 80 percent for many crimes, thus indicating that the courts believe that some kind of supervision will benefit the offender rather than placement in an institution.

For females (Table 6.18) we see that very few offenses result in institutional placement. Institutions are ordered in 19 percent of index crimes and in 21 percent of nonindex. Probation, restrictions, and/or parents' custody are very prevalent for females. These sentences occur in more than one-half of most crimes and range up to 100 percent in others. Thus, for females, the courts quire obviously feel that because the offense is probably a first offense, that supervision is the preferred solution.

Table 6.19 reports sentence data by color. These data repeat the race effect we observed earlier for court disposition. That is, nonwhites are more likely to receive institutional placements (14 percent) than are trigueños (11 percent) and whites (5 percent). Further, nonwhites are more likely to receive the less severe sentences as well. Nonwhites receive probation, etc. 24 percent of the time compared to about 17 percent for trigueños and 14 percent for whites. These data clearly show a tendency for the courts to be more severe with nonwhite delinquents.

TABLE 6.17 Type of Court Sentence By Crime Code for Males

MALES

Crime Code	Custody of Parents N	Custody of Parents %	Probation N	Probation %	Other Restrict. N	Other Restrict. %	Other Conditions N	Other Conditions %	Institution N	Institution %
UCR Index	205	70.7	202	69.7	197	67.9	85	29.3	123	42.4
UCR Nonindex	187	77.6	177	73.4	171	79.9	58	24.1	71	29.5
Homicide, Man.										
Att. Homicide	7	41.2	6	35.3	6	35.3	2	11.8	9	52.9
Rape	—	—	—	—	—	—	—	—	—	—
Robbery	49	54.4	48	53.3	48	53.3	18	20.0	49	54.4
Aggravated Assault	22	91.7	20	83.3	20	83.3	6	25.0	4	16.0
Burglary	72	74.2	73	75.3	70	72.2	31	31.9	43	44.3
Larceny	40	85.1	39	82.9	37	78.7	20	42.6	16	34.0
Vehicle theft	15	93.8	16	100.0	16	100.0	8	50.0	2	12.5
Assault	6	85.7	5	71.4	4	57.1	4	57.1	2	28.6
R.S.P.	36	87.8	36	87.8	36	87.8	13	31.7	12	32.4
Mischief	6	66.7	5	55.5	5	55.5	3	33.3	6	66.7
Weapons	12	66.7	12	66.7	11	61.1	1	5.6	7	38.9
Narcotics	50	86.2	51	87.9	51	87.9	16	27.6	24	41.4
Breach-Peace	17	100.0	17	100.0	17	100.0	4	23.5	3	17.6
Threats	5	55.6	5	55.6	4	44.4	—	—	3	33.3
Other	54	65.9	46	56.1	43	52.4	17	20.7	14	17.1
Sellin-Wolfgang Index	265	71.0	256	68.6	252	67.7	106	28.4	143	38.3
Sellin-Wolfgang Nonindex	127	79.9	123	77.4	116	72.9	37	23.3	51	32.1
Sellin-Wolfgang Injury	61	69.3	57	64.8	55	62.5	19	21.6	32	36.4

Percentages do not sum to 100.0% because categories are not mutually exclusive. All categories that applied were coded.

TABLE 6.18 Type of Court Sentence By Crime Code for Females

					FEMALES					
	Custody of Parents		Probation		Other Restrict.		Other Conditions		Institution	
Crime Code	N	%	N	%	N	%	N	%	N	%
UCR Index	11	52.4	12	57.1	12	57.1	7	33.3	4	19.0
UCR Nonindex	17	58.6	17	58.6	17	58.6	8	27.6	6	20.7
Homicide, Man.										
Att. Homicide	1	100.0	1	100.0	1	100.0	—	—	—	—
Rape	—	—	—	—	—	—	—	—	—	—
Robbery	1	33.3	1	33.3	1	33.3	—	—	2	66.7
Aggravated Assault	2	66.7	3	100.0	3	100.0	3	100.0	—	—
Burglary	1	50.0	1	50.0	1	50.0	1	50.0	1	50.0
Larceny	6	50.0	6	50.0	6	50.0	6	50.0	6	50.0
Vehicle theft	—	—	—	—	—	—	—	—	—	—
Assault	5	71.4	5	71.4	5	71.4	5	71.4	4	57.1
R.S.P.	—	—	—	—	—	—	—	—	—	—
Mischief	—	—	—	—	—	—	—	—	—	—
Weapons	1	100.0	1	100.0	1	100.0	1	100.0	—	100.0
Narcotics	3	100.0	3	100.0	3	100.0	1	33.3	1	33.3
Breach-Peace	5	71.4	5	71.4	5	71.4	1	14.3	3	42.9
Threats	—	—	—	—	—	—	1	100.0	—	—
Other	3	30.0	3	30.0	3	30.0	—	—	2	20.0
Sellin-Wolfgang Index	20	52.6	21	55.3	21	55.3	11	28.9	5	13.2
Sellin-Wolfgang Nonindex	8	66.7	8	66.7	8	66.7	4	33.3	5	41.7
Sellin-Wolfgang Injury	20	60.0	13	65.0	13	65.0	7	35.0	3	15.0

Percentages do not sum to 100.0% because categories are not mutually exclusive. All categories that applied were coded.

TABLE 6.19 Type of Court Sentence by Color

Sentence	Nonwhite N	%	Trigueño N	%	White N	%
Custody of Parents	54	24.2	181	18.2	185	14.5
Probation	54	24.2	173	17.4	181	14.2
With Restrictions	54	24.2	168	16.9	175	13.8
Restitution	16	7.2	83	8.4	59	4.6
Institution	30	13.5	106	10.7	68	5.3

TABLE 6.20 Type of Court Sentence By Crime Code for Nonwhites

	\multicolumn{2}{c}{}	\multicolumn{2}{c}{}	NONWHITE					
	Custody of Parents		Probation		Other Restrict.		Other Conditions		Institution	
Crime Code	N	%	N	%	N	%	N	%	N	%
UCR Index	24	66.7	24	66.7	24	66.7	8	22.2	16	44.4
UCR Nonindex	30	76.9	30	76.9	30	76.9	8	20.5	14	35.9
Homicide, Man.										
Att. Homicide	2	100.0	2	100.0	2	100.0	1	50.0	—	—
Rape	—	—	—	—	—	—	—	—	—	—
Robbery	5	35.7	5	35.7	5	35.7	1	7.1	10	71.4
Aggravated Assault	2	100.0	2	100.0	2	100.0	—	—	—	—
Burglary	8	88.9	8	88.9	8	88.9	1	11.1	5	55.6
Larceny	6	75.0	6	75.0	6	75.0	5	62.5	1	12.5
Vehicle theft	1	100.0	1	100.0	1	100.0	—	—	—	—
Assault	1	100.0	1	100.0	1	100.0	1	100.0	—	—
R.S.P.	3	100.0	3	100.0	3	100.0	2	66.7	1	33.3
Mischief	2	100.0	2	100.0	2	100.0	2	100.0	—	—
Weapons	—	—	—	—	—	—	—	—	2	100.0
Narcotics	7	87.5	7	87.5	7	87.5	1	12.5	3	37.5
Breach-Peace	3	100.0	3	100.0	3	100.0	—	—	1	33.3
Threats	1	100.0	1	100.0	1	100.0	—	—	—	—
Other	13	68.4	13	68.4	13	68.4	1	5.3	6	31.6
Sellin-Wolfgang Index	35	64.8	35	64.8	35	64.8	14	25.9	24	41.4
Sellin-Wolfgang Nonindex	19	90.5	19	90.5	19	90.5	2	9.5	6	28.6
Sellin-Wolfgang Injury	16	72.6	16	72.6	16	72.6	4	18.2	10	45.5

Percentages do not sum to 100.0% because categories are not mutually exclusive. All categories that applied were coded.

Police and Court Dispositions

When we turn to crime-code categories (Tables 6.20, 6.21, and 6.22), we find that type of crime does seem to influence the court sentence by color, the color groups are treated similarly for serious offenses, but the color effect still exists. That is, for serious offenses (UCR index) the courts treat nonwhites (44 percent) and trigueños (48 percent) about the same concerning institutional placement, but whites (31 percent) are given this sentence less often. This difference persists regardless of the specific serious offense that was committed. Nonwhites and trigueños are given institution more often than whites.

The situation surrounding probation and related sentences shows that nonwhites receive supervision type sentences more often regardless of crime code than either trigueños or whites. The nonwhite scores range upward from 68 percent up to 100 percent for many crimes, while the trigueños are given probation less often and whites less often still.

Table 6.23 shows that introducing the offender's sex into the analysis does not affect the results. Nonwhites are given institution more often for males (14 percent) and females (8 percent) compared to their trigueño and white counterparts. Similarly, nonwhites are given probation-type sentences more often for both sex groups, about 25 percent for males and 15 percent for females, compared to trigueños and whites.

Table 6.24 reports the very clear cut result that the courts do let recidivists get off lightly. Recidivists are much more likely to be given every sentence type than are one-time delinquents. Recidivists receive institutional placement 15 percent of the time compared to just 2 percent for one-time delinquents. Recidivists receive the probation-type supervision around 23 percent of the time compared to about 10 percent for the one-time offender.

In addition to the above sentences, the courts can order the delinquent to undergo some kind of treatment program, ranging from medical to vocational. These data are given in Table 6.25 by sex and Table 6.26 by color. Table 6.25 presents the familiar finding that males are more likely to be referred for treatment than are females. The male versus female differences are 9 percent versus 2 percent for medical, 6 percent versus 2 percent for psychiatric, 2 percent versus 1 percent for vocational, and 2 percent versus 3 percent for other unspecified treatment.

The color data are shown in Table 6.26 and do not reveal much of a color effect. That is, except for medical treatment, for which nonwhites (12 percent) are referred more often than trigueños (9 percent) or whites

TABLE 6.21 Type of Court Sentence By Crime Code for Trigueños

Crime Code	Custody of Parents N	%	Probation N	%	TRIGUEÑO Other Restrict. N	%	Other Conditions N	%	Institution N	%
UCR Index	93	61.6	90	59.6	88	58.3	46	30.5	72	47.7
UCR Nonindex	88	73.9	83	69.7	80	67.2	37	31.1	34	38.6
Homicide, Man.	—	—	—	—	—	—	—	—	—	—
Att. Homicide	2	22.2	1	11.1	1	11.1	1	11.1	6	66.7
Rape	—	—	—	—	—	—	—	—	—	—
Robbery	19	40.4	19	40.4	19	40.4	7	14.9	30	63.8
Aggravated Assault	12	92.3	11	84.6	11	84.6	5	38.5	2	15.4
Burglary	35	71.4	34	69.4	33	67.3	17	34.7	22	44.9
Larceny	20	71.4	20	71.4	19	67.9	13	46.4	12	42.9
Vehicle theft	5	100.0	5	100.0	5	100.0	3	60.0	—	—
Assault	4	80.0	3	60.0	3	60.0	4	80.0	1	20.0
R.S.P.	14	77.8	14	77.8	14	77.8	6	33.3	6	33.3
Mischief	3	60.0	3	60.0	3	60.0	—	—	2	40.0
Weapons	6	75.0	6	75.0	5	62.5	1	12.5	2	25.0
Narcotics	28	84.8	29	87.9	29	87.9	13	39.4	10	33.3
Breach-Peace	12	100.0	12	100.0	12	100.0	4	33.3	4	33.3
Threats	2	50.0	2	50.0	1	25.0	—	—	2	50.0
Other	19	54.3	14	40.0	13	37.1	9	25.7	7	20.0
Sellin-Wolfgang Index	118	64.1	112	60.9	110	59.8	58	31.5	73	39.7
Sellin-Wolfgang Nonindex	63	73.3	61	70.9	58	67.4	25	29.1	33	38.4
Sellin-Wolfgang Injury	24	60.0	22	55.0	21	52.5	12	30.0	13	32.5

Percentages do not sum to 100.0% because categories are not mutually exclusive. All categories that applied were coded.

TABLE 6.22 Type of Court Sentence By Crime Code for Whites

Crime Code	Custody of Parents		Probation		WHITE Other Restrict.		Other Conditions		Institution	
	N	%	N	%	N	%	N	%	N	%
UCR Index	99	79.2	100	80.0	97	77.6	38	30.4	39	31.2
UCR Nonindex	86	76.8	81	72.3	78	69.6	21	18.8	29	25.9
Homicide, Man.										
Att. Homicide	4	57.1	4	57.1	4	57.1	—	---	3	42.9
Rape	—	---	—	---	—	---	—	---	—	---
Robbery	26	81.2	25	78.1	25	78.1	10	31.3	11	34.4
Aggravated Assault	10	83.3	10	83.3	10	83.3	4	33.3	2	16.7
Burglary	30	73.2	32	78.0	30	73.2	14	34.1	17	41.5
Larceny	20	86.9	19	82.6	18	78.3	5	21.7	4	17.4
Vehicle theft	9	90.0	10	100.0	10	100.0	5	50.0	2	20.0
Assault	6	75.0	6	75.0	5	62.5	2	25.0	1	12.5
R.S.P.	19	95.0	19	95.0	19	95.0	5	25.0	5	25.0
Mischief	1	50.0	—	---	—	---	1	50.0	2	100.0
Weapons	7	77.8	7	77.8	7	77.8	1	11.1	2	22.2
Narcotics	18	90.0	18	90.0	18	90.0	3	15.0	12	60.0
Breach-Peace	8	80.0	7	70.0	7	70.0	1	10.0	1	10.0
Threats	2	40.0	2	40.0	4	40.0	1	10.0	1	10.0
Other	25	65.8	22	57.9	20	52.6	7	18.4	3	7.9
Sellin-Wolfgang Index	132	76.3	130	75.1	128	73.9	45	26.0	51	29.5
Sellin-Wolfgang Nonindex	53	82.8	51	79.7	47	73.4	14	21.9	17	26.6
Sellin-Wolfgang Injury	33	71.8	32	69.6	31	67.4	10	21.7	12	26.1

Percentages do not sum to 100.0% because categories are not mutually exclusive. All categories that applied were coded.

TABLE 6.23 Type of Court Sentence by Sex and Color

MALES

Sentence	Nonwhite N	%	Trigueño N	%	White N	%
Parents Custody	50	25.4	174	19.6	168	15.6
Probation	50	25.4	166	18.7	163	15.1
With Restrictions	50	25.4	161	18.2	157	14.6
Restitution	12	6.1	81	9.1	50	4.6
Institution	28	14.2	100	11.3	66	6.1

FEMALES

Sentence	Nonwhite N	%	Trigueño N	%	White N	%
Parents Custody	4	15.4	7	6.6	17	8.7
Probation	4	15.4	7	6.6	18	9.2
With Restrictions	4	15.4	7	6.6	18	9.2
Restitution	4	15.4	2	1.9	9	4.6
Institution	2	7.7	6	5.7	2	1.0

TABLE 6.24

Type of Court Sentence by Offender Status

OFFENDER STATUS

Sentence	One-time N	%	Two or more N	%	Both N	%
Parents Custody	138	10.7	282	23.5	420	16.9
Probation	131	10.2	277	23.1	408	16.4
With Restrictions	128	9.9	269	22.4	397	15.6
Restitution	46	3.6	112	9.3	158	6.4
Institution	20	1.6	184	15.3	204	8.2

TABLE 6.25   Type of Court-Ordered Treatment by Sex

Treatment	Males N	Males %	Females N	Females %	Both N	Both %
Medical	194	8.9	7	2.1	201	8.1
Psychiatric	129	5.9	5	1.5	134	5.4
Vocational Program	45	2.1	3	.91	48	1.9
Other Treatment Program	104	2.1	10	3.1	114	4.6

Each type of treatment is a separate program, thus the percentages will not add to 100.0%.

TABLE 6.26   Type of Court-Ordered Treatment by Color

Treatment	Nonwhite N	Nonwhite %	Trigueño N	Trigueño %	White N	White %
Medical	26	11.7	90	9.1	85	6.7
Psychiatric	14	6.3	62	6.2	58	4.6
Vocational Program	8	3.6	26	2.6	14	1.1
Other Treatment Program	8	3.6	52	5.2	5	4.2

Each type of treatment is a separate program, thus the percentages will not add to 100.0%.

(7 percent), the treatment programs are ordered in very similar proportions across the color categories.

In sum, treatments are not ordered very often, and when they are, these treatment programs are more likely to apply to male delinquents than anyone else.

We conclude the disposition chapter with two tables that describe the number of offenses that a delinquent commits while known to the courts or under some kind of supervision. Table 6.27 indicates that 52 males committed 96 offenses while a fugitive from the authorities. Males had 115 offenders commit 195 offenses during the time when they already had charges pending in court. Lastly, males show 77 delinquents who committed 126 offenses while they were on probation status for a prior conviction. Females, on the other hand, do not show this kind of behavior with a maximum of only 12 girls committing crimes while in any of the three statuses.

The color data given in Table 6.28 shows that none of the groups stands out. Each color category has some delinquents who commits offenses while under supervision, etc. But, neither the number of active offenders, nor the number of offenses committed differs in a proportion different from the proportion of the color groups in the total cohort.

DISPOSITION SUMMARY

Our analyses of the dispositions given to the 1970 cohort by the police and then subsequently by the juvenile court may be summarized as follows.

First, the police appear to be using their discretion effectively in referring cases to court. Serious offenses are usually referred, while less serious nonindex offenses are handled informally. Males are referred more often than females; nonwhites are referred more often than trigueños or whites.

Second, the courts are more willing to convict males (42 percent) than females (27 percent); and nonwhites (50 percent) rather than trigueños (45 percent) or whites (34 percent).

Third, if convicted, males are three times more likely than females to receive an institutional sentence than are females. Similarly, nonwhites (14 percent) receive institution dispositions more often than trigueños (11 percent) or whites (5 percent).

In addition to these regular sentences, the courts occasionally order some type of treatment. These treatments are much more likely for males than females. There is no color difference, however.

TABLE 6.27 Offenders and Offenses While Under Supervision by Sex

	MALES		FEMALES	
Status	Offenders	Offenses	Offenders	Offenses
While a fugitive:				
Yes	52	96	5	7
No	1,352	1,964	280	310
With charges pending:				
Yes	115	195	12	13
No	1,289	1,856	273	304
Currently on probation:				
Yes	77	126	2	3
No	1,327	1,929	283	314

TABLE 6.28 Offenders and Offenses While Under Supervision by Color

	NONWHITE		TRIGUEÑO		WHITE	
Status	Offenders/	Offenses	Offenders/	Offenses	Offenders/	Offenses
While a fugitive:						
Yes	6	12	26	49	25	42
No	129	206	609	899	894	1,169
With charges pending:						
Yes	15	26	57	95	55	87
No	120	192	578	846	864	1,122
Currently on probation:						
Yes	11	20	38	66	30	43
No	124	198	597	878	889	1,167

7
Cohort Comparisons

This 1970 Puerto Rican cohort study was modelled after the two Philadelphia birth cohort studies of delinquency. The same cohort design was used--following a group of persons born in the same year through their period at risk for delinquency. The the same measurements and data coding were employed--prevalence, incidence, and severity of delinquency. Finally, the same analyses were utilized to investigate the nature and extent of delinquency. Because of this replication effort, it is desirable to compare this present cohort with its two predecessors (for males only owing to the absence of females in the 1945 Philadelphia cohort). One caution, however, is necessary.

This is a cross-cultural replication. The island of Puerto Rico is different from the urban environment of Philadelphia, Pennsylvania. The cultures are somewhat different, and thus, the societal relations are different. It is possible, therefore, that the pushes toward and the pulls away from delinquency may be different in these two venues. Thus, the delinquency data may be different because of these factors. Nonetheless, a few comparisons are justified.

First, it is quite obvious that the 1970 Puerto Rico cohort is very much less delinquent than its two Philadelphia counterparts. The overall prevalence rate for males was only 11 percent in the 1970 cohort. Compared to this, the two Philadelphia cohorts were about three times more delinquent (1945 = 35 percent; 1958 = 32 percent). This means that for every delinquent in the 1970 Puerto Rico cohort, the Philadelphia studies found three such offenders. This is a very noteworthy statistic.

Second, the difference between the 1970 Puerto Rico cohort and those of Philadelphia pertain not only to the concentration of delinquents, but also extend to the various types of delinquency statuses. That is, the 1970 Puerto rico cohort showed 74 percent of the delinquents as one-time offenders. This is in sharp contrast to the one-time delinquents in the two Philadelphia cohorts, with 46 percent for 1945 and 42 percent for 1958. Effectively, therefore, there were at least twice as many recidivists in the 1945 study (53 percent) and the 1958 study (58 percent) compared to 1970 Puerto Rico with just 26 percent recidivists. Further, the Philadelphia recidivists were much more likely to be chronic than their Puerto Rico counterparts. For 1945, the chronics were 18 percent of the delinquents, and for 1958 the percentage was 23 percent, but in 1970 the chronics comprised only 11 percent of the delinquents (even though the definition was less restrictive in the Puerto Rico Study).

Third, the offense commission rates across the three cohorts point out definitively the vast differences in the extent of delinquent behavior. The 1970 overall offense rate of 173 offenses per 1,000 males was considerably lower than the 1945 rate (1027 offenses per 1,000) and the 1958 rate (1159 offenses per 1,000). The comparison for serious UCR index offenses shows a 1970 Puerto Rico rate of just 67 offenses per 1,000 compared to 274 per 1,000 in 1945 and 455 per 1,000 in 1958. Violent UCR offenses, the most serious of all crimes, are twice as few in 1970 (24) compared to 1945 (47) and six times fewer than 1958 (153). Once again, these offense rates differences are very important in showing the smaller extent of delinquent behavior in Puerto Rico.

The offense rate differences also extend to two other important dimensions--weapons and drugs. Despite the role of handguns in this 1970 study, the comparative data indicate that there were only about 5 weapon offenses per 1,000 population. For Philadelphia the rates were 27 offenses per 1,000 in 1945 and 35 offenses per 1,000 in 1958. Turning to drugs, we reiterate the previous findings from this study that many offenders were drug involved. Despite this, the data indicate that drug offense rates were lower in the 1970 study (12 per 1,000) than in the 1958 cohort (54 per 1,000). The 1945 study had only 1 drug offense, but that was a very different era from either 1958 or 1970.

Fourth, and lastly, there are vast differences in the ways in which the offenders in the various cohorts were handled by the police and the courts. Informal police dispositions were given in 65 percent of the 1945 offenses and 37 percent of the 1958 offenses compared to 32 percent of the 1970 delinquent events. Thus, especially in the 1945, the police rather than the courts were the deciding agency regarding intervention. The 1970 Puerto Rico cohort was much more likely to receive probation sentences (17 percent of the crimes) compared to 13 percent in 1958 and 11 percent in 1945. Moreover, sentences to institutions were used in about 10 percent of the 1970 cases compared to just 6 percent in 1945 and only 2 percent in 1958.

These disposition differences thus indicate two important implications. One concerns the fact that the police in Puerto Rico do not seem to be overstepping their bounds in handling juveniles; they appropriately refer cases to courts for disposition and retain others for administrative resolution at the police stage. The second issue is that the juvenile courts in Puerto Rico seem more willing to order supervision through probation and institutional placements when necessary than did the courts in Philadelphia. We can only hazard a guess, but it is very plausible that the low recidivism rates in the 1970 cohort may be due to the firm intervention that characterizes the Puerto Rico juvenile courts. This issue should be investigated further.

8
Summary and Implications

SUMMARY

We have conducted a longitudinal birth-cohort study of delinquency in three districts of Puerto Rico. The cohort was born in 1970 and consisted of over 24,000 persons. Through a thorough data-collection and coding process we have recorded the delinquency data, from police and court records, pertaining to this birth cohort.

We have used a research design, a measurement approach, and a statistical analysis framework that has been used very successfully in the two well-known Philadelphia birth cohort studies. Our results indicate the following observations.

First, males are more likely than females to be delinquent and to be delinquent recidivists. Delinquents from public residences, and those from urban areas, were more likely to be recidivists. Public schools have more delinquents, and persons not currently enrolled in school were very likely to be delinquent and delinquent recidivists.

Second, males predominate both in overall delinquency and in serious offenses. The violent offenses of homicide, attempted homicide, and manslaughter occurred the most for males, in urban areas, and in barrio-type residences. There was a relation between drugs and delinquency. Twenty-five percent of all offenses were committed by delinquents who were known to be users of drugs.

Third, delinquency does not begin very early or late in the juvenile age span but mostly begins in the middle years. On the other hand, offense rates increase with age up to age 16 and then decline. There did not appear to be an association between beginning a delinquency career early and accumulating a large number of offenses. In fact, delinquents who began in the middle years at risk committed the most offenses.

Fourth, males are much more likely to be recidivists than are females. The chances of continued male recidivism increase as the number of offenses already committed increases. There did not appear to be evidence of offense specialization. Offenders do not usually repeat the type of prior offense at the next offense; they move around and commit a variety of offenses.

Fifth, there were good indications that the authorities have responded successfully to the offenders in the 1970 cohort. The police use their discretion when it seems desirable to do so. When cases do reach the courts, the courts generally favor some kind of supervision, like probation, so that the offender will receive the monitoring he or she seems to deserve. These interventions seem to have worked exceedingly well.

Last, delinquency in the 1970 cohort is a very different phenomenon from that in the two Philadelphia studies. The 1970 cohort contained a smaller concentration of delinquents and a larger share of delinquents who do not go on to be recidivists. The 1970 cohort did have crimes and some were very serious, but the offense rates across the three cohorts revealed an extent of delinquency that was much less in Puerto Rico. Most important, as noted above, the authorities exhibited an earlier and a more effective response to the delinquents in Puerto Rico than was the case in Philadelphia. This last observation may prove to be the most important of all.

POLICY IMPLICATIONS

This cohort study shows that in Puerto Rico the rate of delinquency, both for males and females, is low compared to other jurisdictions where longitudinal birth-cohort studies have been conducted. Because of this, the major social agencies of response to delinquency should surely be financially supported even more than they have been previously; budgets should be increased.

The programs of delinquency prevention deserve acclaim, as do services to juveniles that treat and respond to those delinquents arrested by the police. More attention and more resources should be provided to these services

Summary and Implications

to deter even more first-time offenders from becoming recidivists because the current programs appear to have been very effective.

In the allocation of resources, whether they be money or social service talent, should be concentrated on these first and second-time offenders. Few delinquents become three-time, or chronic offenders. But those few who do become chronic, commit a vast number of offenses, as was also found in the Philadelphia birth cohort studies.

Hence, we recommend that more resources be intensively concentrated on the one-time and two-time offenders, both males and females, in order to prevent their becoming chronic juvenile offenders. This is especially important because chronic juvenile offenders will most likely otherwise become adult offenders whose crimes will be very difficult to deter.

Efforts should be increased to retain juveniles in schools, and the programs that are currently aimed at reintegrating dropouts should be intensified, since school assistance and achievement are deterrents to delinquency. Similarly, prevention programs should concentrate more efforts on public housing, since many delinquents reside in this type of housing.

We recommend a follow up of this 1970 birth cohort in order to determine the cohort's continuation into adult crime. The data files should be retained by the research team. Through a follow up, we can discern who, among juveniles, have the highest probability of continuing their criminal behavior into the adult years. By studying this population, we can develop prediction models that could result in policy implications for treatment and intervention of particular juvenile offenders while they are still juveniles, in order to prevent their becoming adult offenders.

Some juveniles commit homicide and other very serious felonies. They offenders should, at ages 15 and 16, be waived to the adult court in consideration of their very serious violations of the law. Because these offenders are usually recidivists in delinquency, they should be treated by the just deserts model as serious offenders regardless of age. After age 15, juveniles usually have the cognitive capacity to understand the nature and consequences of their actions and should be treated accordingly by the justice system. Thus, juveniles aged 15 and over who commit serious crimes such as homicide, rape, and armed robbery should be transferred to the adult criminal court for trial.

Juvenile police and court records should in general be retained for five years after the eighteenth birthday, but only the records of juveniles who were arrested and adjudicated for serious felonies should be available to

Delinquency in Puerto Rico

The fingerprinting of juveniles arrested for felonies should be considered, as is being done in the States, for purposes of identification that aid in future investigations and, at the same time, provide protection for the defendant against false charges.

The relationship between guns, homicide, and other assaultive crimes causes us to suggest that Puerto Rican legislative bodies consider more restrictive gun control laws, and that law enforcement agencies tighten control of existing laws.

The high proportion of illicit drugs involved in delinquency only confirms what is already assumed about the relation between drugs and crime. Our recommendations can only be for more stringent monitoring of the drug traffic near and around schools and more firm control and supervision of delinquents who are users and possessors of drugs in any form.

Drug usage, weapons, and violent crime form a dangerous triangulation that may not be as severe in Puerto Rico as in many other places, but is this coalescence of criminal deviance that must be controlled in order to make Puerto Rico an even safer society and our future generations of cohorts less delinquent.

Endnotes

1. For a review of delinquency research in Puerto Rico from 1947 to 1969, see Kupperstein and Toro-Calder, 1969.

2. In Puerto Rico, Type I offenses consist of serious felonies (for example, the UCR index offenses); Type II offenses are generally misdemeanors.

3. Some offenses committed by seventeen year-olds were unavailable. Our data collection process occurred mostly during 1987 and was completed by early 1988 to allow sufficient time for data coding and analysis.

4. Percentages were derived from 1980 Census, Puerto Rico, General Population Characteristics, Table 14.

5. The agencies are: Department of Justice, Department of Education, Department of Social Services, Governor's Office of Youth Affairs, Police Superintendency, Office of Demographic Records, and Courts Administration.

6. Because of the strong correlation (.9942) between the core items of the Wolfgang et al. (1985) severity study and the Puerto Rican sample, the national scale scores were used in this research.

7. The results of the 1945 cohort study are given in Wolfgang et al., (1972), while the results for the 1958 cohort can be found in Tracy et al., (1985, 1990).

8. The decline at this age has been reported in many studies, including the two Philadelphia birth cohorts.

References

Bureau of the Census (1983)
   <u>General Population Characteristics</u>. Washington, D.C.: United States Government Printing Office.

Ferracuti, F., S. Dinitz, & E. Acosta (1975)
   <u>Delinquents and Nondelinquents in the Puerto Rican Slum Culture</u>. Columbus, OH: Ohio State University Press.

Kupperstein, L. & J. Toro-Calder (1969)
   <u>Juvenile Delinquency in Puerto Rico</u>. Rio Pedras: University of Puerto Rico (revised edition in Spanish sub. nom. <u>Delinquencia Juvenil en Puerto Rico</u> (1974).

Lopez-Rey, M., J. Toro-Calder, & C. Cedeno-Zavala (1975)
   <u>Extension, Tendencias y Characteristicas de la Criminalidad en Puerto Rico, 1964-70</u>. Rio Piedras: Editorial Universidad de Puerto Rico.

Otero De Ramos, M. (1970).
   <u>Estudio Socio-Ecologico de la Desercion Escolar y de la Delincuencia Juvenil en Puerto Rico</u>. Rio Piedras: University of Puerto Rico.

Tracy, P.E., M.E. Wolfgang, & R.M. Figlio (1985)
   <u>Delinquency in Two Birth Cohorts, Executive Summary</u>. Washington, D.C.: United Sates Government Printing Office.

Tracy, P.E., M.E. Wolfgang, & R.M. Figlio (1990)
   Delinquency Careers in Two Birth Cohorts. New York: Plenum Press.

Vales, P. & E. Ayala (1986)
   Caracteristicas Socioeconomicas de los Menores Ingresados en los Centros de Tratamiento Social por Haber Cometido Faltas contra la Ley. Unpublished paper, Department of Social Services.

Wolfgang, M.E., R.M. Figlio, & T. Sellin (1972)
   Delinquency in a Birth Cohort. Chicago: University of Chicago Press.

Wolfgang, M.E., R.M. Figlio, P.E. Tracy, & S.I. Singer (1985)
   The National Survey of Crime Severity. Washington, D.C.: United States Government Printing Office.

Appendices

APPENDIX 1.
Order of the Court Authorizing Access to Juvenile Records

(Orden y Solicitud de Análisis y Estudio al Amparo del Art. 37(d) de la Ley 88 de 9 de Julio de 1986).

EN EL TRIBUNAL SUPERIOR DO PUERTO RICO
SALE DE

Ex-Parte:
ESTUDIO LONGITUDINAL   NUM: PE87-1
DE DELINCUENCIA

ORDEN

Vista la solicitud de Análisis y Estudio al amparo del Artículo 37 (d) de la Ley Núm. 88 de 9 de julio de 1986, presentada por el peticionario, se dispone lo siguiente por entender que se trata de un estudio oficial cubierto bajo la citada disposición cuyos resultados serán utilizados en la formulación de política pública en Puerto Rico en el área de menores.

1. Los directores del estudio, Dr. Marvin Wolfgang y Dra. Dora Nevarez de Aponte y los asistentes de investigación; estos últimos previa identificación por el Juez Administrador, podrán tener acceso a los expedientes del Tribunal de Menores intervenidos al

Tribunal de Menores, Sala de San Juan. Asimismo, podrán fotocopiar aquella información necesaria para ser codificada posteriormente. A saber, el informe social, la querella, informe de intervención, algunas mociones que incluyen como parte de la misma un recuento de datos petinentes y la orden del Tribunal al efecto. Los Asistentes de Investigación del estudio podrán, además, revisar el expediente completo y levantar la información que sea necesaria.

2. Se dispone que el personal, al fotocopiar la información descrita en el párrafo número 1, arriba, cubrirá la referencia al nombre del menor intervenido y en su lugar se pondrá un número de indentificación clave previamente determinado. De manera que, las fotocopias de materiales de los expedientes de menores que salgan del Tribunal para efectos del estudio de delincuencia juvenil no tendrán el nombre de los menores sino números de indentificación.

3. Las fotocopias que se hagan de los documentos que obren en el expediente del menor, así como la información que se recopile, será colocada en la oficina del estudio, ubicada en el Senado, en archivos bajo llave. La misma se mantendrá en esa oficina mientras dure la codificación y análisis de la data recopilada. Una vez se termine esta fase del estudio, se devolverán las copias al Tribunal.

4. Para trasladar los documentos fotocopias del Tribunal a la oficina del estudio se tormarán las previsiones pertinentes, incluyendo escolta al asistente de investigación de parte de un alguacil hasta entregar la información en la oficina del estudio.

5. El personal del estudio podrá ubicar una fotocopiadora del Senado en la Secretaría del Tribunal y alimentará la misma con papel que traiga para ello. Una vez termine la fase de la recopilación de la data, deberá llevarse la fotocopiadora.

Registrese y notifiquese.

En   , Puerto Rico, a   de   de 1987.

JUEZ SUPERIOR

Appendix

EN EL TRIBUNAL SUPERIOR DE PUERTO RICO
SALA DE

Ex-Parte:
ESTUDIO LONGITUDINAL   NUM:
DE DELINCUENCUA JUVENIL

SOLICITUD DE ANALISIS Y ESTUDIO AL AMPARO DEL
ARTICULO 37 (d) DE LA LEY NUM. 88 DE
9 DE JULIO DE 1986

AL HONORABLE TRIBUNAL:
Comparece la Comisión Especial del Senado sobre Problemas de Incidencia Criminal y el Hon. Miquel A. Hernández Agosto, Presidente del Senado y de la referida Comisión, representada por la Dra. Dora Nevarez de APonte, quien respetuosamente expone y solicita lo siguiente:

1. El 29 de fedrero de 1986, el Senado de Puerto Rico aprobó la Resolución del Senado Núm. 329 (R. del S. 329), que crea la Comisión Especial del Senado Sobre Problemas de Incidencia Criminal para que, "...examine profunda, serena y objectivamente el problema de la incidencia criminal que afecta el Estado Libre Asociado de Puerto Rico..." Se acompaña certificación del Secretario del Senado sobre la aprobación de dicha Resolución, así como la R. del S. 329 y se identifica como Exhibit 1.

2. Como parte de la encomienda descrita en el párrafo primero de esta moción la Comisión Especial del Senado sobre Problemas de Incidencia Criminal está realizando un estudio longitudinal de delincuencia juvenil en Puerto Rico, bajo la dirección del Dr. Marvin Wolfgang y la Dra. Dora Nevarez de Aponte, cuyos objectivos y metodolgía se desriben extensamente en el Exhibit 2 que se acompaña.

3. Dicho estudio está diseñado para determinar los patrones de delincuencia juvenil en Puerto Rico y la probabilidad de ser arrestado como delincuente un menor antes de llegar a su mayoría de edad. La muestra del estudio consiste de todos los varones nacidos en 1970 que han sido intervenidos como menores por la Policía en las áreas de San Juan, Carolina y Bayamón. El estudio contestará preguntas como las siguientes: ¿Cuál es la edad promedio para iniciarse en la delincuencia? ¿Existe una tendencia de pasar de delitos menos severos a los más severos a medida que aumenta la edad del joven y la frecuencia de su conducta delictiva? ¿Hay especialización en patrones de delincuencia? ¿Son la

mayoría de los delitos cometidos por un número pequeño de delincuentes? ¿Cuáles son las probabilidades que tiene un menor de cometer una primera, segundo o tercera falta antes de llegar a los dieciocho años? ¿Cuáles son las condiciones que propician que un menor se convierta en un delincuente crónico? ¿Cuáles son las condiciones adecuadas para prevenir que un menor incida en conducta delictiva?

4. Los resultados del referido estudio serán utilizados en la formulación de política pública en el área de menores.

5. El estudio cuenta con la cooperación de las siguientes agencias de la Rama Ejecutiva: Departamento de Justicia, Departmento de Instrucción Pública, Departmento de Servicios Sociales, Superintendencia de la Policía, Oficina de Ausntos de la Juventud y la Oficina de Administración de Tribunales, a cuyos fines han firmado el acuerdo cooperativo que se incluye como Exhibit 3.

6. El personal del estudio, asistentes de investigación y directores del estudio, han sido investigados por la Policía de Puerto Rico, a los fines de cualificarlos y autorizarlos a tener acceso a los expedientes de menores que obran en la Policía.

7. Como parte del estudio será necesario tener acceso a los expedientes de menores intervenidos que formen parte de la muestra del estudio y que fueron referidos al Tribunal de San Juan. Asimismo, será necesario fotocopiar aquella información necesaria para ser codificada posteriormente, a saber, el informe social, la querella, informe de intervención, algunas mociones que incluyen, como parte de la misma, un recuento de datos pertinentes y la orden del Tribunal al efecto. Los Asistentes de Investigación necesitarán, además, revisar el expediente completo y levantar la información que sea necesaria.

8. El personal del estudio se compromete a que, al fotocopiar la información descrita en el párrafo número 7, arriba, se cubrirá el nombre del menor intervenido y en su lugar se pondrá un número de indentificación clave previamente determinado. De manera que, las fotocopias de materiales de los expendientes de menores que salgan del Tribunal para efectos del estudio de delincuencia juvenil no tendrán nombres de menores sino números de identificación.

Appendix

9. Las fotocopias que se hagan de los documentos que obren en el expediente del menor, así como la información que se levante, será colocada en la oficina del estudio, ubicada en el Senado, en archivos bajo llave. La misma se mantendrá en esa oficina mientras dure la codificación y análisis de la data recopilada. Una vez se termine esta fase del estudio, se devolverán las copias al Tribunal.

10. Para trasladar, los documentos fotocopiados del Tribunal a la oficina del estudio se tomarán las previsiones pertinentes, incluyendo escolta al asistente de investigación de parte de un alguacil hasta entregar la información en la oficina del estudio.

11. Se trata de un estudio oficial auspicado por el Senado de Puerto Rico, varias agencias de la Rama Ejecutiva y la Administración de los Tribunales, llevado a cabo bajo la dirección de personas de probada reputación científica y de asistentes de investigación debidamente cualificados, donde se mantendrá estricta confidencialidad de los menores de la muestra, y cuyos hallazgos serán utilizados en la formulación de politica pública en Puerto Rico.

POR TODO LO CUAL, respetuosamente solicitamos que al amparo del párrafo número 2, letra d, del Articulo 37 de la Ley Núm. 88 de 9 de julio de 1986, se permita al personal del estudio de referencia tener acceso a los expedientes de menores que formen parte de la muestra bajo las condiciones antes señaladas.
Respestuosamente sometido.
En   , Puerto Rico, a de   de 1987.

>Dora Nevarez de Aponte
>Oficina 5 y 6
>Anexo Medicina Tropical
>Senado de Puerto Rico
>Tel. 724-2030 (x258)
>ó 722-4012

APPENDIX 2.
Form PPR36, Police Juvenile Records Card

(Tarjeta de Record de Menores en la Policia)

Appendix

FPR-36
1-80

ESTADO LIBRE ASOCIADO DE PUERTO RICO
POLICIA DE PUERTO RICO
RECORD DE MENORES

Unidad de Trabajo

Apellido Paterno	Apellido Materno	Nombre	Apodo
Edad	Sexo	Color	Dirección		
Pueblo		Sitio de Nacimiento		Fecha de Nacimiento	
Nombre del Padre		Vive Si ☐ No ☐	Dirección		
Nombre de la Madre		Vive Si ☐ No ☐	Dirección		
Reside con			Parentesco	Motivo	
Estudiante Si ☐ No ☐	Nombre de la Escuela			Grado Cursa	Grado Curso
Trabaja Si ☐ No ☐	Ocupación			Patrono	

FALTA COMETIDA	Fecha Falta	Sitio de los Hechos	Núm. de Querella	DISPOSICION

APPENDIX 3.
Form OAT110, Index Juvenile Card

(Tarjeta de Indice Juvenile en el Tribunal)

Appendix

APELLIDO PATERNO	APELLIDO MATERNO	NOMBRE
DIRECCION		NUM. DE CASO
FECHA DE NACIMIENTO PADRE		ASIG. A
MADRE		

CONTRAREFERIDO CON

ANTECEDENTES EN CORTE

FECHA	QUERELLA NO	QUERELLA SI	NUMERO	FALTAS	DISPOSICION	P	F

TARJETA INDICE JUVENIL
OAT FORM 110

FECHA	QUERELLA NO	QUERELLA SI	NUMERO	FALTAS	DISPOSICION	P	F

APPENDIX 4.
Form PPR116, Police Intervention Report

(Intervención con Menor)

PPR-116
REV. 11-74

ESTADO LIBRE ASOCIADO DE PUERTO RICO
POLICIA DE PUERTO RICO
INTERVENCION CON MENOR

AREA

UNIDAD DE TRABAJO

SEG. SOC. DEL INTERVENIDO

NUM. DEL INFORME

NUM. DE QUERELLA

1. FALTA COMETIDA | 2. Distrito Informe El Delito (Tipo 1) | NUM. DEL DELITO | 3. FECHA DE LA FALTA | 4. FECHA Y HORA DE LA INTERVENCION | 5. SITIO DE LA INTERVENCION

6. NOMBRE DEL MENOR | SEXO | COLOR | 7. DIRECCION | 8. TEL. RESIDENCIA

9. APODO | 10. SITIO DE NACIMIENTO | 11. FECHA DE NACIMIENTO | 12. ARMAS USADAS | 13. ¿NARCOTICOS ENVUELTOS? ☐ SI ☐ NO

14. NOMBRE DEL PADRE | ¿VIVE? ☐ SI ☐ NO | 15. DIRECCION

16. NOMBRE DE LA MADRE | ¿VIVE? ☐ SI ☐ NO | 17. DIRECCION

18. CONVIVENCIA
 1 ☐ CON AMBOS PADRES
 2 ☐ CON PADRE Y MADRASTRA
 3 ☐ CON MADRE Y PADRASTRO
 4 ☐ SOLAMENTE CON: ☐ PADRE ☐ MADRE
 DEBIDO A: ☐ ABANDONO ☐ MUERTE DE: ☐ PADRE ☐ MADRE
 ☐ RECLUSION ☐ OTROS
 5 ☐ CON FAMILIARES POR
 6 ☐ CON OTROS
 7 ☐ SOLO
 8 ☐ AMBULANTE

19. ¿ASISTE A ESCUELA?
 SI ☐ CURSA 1, 2, 3, 4, 5, 6, 7, 8, 9, 10, 11, 12
 NO ☐ CURSO HASTA 1, 2, 3, 4, 5, 6, 7, 8, 9, 10, 11, 12.
 ☐ NUNCA HA ASISTIDO A

20. NOMBRE DE LA ESCUELA | 21. DIRECCION ESCUELA

22. ¿TRABAJA? SI ☐ NO ☐ | 23. OCUPACION

24. NOMBRE Y DIRECCION DEL PATRONO

25. NOMBRE DEL QUERELLANTE O PERJUDICADO | EDAD | SEXO | COLOR | 26. DIRECCION | 27. TEL. RESIDENCIAL

28. TESTIGOS | NOMBRE | 29. DIRECCION | 30. TEL. RESIDENCIAL
 1-
 2-

31. MIEMBRO(S) QUE EFECTUO (UARON) LA INTERVENCION | NUM. SERIE | 32. DIVISION O DISTRITO A QUE PERTENECE(N)
 1-
 2-

33. ACCION TOMADA:
 ☐ RESUELTO ADMINISTRATIVAMENTE
 REFERIDO A:
 ☐ D.A.J.
 ☐ BIENESTAR PUBLICO
 ☐ OTRA AGENCIA
 ☐ INTAKER

34. MIEMBRO(S) A QUIEN(ES) SE LE ENTREGO EL MENOR | NUM. SERIE | 35. DIVISION O DISTRITO A QUE PERTENECE(N)
 1-
 2-

USE LA HOJA DE CONTINUACION PARA RELATAR BREVEMENTE LAS CIRCUNSTANCIAS DE LA INTERVENCION

AYUDA JUVENIL DEL AREA

PPR 118
REV 11/74

ESTADO LIBRE ASOCIADO DE PUERTO RICO
POLICIA DE PUERTO RICO

HOJA DE CONTINUACION

NUMERO Y CLASE DE INFORME		AREA
NUMERO DE QUERELLA		UNIDAD DE TRABAJO

1 PREPARADO POR	NUM DE SERIE	2 SUPERVISOR	NUM DE SERIE

CIC DEL AREA

APPENDIX 5.
Form PPR113, Supplementary Police Report

(Supplementario de Intervención)

PPR-113
Rev. 11-74

ESTADO LIBRE ASOCIADO DE PUERTO RICO
POLICIA DE PUERTO RICO
SUPLEMENTARIO DE _____

AREA
UNIDAD DE TRABAJO

NUM. DE INFORME ORIGINAL _____
NUM. DE QUERELLA ORIGINAL _____

1. UNIDAD DE TRABAJO DE INFORME ORIGINAL | 2. FECHA DE INFORME ORIGINAL | 3. FECHA Y HORA DE ESTE INFORME | TIPO DE INFORME

4. PROPOSITO DE ESTE INFORME:
☐ AMPLIAR INVESTIGACION   ☐ CAMBIAR CLASIFICACION DE DELITO   ☐ ESCLARECIMIENTO EXCEPCIONAL
☐ DELITO INFUNDADO   ☐ CERRAR CASO   ☐ OTRO _____ INDIQUE

5. CLAVE: Q - QUERELLANTE   T - TESTIGO
           P - PERJUDICADO   A - ACUSADO

UTILIZANDO ESTAS CLAVES, INDIQUE EL NOMBRE Y DIRECCION DE LAS PERSONAS CORRESPONDIENTES.

CLAVE	NOMBRE	DIRECCION	TEL. RES.	TEL. NEG.	CLAVE

6. INFORME LAS RAZONES PARA ACCION TOMADA:

_____
_____
_____
_____
_____
_____
_____
_____
_____
_____
_____
_____
_____
_____

DE SER NECESARIO USE HOJA DE CONTINUACION.

7. PREPARADO POR:	NUM. SERIE	8. SUPERVISOR	NUM. SERIE

CIC DEL AREA

APPENDIX 6
Offender Demographic Form

1. Offender ID Number   - / - - - -
   (using police district)

2. PRAJJIS Number   - - - / - - / - - - - -

3. Date of Birth   - - / - - / - -

4. Place of Birth   - -
   (codes: PR = Puerto Rico; DR = Dominican Republic; for the 50 US states, use 2 digit postal codes-- NY = New York; PA = Pennsylvania; etc).

5. Sex of Offender   -

6. Color of Offender   -
   (W = White; N = Nonwhite; T = Trigueno)

APPENDIX 7
Offense Form

Offender ID Number (using police district)   - / - - - -

PRAJJIS Number   - - - / - - / - - - - -

8. Offense Number   - -

9. Sources of Household Income (check all that apply)
a) father   -   g) the juvenile   -
b) mother   -   h) the juvenile's spouse   -
c) stepfather   -   i) voc./rehab. program   -
d) stepmother   -   j) social security   -
e) other relative -   k) nutritional assistance   -
f) legal guardian -   l) other.   -

10. Number of siblings   - -

11. Mental retardation (Y = Yes, N = No)   -

12. Insanity (Y = Yes, N = No)   -

Offense Variables:

13. Court Number   - - / - - / - - - -

14. Case Number   - - - - - - - - - -

15. Date of Offense   - - / - - / - -

Appendix

16. Age at Offense   \- \-
17. Type of Offense (use crime code list)   \- \- \- \-
18. Number of Victims   \- \-
19. Victim Characteristics:

	Sex (M/F/U/)	Color (W/N/T/U)	Age	Injury (N/M/T/ H/D/U)	Forcible rape
a) victim 1	-	-	--	-	-
b) victim 2	-	-	--	-	-
c) victim 3	-	-	--	-	-
d) victim 4	-	-	--	-	-
e) victim 5	-	-	--	-	-
f) victim 6	-	-	--	-	-
g) victim 7	-	-	--	-	-
h) victim 8	-	-	--	-	-
i) victim 9	-	-	--	-	-
j) victim 10	-	-	--	-	-

20. Weapons Present (check all that apply)
    a) handgun   \-   d) blunt instrument   \-
    b) other gun   \-   e) other weapon   \-
    c) sharp instrument   \-

21. Dollar Value of Theft $ \- \- \- \- \- \-
22. Dollar Value of Damage $ \- \- \- \- \- \-
23. Number of Premises Forcibly Entered   \- \-
24. Type of Premises Forcibly Entered
    (check all that apply)
    a) Commercial \-   b) Private \-   c) Public \-

Delinquency in Puerto Rico

25. Number of Co-offenders   --

26. Co-offender Characteristics: Sex   Color
                                    (M/F/U/)   (W/N/T/U)   Age

    a) victim 1   -   -   --
    b) victim 2   -   -   --
    c) victim 3   -   -   --
    d) victim 4   -   -   --
    e) victim 5   -   -   --
    f) victim 6   -   -   --
    g) victim 7   -   -   --
    h) victim 8   -   -   --
    i) victim 9   -   -   --
    j) victim 10   -   -   --

27. Possession of Drugs (check all that apply)

    a) marijuana   -   b) heroin   -
    c) cocaine   -   d) other   -

28. User or Under Influence of Drugs/Alcohol
    (check all that apply)

    a) marijuana   -   b) heroin   -
    c) cocaine   -   d) alcohol   -
                                    e) other   -

Disposition Variables

29. Date of Arrest   -- / -- / --

30. Disposition by Police   -
    (A = administrative; R = referred to court)

31. Date of Pre-trial Detention   --

32. Days of Pre-trial Detention   --

33. Date of Court Disposition   -- / -- / --

34. Type of Court Disposition   -

    1 = Dismissed   4 = Diversion
    2 = Acquitted   5 = Sentenced
    3 = Waived Jurisdiction   6 = Pending

Appendix

35. Reason for Jurisdiction Waiver (check all that apply)

    a) gravity of offense -   b) prior record -
                    c) other -

36. Disposition by Adult Court   -

    1 = Dismissed   2 = Acquitted   3 = Sentenced

37. If Sentenced, Type of Sentence   -

a) nominal sentence   g) private institution
b) custody of parents h) maximum security institution
c) probation   i) intermediate security inst.
d) restrictions   j) vocational/agricul. inst.
e) restitution   k) minimum security homes
f) other conditions   l) mental institution
                     m) other institution

38. Weeks Served on Probation   - - -

39. Weeks Served in Diversion Program   - - -

40. Weeks Served in Custodial Institution - - -

41. Type of Treatment (check all that apply)

a) medication   -   c) vocational program -
b) psychiatric treatment -   d) other   -

42. Amount of Fine (in dollars) $- - - - -

43. Amount of Restitution (in dollars) $- - - - -

44. Date of Discharge   - - / - - / - -

45. Was Juvenile a Fugitive at time of Current Offense?

    (Y = YES; N = NO)   -

46. Did Juvenile Have Pending Charges at

    Time of Current Offense? (Y = YES; N = NO)   -

47. Was Juvenile on Probation at time of

    Current Offense? (Y = YES; N = NO)   -

Delinquency in Puerto Rico

Crime Code List

Offense	Code	Offense	Code
Homicide or Murder	0100	Lewd & lacivious acts	2006
Attempted homicide	0120	Indecent exposure	2007
Forcible rape	0200	Obscenity	2008
Robbery	0300	Participation in obscene show	2009
Aggravated assault	0400	Incest	2011
Burglary	0500	Drugs & narcotics	2100
Aggravated larceny	0600	Illegal gambling	2200
Auto theft	0800	Automobile laws	2400
Negligent manslaughter	1000	Disorderly conduct	2700
Simple assault	1100	Kidnapping	3301
Mayhem	1110	Explosives laws	4400
Arson	1200	Law #21—to spoil a public or private property	4500
Forgery	1300		
Fraud	1400		
Receiving, transporting, selling stolen property	1600	Law #30—school trespassing	4600
		Unnecessary noise	5000
		Municipal violations	5400
Malicious mischief	1700	Escape	6000
Weapons laws	1800	Status Offenses:	
Prostitution	1900	runaway	8801
Statutory rape	2001	truancy	8802
Adultery	2002	incorrigibility	8803
Seduction	2003	disrespect authority	8804
Bestialism	2004		
Sodomy	2005	Libel	9905

If the offense is not included in the codes listed above:

Offenses against civil rights	3300
Offenses against due care of juveniles	3500
Other property offenses	3600
Offenses against the judiciary	4000
Offenses against the public authority	4200

If the offense is an attempt, a number 2 is written as the third digit of the completed offense code. For example, attempted robbery = 0320.

**APPENDIX 8. Coding Instructions
Instrucciones Generales:**

(Instrucciones para Codificación)

Toda codificación deberá a hacerse a lápiz.

<u>SI DESCONOCE EL DATO</u>

Dejar en blanco todo espacio para el cual no tenga información; con excepción de los espacios en las preguntas 19 y 26 del <u>offense</u> <u>form</u> donde cuando se desconoce el dato, la propia forma indica que ponga "U".

Iniciar la última pagina del <u>offender form</u> y del <u>offense form</u> al margen inferior derecho.

EN CASO DE DUDA CONSULTAR CON SU SUPERVISOR O CON LA DOCTORA NEVARES; NO SUPONER NI INVENTARSE DATOS QUE NO SURGEN DE LA DATA QUE TIENE DISPONIBLE.

<u>EXPEDIENTE INCOMPLETO</u>

Hay varios expedientes que están incompletos. Unos por estar pendientes ante el tribunal a la fecha en que se recopiló la data; otros porque el expediente policíaco no concuerda con el de tribunales o viceversa; otros por inadvertencias en el proceso de recopilar la data. En cualquiera de esos casos, anote en un papel el número de

Delinquency in Puerto Rico

identificación del ofensor, el número del expediente juvenil del menor, y el número de la querella con relación a la cual falta información, y una referencia al dato especifico a buscar. Si ha podido llenar parcialmente el "offense form" indique a que "offense number" se refiere la información que falta y el número del item que está pendiente. Una vez haga esa anotación, se la entrega junto con el expediente a Supervisor o a la Doctora, quienes le daran instrucciones al efecto.

OFFENDER DEMOGRAPHIC FORM

Debe comenzar la codificación de cada expediente llenando primero esta forma. La cual deberá tener a mano para hacer el cómputo de la edad en que se cometió la falta, a que hace referencia el item #16 de la "offense form."

1. Tan pronto inicie la codificación de un expediente de un menor, VERIFIQUE SI ESE MENOR APARECE EN LAS LISTAS DE LOS OTROS DOS DISTRITOS PolicíaCOS. Esta labor es importantísima, y no puede ser omitida, por cuanto si estuviera repetido, lo estaríamos codificando como si fueran dos personas distintas, cuando en realidad se trata de un reincidente.

2. Busque las hojas que PRAJJIS envió e identifique si hay una hoja para el menor que habrá de codificar. Si la hay, póngala en el expediente del menor y utilícela durante la codificación. A esa hoja de PRAJJIS le escribe en el número superior derecho nuestro número de indentificación.

3. No estará listo para comenzar la codificación hasta que haya llevado a cabo los pasos 1 y 2 de arriba.

Instrucciones sobre Items Específicos

En el item #3, fecha de nacimento, deberá verificar adecuadamente la misma. Recuerde que hay expedientes donde la fecha de nacimiento según el informe policíaco no concuerda con la del tribunal. En tal caso se necesita el acta de nacimiento o verificar el dato en las listas que nos porveyó el Registro Demográfico; en su defecto (e.g., si fuera extranjero, dejarse llevar por la fecha que da el tribunal y, en su defecto, la del informe social).

En el item # 4, lugar de nacimiento, poner las iniciales que correspondan según la tabla OD-4 que se aneja a estas instrucciones.

En el item # 6, color del ofensor, dejarse llevar en primera instancia por el dato que aparece en el informe social y en su defecto por el que da el informe policíaco. En caso de discrepancia, dejarse llevar por el del informe social.

Si en el caso bajo estudio se diera la situación que el menor ha vivido en los Estados Unidos durante alguno de los cinco años anteriores a cometer la falta, y ese menor nació en Puerto Rico, poner un numero 7 que diga "migrant (y el lugar)."

OFFENSE FORM

Deberá LLENAR UNA FORMA PARA CADA DELITO O CURSO DE CONDUCTA.

Tenga en cuenta que la información demográfica, items # 1 al 12, puede variar con los diferentes delitos o eventos delictivos a través del transcurso del tiempo. De manera que, no se limite a copiar de una forma a otra.

OFFENSOR REINCIDENTE

Cuando se trata de un ofensor reincidente, antes de comenzar a llenar las formas haga lo siguiente:

1. organice el expediente;

2. identifique el orden en que se sometieron las querellas y póngale el número correspondiente, comenzando con 01 para la primera intervención o querella;

3. identifique la fecha en que se hizo el informe social, léalo y relaciónelo con la data que irá obteniendo al llevar a cabo el paso (4) que sigue;

4. una vez identificadas las faltas y organizado el expediente proceda a analizar las faltas en el orden en que se sometieron (01 al On) en el siguiente orden: informe de intervención policíaca, informe suplementario, querella, minuta de vista de hechos, órdenes del tribunal según la fecha;

5. indique en un papel que pegará al frente del expediente, la información, si alguna, que le hace falta para llevar a cabo la codificación. Si, por el

Delinquency in Puerto Rico

contrario, terminó de codificar el expediente, inicie el "folder" en la carpeta y ponga la fecha en que lo codificó. Lo archiva en el lugar seleccionado para ello y en la lista maestra pone la fecha en que lo codificó y su inicial.

Instrucciones Específicas por Items

Offender ID Number--
se refiere al número de identificación que previamente le dimos a los miembros de nuestro cohorte.

PRAJJIS Number--
lo tendrá que dejar en blanco, pues PRAJJIS no nos proveyó la información, a pesar de que se solicitó.

Offense Number--

número de la ofensa (incluye un solo delito o un curso de conducta o evento delictivo) en el orden en que se le sometió el caso a un mismo ofensor, e.g., 01, 02, 03, 04,...On).
Nota: La información del "Offender ID Number" y del "Offense Number" DEBE LLENARLA EN CADA UNA DE LAS 6 PáGINAS DEL OFFENSE FORM.

Item # 1--

1 = Public-- se refiere a cualquier escuela adscrita al sistema de instrucción pública. Ver listado de escuelas en caso de duda. Incluye escuelas publicas especiales y las llamadas de adultos o estudios libres o vocacionales.

2 = Private denominational-- se refiere a escuelas privadas administradas por alguna religión institucionalizada: e.g., católicas, bautistas, evangélicas, etc.

3 = Private non-denominational-- se refiere a escuelas privadas laicas.

Item # 2--

Está información la obtiene del informe social y en su defecto del informe policíaco. Tenga en cuenta que la pregunta se refiere a si a la fecha de los hechos delictivos estaba aistiendo a la escuela o no lo estaba.

Item # 3--

Appendix

Se refiere al último grado escolar aprobado. Esto significa que cuando el menor está en la escuela usted restará un grado al que aparece en el informe de la policía (item 19 (a)) pues ese item se refiere al grado que está cursando.

Ahora bien, <u>si el menor no está en la escuela</u> entonces en el informe de la policía (item 19 (b)) aparecerá el ultimo grado que cursó. En este caso escribe ese número.

En aquellos donde no hay un informe social con tal información al momento del delito, ponga el número que aparece en el informe de la policía.

Item # 4--

Si el menor no trabaja déjelo en blanco. Si trabaja, refiérase a la occupación según aparece en la tabla OF-8 que se aneja.

Item # 5--

Para determinar si la residencia es úrbana o rural déjese llevar por el informe social. Si el expediente no tiene informe social, examine en la lista de las escuelas si la escuela a que ese menor asiste está en zona urbana o rural. Tenga presente que por norma si el menor va a escuela pública asistirá a la más cercana a su residencia.

En ocasiones he encontrado discrepancia entre el informe de PRAJJIS y el dato real sobre si la residencia es urbana o rural. En ese caso busque en el mapa, luego consulte con su Supervisor o la Dra. antes de tomar una decisión.

Item # 6--

1 = Barrio/Barriada-- se refiere a residencias en barrios (barrios rurales, rescates de terrenos, campos) o barriadas (por lo general son los arrabales úrbanos o sectores de los pueblos que no constituyen urbanizaciones).

2 = Private-- se refiere a residencias privadas, alquiladas o de propiedad, en las calles de los pueblos, en urbanizaciones o condominios. Incluye viviendas subsidiadas por el Banco de la Vivienda, por la Farmer's Home o por la Sección 8 del Gobierno Federal, y las cooperativas.

3 = Public-- se refiere a los residenciales públicos.

Item # 7--

Se refiere a la naturaleza del hogar o tipo de convivencia. Si tuviera la hoja de PRAJJIS, allí se le domina "cohabitation."

Si el menor convive con los padres, marque la (a) y la (b). Si en ese hogar hay hermanos que conviven con el ofensor, no marque la (e); pues la información sobre los hermanos se incluye en el item # 10.

Si el menor vive en casa de su abuela, marque la (e) y ponga entre paréntesis (grandmother). Asimismo, marque la (e) si el menor vive en la casa de cualquier otro familiar, incluyendo hermanos, tios, primos, etc.

La (c) se refiere al padrastro; y la (d) a la madrastra.

La (f) se refiere al tutor legal; la (g) al hogar sustituto o de crianza donde un menor es colocado por Servicios Sociales o una agencia autorizada para colocar niños; la (h) se marca cuando el menor vive con su cónyuge; La (i) cuando el menor está en una institución del estado o privada y la (j) en otro tipo de convivencia, como podria ser: si vive errante (escriba "runaway"), en casa de algún amigo no relacionado por parentesco (escriba "friends").

Item # 8--

Identifique la persona que es el jefe de la casa donde convive el menor. Esto surge por lo general del informe social; en su defecto en el informe de la policía lo puede identificar del item # 18 (convivencia); mientras que en la hoja de PRAJJIS lo indentifica bajo "responsible adult."

Si vive con ambos padres por lo general es el hombre, excepto que éste no genere ingresos y en su lugar los genere la mujer.

Refierase a la tabla OF-8 y escriba el nombre del la ocupación.

Si desconoce la ocupación, ponga "unknown."

Si tiene alguna ocupación pero al momento está desempleado ponga la ocupación y entre paréntesis "unemployed."

Appendix

Si está pensionado por edad o incapacidad, se pone la ocupación y entre paréntesis "retired."

Si no trabaja porque no quiere o dejó de buscar empleo, escriba "not in the labor force."

Si es empleado de gobierno, ponga "government employee" y entre paréntesis "la ocupación."

Si está preso, ponga la ocupación y entre paréntesis "in jail".

Item # 9--

Se refiere a las fuentes de ingreso familiar. Marque todas las aplicables a la fecha en que el menor cometió la ofensa.

Las letras (a) a la (h) se refieren a ingreso obtenido mediante algún tipo de trabajo.

Bajo "other," puede escribir cualquiera de los siguiente si aplicaran:

DSS (se refiere al la ayuda de bienestár publico o asistencia pública que da Servicios Sociales; esta ayuda no coresponde a los cheques de alimentos, que están incluidos en la (k);
Alimony (se refiere a la pensión alimenticia;

Workmen's Compensation (i.e., Fondo de Seguro del Estado);

Unemployment Insurance (i.e., cobrando el seguro por desempleo);

Veteran's Pension (i.e., pensión como veterano);

Private Retirement income (i.e., pensiones por trabajo o incapacidad que no sean el seguro social).

Item # 10--

Number of Siblings se refiere a número de hermanos y hermanas, de doble vinculo o sencillo que tiene el miembro del cohorte y que son parte del núcleo familiar. En el conteo no incluya al ofensor.

En las hojas que PRAJJIS suministró incluyó erróneamente la palabra "brothers" como sinónimo de siblings. No

211

obstante puede usar el dato por cuanto se refiere al número de hermanos y hermanas.

Item # 11--

La información de si el menor es retardado, la puede encontrar en el informe social o en las evaluaciones sicológicas si las hay. De no haberlas, si lo que tiene es el informe de la policía y el menor está en un grado muy bajo para su edad, y matriculado en un curso de educación especial, posiblemente se deba a retardación, por lo que puede marcar yes = "Y."

Si el menor está en un grado razonable para su edad y no hay información al efecto de que es retardado, y razonablemente puede inferir que no lo es, ponga "N."

Si desconoce el dato, déjelo en blanco.

Item # 12--

Esta información la obtendrá del informe social y con más seguridad del informe siquiátrico.

Item # 13--

<u>Court Number</u> se refiere al número del expediente del menor que se le asigna en el tribunal y que corresponde al de su primer caso ante el tribunal.

Item # 14--

<u>Case Number</u> = Dependiendo del caso se referirá a:

Si el caso se resolvió administrativamente o si se refirió al tribunal, escriba el número del informe de intervención policíaca.

Si se renunció jurisdicción, entonces escriba el número del caso ante el tribunal de adultos.

Si se trata de un indisciplinado o un caso de DESCA que no fue al tribunal, ponga el número que le asignaron en PRAJJIS.

Item # 15--

Fecha en que cometió el delito o evento delictivo. Esta fecha la obtiene del informe de intervención policíaca o de la querella.

Appendix

En los casos de indisciplinados, se pone la fecha en que el caso fue referido a Servicios Sociales. En los casos de DESCA, se pone también la fecha en que fue referido a la agencia.

Item # 16--

Edad cuando se cometió el delito. Escriba el año cumplido al momento de los hechos delictivos. Aún cuando le falte uno o dos días, si todavía no ha cumplido el año, no puede redondear a la fecha más cercana.

Cuando haga este cómputo tenga a mano la hoja titulada: offender demographic form" donde el item # 3 tiene la fecha de nacimiento.

Item # 17--

Refiérase a la tabla OF-17 para el número correspondiente al nombre legal de la falta.

Si se trata de una serie de delitos que forman parte de un curso de conducta, clasifíquelos bajo el delito más severo o que por lo general es el primero que aparece en la querella.

Por favor, dejese llevar por la classificación que da el tribunal y en su defecto la policía. Si hubiera un error manifiesto en la clasificación del delito que hizo la policía, consulte con su Supervisor o la Dra. antes de codificar el dato.

Item # 18--

Se refiere al número de víctimas de violencia personal donde hay algún contacto personal. Esto aplica a delitos como los siguientes: homicidios, delitos sexuales, agresiones, robos, secuestros, choques atomovilísticos, etc.

Por el contrario, no aplica en delitos como alteración a la paz, daños a la propiedad, etc.

Si quien sufre daño personal es el menor ofensor o uno de sus coautores no puede incluirlos aquí, pues ellos no se consideran victimás.

Si el item # 18 es 00, entonces no conteste la item # 19.

Item # 19--

Delinquency in Puerto Rico

Se refiere a las víctimas de violencia personal que incluyó en el número 18. En todos los grupos "U" significa "unknown" o que desconoce la información.

Sex: M= másculino; F = femenino; U = se desconoce

Color: W = blanco; N = negro; T = trigueño; U = no sabe

Age: ponga la edad; si la desconoce la deja en blanco, excepto que sepa que es un menor (juvenile) o adulto (adult)
Injury = daño personal o al cuerpo

N = ningun daño personal

M = daño menor = Como resultado de violencia física ejercida contra la víctima, ésta recibe un daño personal que no requiere atencion médica. E.g., un empujón, un rasguño, tumbarla, un moratón, una agresion que no requiere atención médica

T = tratamiento médico ambulatorio = La víctima requiere atención médica a consecuencia del daño sufrido; pero no requiere ser hospitalizada, ni tratamiento ambulatorio prolongado

H = hospitalización = La víctima requiere ser hospitalizada para recibir tratamiento, o requiere tratamiento ambulatorio durante tres o más visitas médicas

D = muerte = La víctima muere a consecuencia del daño que se le infligió por el ofensor

U = se desconoce

Forcible Rape

Se refiere a la violación mediante la fuerza o por intimidación, fraude o engaño. Conteste si (Y) o no (N). En estos casos debe contestar si además hubo daño personal (injury) o no y el tipo. Por lo general, el solo hecho de la penetración por la fuerza (aunque no sufra un daño mayor) que requiere examen médico para ver si hay enfermedad venérea, requerirá que marque también la M bajo "injury."

Si en lugar de violación, lo que hubo fue otro delito sexual mediante violencia o intimidación: e.g., incesto, sodomía, escriba tal nombre encima de "rape," y conteste

Appendix

y. Además como hubo contacto físico llene la parte correspondiente a "injury."

Si hay una víctima y no hay violencia sexual, ponga N.

Item # 20--

(a) = handgun = pistola o revólver, escopeta de mano, escopeta de cañón corto, de fabricación comercial o casera, arma de fuego de cañón corto o aire;

(b) = other gun = otra arma de fuego o aire, e.g., rifle que se dispara desde el hombro;

(c) sharp instrument = armas blancas que tienen punta o filo; incluye botella rota utilizada como objeto de agresión capaz de cortar;

(d) blunt instrument = instrumentos o armas que no tienen filo, y son botas, e.g., garrón, culata, tubo, etc.;

(e) other = otra arma que no caiga bajo las anteriores u objeto que se use como tal.

Item # 21--

Dollar Value of Theft = se refiere a valor de la propiedad apropiada ilegalmente o robada.

Este item es aplicable en delitos de robo, apropiación ilegal, recibo y disposición de bienes objeto de delito contra la propiedad, extorsión, fraude, escalamiento si se llevaron propiedad.

Si el valor está en el informe policíaco o en la querella, incluyalo en dólares. Si el valor no está pero se describe el objeto, estime el valor, pongalo en el espacio y entre paréntesis ponga (est.). Refiérase a la tabla de valores estimados, OF-21.

Si no sabe la cantidad ni hay datos para estimarla, lo deja en blanco, o si el item no es aplicable.

El que la propiedad se recupere, o no no tiene importancia para efectos de la codificación de este item.

Item # 22--

Dollar Value of Damage = se refiere a valor de la propiedad que recibió daño.

Delinquency in Puerto Rico

Si el valor está en el informe policíaco o en la querella, incluyalo en dolares. Si el valor no está pero se describe el daño, estime el valor, pongalo en el espacio y entre paréntesis ponga (est.). Refiérase a la tabla de valores estimados, OF-22. Si no sabe la cantidad, lo deja en blanco, o si el item no es aplicable.

Este item deberá llenarlo siempre en casos del delito de daños. Si hubo un escalamiento o cualquier otro delito contra la propiedad deberá determinar si ésta sufrió daño, en cuyo caso deberá llenar este item.

Item # 23--

Se refiere al número de lugares objeto de escalamiento.

Incluye forzamiento en la penetración--en cuyo caso si hay daño a la propiedad deberá llenar también el item # 22--y entrada ilegal con itención de escalar a un lugar donde no hay libre acceso.

Si además hay apropiación ilegal deberá también llenar el item # 21.

Item # 24--

Marque el tipo de lugar objeto del escalamiento, i.e., establecimiento comercial, lugar privado, lugar público.

Recurde que el delito de escalamiento se comete con tan sólo entrar a un lugar--incluye cualquier estructura, edificio, casa, o sus dependencias o anexos--con la intención de cometer un delito grave o apropiación ilegal.

Item # 25--

<u>Numero de coautores</u> = en este número no incluya al menor del cohorte.

Item # 26--

Se refiere al sexo, color y edad de los otros coautores.

Si se trata de un adulto y no se sabe la edad, ponga "adult."

En esta parte <u>debe verificar</u> con las listas maestras para ver si el coautor es de nuestro cohorte. En ese caso será facil obtener la información de la edad y color.

Appendix

Item # 27--

Se refiere a la posesión de drogas al momento de la comisiin del delito.

Para "other" refiérase a la tabla OF-27.

Item # 28--

Subraye la aplicable si al momento de cometer el delito estaba bajo la influencia de drogas o alcohol (under influence) o si era usuario conocido (user of) de drogas o alcohol.

Indique además la apropiada. Para "other" refiérase a la tabla OF-27.

Item # 29--

Fecha del arresto o intervención policíaca.

Item # 30-- Disposición por la Policía o el Fiscal

A = resuelto administrativamente. Incluye servicios breves por la policía, enviado al fiscal y éste decide no semeter, casos en que el querellante desiste, o cualquier otra resolución de naturaleza administrativa.

R = referido al tribunal.

Item # 31-- Fecha de detención preventiva

Esto lo llenará únicamente si fue detenido preventivamente.

Item # 32-- Dias en detención preventiva

Si no pasó tiempo en detención preventiva, deberá poner 00.

Item # 33-- Fecha de la Decisión del Tribunal

Se refiere a cuando el caso es referido al tribunal y éste lo resuelve a base de una de las siguientes: no causa probable o desestimación por algún otro fundamento, no incurso, renuncia de jurisdicción, desvío, incurso, pendiente porque el menor se evadió de la jurisdicción o está fugitivo.

La fecha que se escribe es la de la decisión del tribunal para el caso aplicable, de los indicados en el párrafo anterior.

Item # 34--

1 = Dismissed = se refiere a no causa probable, desestimación por otro fundamento, archivo, o "no asumir jurisdicción, dispuesto por el tribunal.

2 = Acquitted = no incurso.

3 = Waived Jurisdiction = tribunal renunció jurisdicción.

4 = Diversion = Desvío.   Incluye los casos de Sydma.

5 Sentenced = Incurso.

6 = Pending = Pendiente por orden del tribunal porque el menor se evadió de la juridicción o no aparece pese a los esfuerzos para traerlo ante el tribunal. Se refiere únicamente a cuando el caso se deja pendiente por el tribunal porque la persona se evadió de la jurisdicción antes de la vista adjudicativa.
La fecha en que se lleva a cabo la decisión por el tribunal a que hace referencia este item es la fecha que se pone en el item anterior # 33.

Items # 35 y 36--

Estos dos items se llenan únicamente cuando el tribunal de menores renuncia a la jurisdicción para que el menor sea tratado como un adulto.

Items # 37--

Se refiere a la sentencia impuesta por el tribunal de menores si se le trató como menor o por el tribunal de adultos si se renunció jurisdicción.

Se llenará únicamente si el menor ha sido sentenciado. Entiéndase, usted marco 5 en el item # 34, o si se renunció a la jurisdicción y usted marco 3 en el item # 36.

<u>Debe marcar todas las que apliquen</u>.

   Nominal Sentence -- Se trata del regaño y amonestación que contempla la nueva Ley de Menores.

Custody of Parents or others -- Debe marcarla cuando el menor se deja en probatoria bajo la custodia de los padres o encargados.

Probatoria -- Debe marcarla cuando el adulto se deja en probatoria o cuando el menor se deja en probatoria.

Restrictions -- Debe marcarla si como condiciones para la probatoria le imponen restricciones.

Restitution -- Si es menor debe marcarla si lo asignaron a un programa de restitución como <u>Carisma, Hogar sultana en Aguadilla</u>.

Si se renunció jurisdicción y como adulto salió convicto, la marca si le impusieron pena de restitución.

Other conditions -- Cualquier condición distinta a la de la forma impresa, para aquella persona que dejan bajo la custodia de los padres o en probatoria, como por ejemplo ingresar en programa vocacional, recibir tratamiento médico, etc. En tal caso indíquela escribiendo el nombre del programa. Aquí caen los casos en que refieran a <u>CREA, SEMYT, CEDAS, RJ</u> (reto juvenil) etc. y el tratamiento es ambulatorio.

Private institution -- Reclusión en institución privada o bajo la custodia de ella. Incluye cuando le entregan la custodia a <u>CREA</u>.

Maximum security institution -- <u>Escuela industrial de Mayaguez para varones; Escuela industrial de mujeres en Ponce</u>.

Intermediate security institution -- <u>Centro de Tratamiento Social de Ponce para varones</u>.

Vocational/agricultural institutions -- <u>Campamento Santana para Varones en Maricao</u>.

Minimum security homes -- se refiere a los hogares de grupo: <u>Sultana en Aguadilla; Caribe; Hogares para jovenes embrazadas</u>.

Mental institution -- Incluye el <u>hospital siquiatrico de Bayamón para jovenes y adolescentes</u>; y cualquier institución mental como la <u>Julia</u>.

Other institution --

Delinquency in Puerto Rico

Nota: En el item #37, si se le revocó la probatoria o el desvío y se recluyó o si primero se recluye y luego sale en probatoria, al marcar la condición que ocurre luego, ponga entre paréntesis la fecha.

Item # 38--

Si estuvo en probatoria y ya terminó la misma, o si se le revocó, compute el número de semanas y escríbalo.

Item # 39--

Si fue referido a un programa de desvío y ya se cerró el caso definitivamente, o si fue revocado el desvío, haga el computo de semanas en desvío y escríbalo.

Item # 40--

Si estuvo recluido en alguna institución y ya salió de ella, haga el computo en reclusión y escríbalo.

Item # 41--

    a) medication = se refiere a terapia médica para dejar adicción a drogas, alcohol o cualquier otro tratamiento que requiera medicinas.

<u>Si lo refirieron a Semyt, Cedes, Ceda, o algun centro del DESCA, marque esta</u>.

Si lo refirieron a UPA o Unidad Siquiátrica de Niños y Adolescentes en Bayamon o a un Centro de Salud mental, determine antes que tratamiento se le dio.

    b) psychiatric treatment = incluye tratamiento siquiátrico o sicologico.

<u>Si lo refirieron a UPA o unidad siquiátrica de niños y adolescentes, o a un Centro de Salud Mental, CEDES o CEDA, marque esta</u>.

    c) vocational program = cualquier tratamiento vocacional o académico.

Incluye, Campamento Santana en Maricao.

    d) other = e.g., <u>escriba</u> family therapy DSS (se refiere a los servicios a la familia que prove Servicios Sociales como parte del plan de tratamiento del menor): RJ (se refiere a Reto Juvenil, tratamiento cristiano a usuarios de drogas).

Items # 42 y 43--

Estos items se llenarán únicamente si el menor fue tratado como adulto y resultó convicto y se le impuso multa o restitucion en dólares; o si al menor se le imputó un caso de Transito y optó bajo la nueva Ley de Menores por el procedimiento que dispone la Ley de Tránsito.

Item # 44--

Se refiere a cuando el caso se cierra definitivamente para el menor.

Se llenará únicamente en los siguientes casos:
Fecha en que se resuelve administrativamente por la policía o el fiscal.

Fecha en que se cierra definitivamente un caso de desvío por el tribunal.

Fecha en que cumplió la sentencia impuesta.

En casos de Servicios Sociales o DESCA, cuando termina el servicio.

Nota: No aplica cuando el caso .fue archivado o desestimado por el tribunal o dejado pendiente por el tribunal.

Item # 45--

Si el menor estaba evadido--de una institución--el momento de cometer este delito, escriba Y.

Item # 46--

Escriba "Y", si el menor tenia casos pendientes de resolución o de someter al momento de cometer este delito; o cuando el caso previo se desvió y todavía el caso no estaba cerrado definitivamente.

Item # 47--

Escriba "Y", si el menor estaba en probatoria por otro delito cuando cometió este delito.

Nota: MENORES EVADIDOS DE INSTITUCIONES O FUGITIVOS

Delinquency in Puerto Rico

Si el menor se fuga de una institución mientras está cumpliendo sentencia, se le debe llenar un offense form para ese delito de fuga. <u>La fuga que se va a codificar como un nuevo delito es aquella que se anota en el expediente como evasión</u>.

En la hoja para esa fuga los items siguientes se llenarán como sigue:
 # 7   marque 1)
 # 13 número de expediente juvenil del menor
 # 15 fecha de la evasión
 # 16 edad que tenga en ese momento
 # 17 6000
 # 29   fecha de regreso a la Institución o fecha del arresto
 # 30: A) si se resuelve por el fiscal o la institutción sin radicarle caso criminal por la fuga.
 # 34 marque el 6 si al codificar, la persona no ha podido ser arrestada.
 # 45 y
 # 46   n, si no se le ha imputafo delito alguno distinto de la evasión o fuga.

APPENDIX 9.
Definition of Coded Variables

Offender ID Number--

The first digit is a letter (B, S, C) corresponding to the police district in which the intervention took place, Bayamón, San Juan, or Carolina.

The next four digits are numbers.

The second digit from left to right is:
   number 9 when the offender is female;
   number 8 when the ID # corresponds to a male, pure
      status offender; and
   number 0 when the offender is male.

If the offender was born in Puerto Rico, but lived in the United States during at least one of the five years prior to the commission of the current offense, a number 7 was added at the end of the offender form; the word "migrant" and the postal code of the state were handwritten.

Offense Form

Offense Number--

Includes a single offense or single event, according to the order in which the arrests took place, and the cases

Delinquency in Puerto Rico

were either administratively resolved by the police or submitted to court (e.g., 01, 02, 03, 04, and so on).

Item # 6--

1 = Barrio/Barriada. Barrio refers to residences in rural barrios, land squatters, or houses in the countryside. Barriada refers to urban ghettos, sectors of the cities which are not urbanizations or suburban communities.

2 = Private. Refers to private residences, rented or owned, located in the cities, main streets of towns, urbanizations, and condos. Includes subsidized residences in the above areas and cooperative housing.

3 = Public. Refers to public housing.

Item # 7--

We are checking all those letters that describe the nature of the household in order to code it similarly to PRAJJIS that refers to it as a type of cohabitation.
For example, if the juvenile was living with his or her parents, we checked (a) and (b). If there were other siblings in the household, we did not check letter (e), since that information was included in item #10. Letter (e) was checked when the juvenile was living with his or her grandfather/grandmother, sister/brother, or other relative. Letter (j) includes: living with friends or when the juvenile had runaway.

Item # 8

See Table OF-8 entitled List of Occupations. This table includes a list in English and Spanish of all the occupations coded.

In addition, we included the following information. If the occupation is unknown, we coded "unknown". If the head of the household was unemployed, we wrote it in parentheses next to the occupation. If the person was retired by age or disability, we wrote the former occupation and "retired" in parentheses. If the person was not in the labor force, we wrote this. If the head of the household was in jail, we wrote the occupation and "jail" in parentheses.

Appendix

In the case of "government employees," we wrote it down and the occupation was included in parentheses.

Item # 9--

Categories (a) to (h) refer to salary income (i.e., salary or wages) received by the named person. Category (1) "other" includes the following:

DSS / SS / SSS / Welfare-- refer to the public welfare given by the Commonwealth's Department of Social Services. This assistance is different from category (k) which is also sponsored by Social Services;
Alimony; Workmen's Compensation; Unemployment Insurance; Veteran's Pension; and Private Retirement Income (when the source of the income (local or federal is unknown)).

Item # 13 Court Number--

Refers to the juvenile record number assigned bu the Juvenile Court to this offender. All court cases against this juvenile are filed under this number.

Item # 14-- Case Number

Refers to the police record number for this offense if the case was either administratively resolved or referred to court.

Refers to the adult court case number when the Juvenile Court waived jurisdiction.

Refers to the PRAJJIS case number if the juvenile was either a status offender or received anti-addiction services, but was not referred to court.

Item # 15-- Date of Offense

In the cases of status offenders or anti-addiction referees, we wrote the date in which the juvenile was referred to the agency.

Item # 16

Refers to attained age.

Item # 17

Refers to Table OF-17, included herewith, sub. nom. legal offenses.

Delinquency in Puerto Rico

Items # 18 - 24

To code these items we followed, when applicable, the instructions given in the National Survey of Crime Severity (Wolfgang et al., 1985: 130-133). For Item 19 (victim characteristics), when forcible (i.e., violence or intimidation) incest or sodomy occurred, we wrote it instead of rape. For items 21 and 22, we included in the first instance the value estimated in the offense report; when unavailable, we estimated the value according to table OF-21. This table includes a description of the items whose value was estimated.

Item # 28

We added 'User of or" to cover cases where the social report indicates that the juvenile was a drug user, but there was no evidence that when he or she committed the offense, he or she was under the influence of drugs. The coder should underline the applicable choice.

Item # 27 (d) and Item # 29 (d)

Included under heading other are the following: valium, morphine, altane, thinner, popper, LSD, and glue sniffing.

Item # 30

Category (a) administrative resolution includes also those cases in which the juvenile's Public Prosecutor disposes of the case administratively.

Item # 34

We added number "6) pending" to refer to those cases in which the juvenile escaped before the trial, was declared a fugitive, and the court postponed the case until the juvenile was re-arrested and brought to court.

Item # 37

Category (f), other conditions, refers to cases on probation and includes:

CREA — abulatory drug rehabilitation program sponsored by a private institution. This is included in category (g) of Item # 37;

SEMYT or SEMIT — ambulatory drug rehabilitation program for the treatment of juvenile

Appendix

offenders on probation, sponsored by the government;

CEDES or CEDA an evaluation program to which the juvenile offender was referred for evaluation and recommendations concerning the type of drug rehabilitation adequate for this juvenile;

RJ or RETO JUVENIL ambulatory drug rehabilitation program sponsored by a private Christian organization and oriented to their religious ideology;

DSS or SSS family therapy abulatory program sponsored by the Department of Social services;

CSM ambulatory treatment at the local centers of mental health for juveniles with psychiatric problms;

Treatment refers to a rehabilitation treatment program, mostly for drugs, in which the offender should participate. The generic name of treatment is used, since we could not determine to which of the available programs the juvenile had been admitted;

SYDMA ambulatory program for juveniles involved in drugs; includes a restitutive component through the performance of specific hours of public service;

DSCA Ambulatory treatment to drug or alcohol usuaries given by the Department of Anti-Addiction Services;

Fine These are the cases where, in addition to a probation sentence, a fine was imposed and the coder incorrectly did not file this information in Item # 42.

Job Corps refers to a government program for offenders who are provided the opportunity to work as voluntaries in certain government jobs; among them, agriculture;

Carisma program of restitution in cases where the offense involved property damage;

Delinquency in Puerto Rico

USEM　　　　　　this is the Division of the Department of Social Services that takes care of juvenile offenders who live in the community and need services; also provides services to status offenders.

Note: category (f) of Item # 37 refers to cases where the sentence is probation and the person receives ambulatory services. Could include institutionalization treatment, but on a voluntary basis.

Item # 37 (m)

Refers to cases in which a sentence of incarceration was imposed. The following abbreviations were included for category (m):

DSS / SSS / SS-- refers to the Department of Social Services, which would evaluate the juvenile to determine to which of their institutions he or she shoud be committed. The procedure is appropriate for offenses that occurred after 1987, since as part of the new JUvenile Law, the judge cannot sentence a person to a particular institution, as was done before the new law, but only to an Evaluation Center Institution of the Department of Social Services;

Pre-Trial Dentention Center-- this information was given for cases where the person was on probation, but was institutionalized pending probation repeal;

DSCA-- institutionalized treatment by the Department of Anti-Addiction Servicves;

Hogar Estatal or Hostel--this is an institution for status offenders.

For **Item # 37** there are cases in which probation was repealed and a custodial sentence was imposed; or after serving a custodial term, the offender was released on probation. In any of these cases, we checked all applicable types of sentences and put in parentheses the date of the condition which occurred later.

Item # 41

Category (d), <u>other type of treatment</u>, includes:
　　Study programs-- Vocational program
　　Education-- Vocational program
　　DSCA-- Medication and Psychiatric
　　CREA-- Medication and Psychiatric

Appendix

Below are the explanations of the other items where a type of treatment was different from the one provided in the Offender Form.

CEDE, or CEDAS,-- see **Item # 37**, category (f)

Family Therapy-- program of services to the whole family sponsored by the Department of Social Services

Semit,
  or Semyt,-- see **Item # 37**, category (f)

Sydma-- see **Item # 37**, category (f)

Open Residential-- refers to treatment of status offenders institutionalized in open facilities sponsored by the Department of Social Services.

Item # 44

The date of discharge refers to the date on which the case of the offense being coded was finally resolved. The codes are as follows:

Date at which the case was administratively resolved, either by the police or by the juvenile's public prosecutor.

Date at which a diversion case is finally dismissed by the court.

Date at which the juvenile completed serving the sentence.

In cases of status offenders or Anti-Addiction services, the date at which the social service ended.

Note: Instructions for coding cases where the juvenile became a fugitive while serving sentence.

Once the court issues an order declaring that the juvenile is a fugitive, a new offense form should be coded for that offender. In the new offense form, the following items shouls be coded as follows:
```
# 13--   juvenile court identification number
# 15--   date at which he escaped from institution
# 17--   6000
# 45--   Y
# 46--   N, if no other offense has been charged
# 47--   N
```

Index

Acosta, Esperanza, 2, 183
Age-at-Offense: by color, 109, 113, 118-19; by sex, 107, 112-13, 118-19
Age-at-Onset: by color, 95, 100, 105; 118-19; by sex 93-95, 100, 105, 118-19
Alcohol, 202, 216-17, 220; drug offenses and, 66-67; users of, 73; violent offenses and, 58
Ayala, Efrain, 3, 183
Birth cohort of 1970: compared to 1945 and 1958, 173-75, 178; defined, 7; follow-up of, 179, population base for, 19-20;
Bureau of the Census, 19,
Cedeno-Zavala, Caferina, 2, 183
Chronic delinquency: defined, 21; area and, 29; color and, 26-27; recidivism and, 121-22, 124; sex and, 25; violent offenses and 54

Cocaine: demographic factors and 77, 82; measurement of, 202; offenses and 66-67, 73; violent offenses and 58
Color breakdown, 26
Court dispositions, 145, 147, 149, 170
Court sentences, 150-51, 154, 158-59, 160, 170
Defining the cohort, 7
Delinquency status, categories of, 23, 28-29, 36, 121, 143
Delinquent recidivism, probabilities of, 124, 128, 133;
Dinitz, Simon, 2, 183;
Dollar loss: damage offenses and, 51-53; theft offenses and, 51
Drug possessions, 58, 73, 77, 82
Ferracuti, Franco, 2, 3, 183
Figlio, Robert, 183
Heroin: demographic factors and 77, 82; measurement of, 202; offenses and 66-67;

Heroin: violent offenses and 58
Highest grade attained, 36, 37
Household composition, 16, 38, 40-43, 200, 224
Kupperstein, Lenore, 1, 2, 5, 181, 183
Layout of cohort 22
Lopez-Rey, Manuel, 2, 183
Marijuana: demographic factors and 77, 82; measurement of, 202; offenses and 66-67, 73; violent offenses and 58
Master subject file, 12-14, 15
Municipalities, 8, 10
Narcotics Offenses, 66, 82
Offender demographic form, 15, 199, 206, 213
Offense form, 16, 200, 205-8, 221, 223, 229
Offense probabilities, 124, 128, 133
Offense specialization, 134-5, 138, 178
Offense transitions, 134-43
Official statistics, delinquency and 3, 6
Otero de Ramos, Mercedes, 2, 183
Philadelphia birth cohorts, 16-17, 21, 135, 173-5, 177-9, 181
Police dispositions, 145, 149, 175
Policy implications, of 1970 cohort, 178-9
PRAJJIS file, 13, 16, 17, 199-200, 206, 208-12, 224-5
Prevalence: areas and 28; color and, 26-28; other factors and, 29-30, 33, 36, 38-41; sex and, 23, 25-28

Private school, 19, 33, 42, 67, 77
Public residence, 29, 30, 67, 77, 82
Public school, 19, 33, 42, 67, 77, 82
Recidivism probabilities, 17, 124, 128, 131, 133, 137, 143
Rural area, 1-10, 30-33, 55, 209, 224
Sellin, Thorsten, 17, 113, 116-118, 130, 133, 134, 143, 146, 183
Seriousness, of offenses, 16, 45, 48, 53, 54, 130, 159, 181, 183, 225
Supplementary intervention report, 15
Toro-Calder, Jamie, 1, 2, 5, 181, 183
Tracy, Paul, 1, 17, 181, 183
Treatment program, 165, 227
UCR offenses: age at, 100, 105, 109, 122; chronic delinquents and, 124; cohort comparisons for, 173-4; court handling of, 151, 154, 158, 165; drugs and, 67, 77; incidence of, 45, 48, 51, 91, 143; police handling of, 147; probability of, 128-33
Urban area, 1-10, 30-33, 42, 54-55, 224
Vales, Pedro, 3, 183
Violent offenses, 53-54, 56, 58, 91, 113, 130, 133, 177
Weapon use, 59, 174
Wolfgang, Marvin, 1, 16, 17, 113, 116-118, 130, 133, 134, 135, 143, 146, 181, 183, 185, 187, 225

About the Authors

DORA NEVARES is Professor of Law at Inter-American University in Hato-Rey, Puerto Rico. She has published four books in Puerto Rico and various journal articles in the United States and Puerto Rico.

MARVIN E. WOLFGANG is a Professor of Criminology and Law at the University of Pennsylvania. He is the author of the books *From Boy to Man* and *Delinquency in a Birth Cohort,* as well as numerous articles and reviews.

PAUL E. TRACY is Associate Professor of Criminal Justice at Northeastern University in Massachusetts. He has numerous publications to his credit, has been an expert witness at many trials, and is a member of several professional organizations relating to crime, delinquency, and sociology.